Yes, You're Pregnant, But What About Me?

Yes, You're

Kevin Nealon

Pregnant,
But What About Me?

HARPER

ENTERTAINMENT
An Imprint of HarperCollinsPublishers

A portion of this book was previously published, in somewhat
different form, in the *New York Times*.

HarperCollins books may be purchased for educational, business,
or sales promotional use. For information please write: Special
Markets Department, HarperCollins Publishers, 10 East 53rd
Street, New York, NY 10022.

FIRST EDITION

Designed by Judith Stagnitto Abbate/Abbate Design

Library of Congress Cataloging-in-Publication Data

Nealon, Kevin, 1953–
   Yes, you're pregnant, but what about me?/Kevin Nealon.–1st ed.
     p. cm.
   ISBN 978-0-06-121520-9
1. Nealon, Kevin, 1953– 2. Actors–United
States–Biography.   3. Comedians–United States–Biography.
4. Fatherhood–Anecdotes. I. Title.
   PN2287. N34A3 2008
   729.702'8092–dc22
   [B]   2007051372

08 09 10 11 12 OFFICETIGERS/RRD 10 9 8 7 6 5 4 3 2 1

For Susan

Contents

Prebirth

Ever since I was a little girl I dreamed of being pregnant. When it finally happened, I couldn't have been happier. I suffered no morning sickness and had a relatively easy pregnancy. I loved every aspect of those nine months. I enjoyed shopping for maternity clothes, reading all the books on child rearing, and exchanging information with other soon-to-be-mothers. My appetite increased, as expected, as did my waistline, but I didn't care. I was just enjoying the freedom to eat whatever I wanted. We now have a beautiful two-year-old boy. We are so blessed!

—MONICA HACKFORD
(29 YEARS OLD), HOMEMAKER

• • •

I was worried about falling behind at work. The pregnancy came as a surprise, but a welcome one. I had never really thought about being a mother, but fortunately, it fit me well. Sometimes I wonder if I should have waited longer before having children, but this is the way it worked out, and I'm glad. I still miss people doting over me and my 38DD's. This pregnancy taught me patience and the ability to shift with change. Jonas and I got married shortly after little Sophia arrived, and I was able to pick up my career where I left off.

—NOELLE ROSSMAN
(24 YEARS OLD), COMPUTER PROGRAMMER

• • •

During the pregnancy I gained twenty-five pounds, lost many nights' sleep, and suffered months of anxiety and insecurity. What can I say? I was nervous and felt out of control. I understand the weight gain, and I am determined to lose it over the next three months so I can fit back in to my favorite prepregnancy clothes. Right now I still can't even get into my "fat jeans"! Starting yesterday, I put myself on a strict running program and have only missed one day so far.

I have to accept that my body has changed. The stretch marks are just something I am going to have to live with. At my age it may be difficult, but my hope is to get back down to my prepregnancy weight of two hundred and five pounds and to finally catch up on some sleep.

In the meantime, I have written this book about my journey through my wife's pregnancy, how it affected me, and how I got here in the first place.

—KEVIN NEALON
(53 YEARS OLD), COMEDIAN

Yes, You're Pregnant, But What About Me?

One-twenty over Eighty

I've always been a late bloomer. I didn't start dating until college. I didn't move away from home until twenty-three. I was in my mid-forties when I started to shave, and I think only last month I started using the term, "dude."

I'm not proud of being a late bloomer, but at this point, it's a reality I've come to terms with. It wasn't so much that I was unprepared for any of these life events, it was more that the time never really seemed right. I mean come on, who ever "wants" to learn how to balance a checkbook? Or invest in stock or buy life insurance? Or unclog a toilet with a plunger? These are not things that most people do for fun . . . except of course using a plunger.

Given this slow trend on my part, it should not come as a shock that I came to fatherhood late in life too—at age fifty-three to be precise. Unlike most of my late blooming, I actually wanted to become a father. I couldn't say why, it was just always something that I knew. Of course in practice the thought was terrifying, but still I liked the idea of it. I thought the word *dad* had a nice ring to it and I wouldn't mind if someone used it in reference to me, preferably my child. Like most men who decide to become fathers I thought, How hard could it be? You walk through the supermarket and look all the other people with kids and think, Okay if he's a "dad" and he's wearing a wallet chain and carrying a skateboard, then I can probably pull this off too.

Everyone has different reasons for wanting to be a parent, and everyone's journey is unique. For some it began on a honeymoon, for others in a petri dish, and for some perhaps it was merely the result of a wardrobe malfunction. As for me, my journey to child rearing began in a far less scandalous way and in a far more scandalous place: on a chance visit to a gypsy palm reader in Atlantic City.

I was newly single and reeling from my divorce with my former wife. Like most stories that involve gypsies, this one took place on a blisteringly cold night as I strolled numbly along the desolate Atlantic City boardwalk. In a few short months, this very spot would be crawling with obese, sunburned, drunk tourists eating crisp, greasy summer food. Screaming kids would be whipping around on the Tilt-a-Whirl in the nearby amusement park, while teenagers would stand idly by intimidating adults with their sarcasm, chain-smoking packs of American Spirit and trying to convince members of the opposite sex that they were cool.

Maybe if I were to walk this same stretch in a few months, the Miss America pageant would be taking place. Maybe as I walked by the venue, Miss Idaho or Miss New Jersey would be outside on a break, smoking a butt or sticking a finger down her throat. Maybe she would ask me if I had a light or a mint, and then maybe we would have struck up a conversation about world peace. Maybe I would have impressed her with my worldliness by flashing the ten euros I had in my wallet from a trip to Euro Disney two years earlier. Maybe we would have talked about teeth whiteners and the merits of flossing.

But it wasn't July. It was February. And in Atlantic City in February there's none of that. Instead of summer sand blowing across the sunbaked wooden planks of the boardwalk, it was now dry snow and sleet whipped into a frenzy by an offshore gale. Most of the small, crappy tourist shops that sold the summer crap food and crappy T-shirts were boarded up for the season and the wooden walkway was now covered with a thin sheet of dark ice. In hindsight, I guess I should have told someone I was venturing off on this bleak and ominous excursion, so that they could have stopped me, but I didn't, and so here I was. This may have been why I ducked into a hole in the wall with a small flickering neon sign outside that read "Miss Edana's Palm Reading," but to tell you the truth, I really have no idea what made me go in there. Perhaps it was just to have someone to talk to. Someone to tell me some good news, someone to give me hope and encouragement that I would meet someone else and be happy again. And if none of that, maybe just someone to assure me that my hands weren't really frostbitten.

In retrospect, I'm not entirely sure why I thought a gypsy would bring me good news. Movies, which form the bulk of my preconceived notions about things and the basis for all of my cultural stereotypes, always seem to portray gypsies as the bearers of *bad* news. They are the soothsayers and prophets whose visions are always the grimmest and least pleasant. Not to mention the fact that they steal babies and con unsuspecting tourists (or so I've heard).

From Miss Edana's demeanor, I assumed she might be an Irish gypsy. She was wearing a lot of "wrapped" garments—stuff you would normally find draped over the back of a couch at your grandmother's: an afghan, a shawl, a half-knitted sweater, two cats, and various other laundry that was not put away. Her looped earrings were so big I expected a Cirque du Soleil performer to land on one at any time, and makeup covered every inch of her face. With an eyebrow pencil she had colored on a fake beauty mark just off the left side of her nose and above the corner of her mouth. It's really the only good place for a beauty mark. One would not look good placed directly under the eye or on the chin. It would look more like a fly had landed on your face.

As I was sizing her up, she was doing the same to me. I shut the door behind me, and she peered out into the blackness, almost as if she was checking to see if anyone had followed me. When she spoke, there was a husk to her voice that sounded as though she had been smoking cigarettes for quite some time, a practice that no doubt created quite the unfit environment for her latest crop of stolen babies.

To make a long story short, but still longer than it was, the gypsy looked at my palm and without hesitation informed me that I had three kids I didn't know about. So much for my good news. She cut right to the chase. There wasn't even any verbal foreplay with my palm. She might have suggested that I would be coming into some money soon, or possibly even be losing some fingers due to frostbite. She could have broken it to me more gently by fixating on my palm and suggesting the possibility that someone I had been with may have missed her period, and then gradually broken the news. But no, she just spouted out that I had three kids that I didn't know about and then surreptitiously glanced at me for a reaction. I don't remember too much else about her reading, because in my head I had started going through my list. An image of a slightly used Rolodex emerged, and the small number of cards flipped by one at a time: there was the one with only the first name, Stacey, while another contained just a description, "The girl from San Diego at that Irish bar." A minute or so later,

Miss Edana handed me back my palm and charged me eighty-five dollars, which I later wrote off as child support.

Miss Edana might have been a certified gypsy palm reader, but I was fairly certain that she made up the tale about the three kids. The likelihood of my having children I didn't know about was, well, highly unlikely. "Don't get anyone pregnant" was my mantra throughout my high school and college years. I'm surprised that I never got it tattooed on my arm. When I was younger, I was never a wild partyer, but more significant was the fact that I was raised a Catholic. I'm paraphrasing a few of the popes here when I say that the central tenant of Catholicism for postpubescent males is, Don't get anyone knocked up out of wedlock. My teenage years were consumed by the fear that I would accidentally impregnate someone, and most likely, it would be a woman. My parochial high school upbringing had ingrained in me that not only would God disapprove of my premarital sex, but also my life would be ruined. It didn't matter whether you accidentally got someone pregnant—perhaps it was a drunken one-night stand, a short relationship, a crush, staring too long, or brushing up against a stripper at a bachelor party in Tijuana—it didn't matter, that would be the person you would *have* to marry.

If letting God down wasn't enough, I was also made aware that I would not have the free young man's life that other free young men would be having. Not only that, but I would be stuck with that baby's mother for the rest of my life. When the right girl came along, I would have this baggage, and be unavailable, not to mention undesirable.

This being a lot of fear and guilt for a teenager to bear, I had always worked hard at not getting anyone pregnant. Luckily for me, this hard work seems to have paid off, since no kid has shown up claiming me as its dad in the last several decades.

One indication of Hollywood success is when an alleged

illegitimate child or its mother shows up on your front doorstep, demanding reparations and support. Though I'm still not sure what constitutes real Hollywood success, as a precaution I had my front doorstep removed. Maybe somewhere, some woman was following my career and waiting for me to really make it big before she came a-knockin'. By the way, this is why I have purposely stayed away from doing the big blockbuster action movies. Either way, if that day comes and someone does show up standing in the dirt where my doorstep used to be, it will be a mixed blessing. On one hand, I'll know that I've truly made it, but I'll also have to pay a lot more than Miss Edana's eighty-five dollars.

A couple of years after my run-in with Miss Edana, I met my current wife, Susan, and finally found the hope and happiness that I'd been looking for when I went to visit the pessimistic gypsy. Susan and I got married and moved into a house several thousand miles from Atlantic City, but decided once again to remove the doorstep for safe measure. Our house was situated across the street from another that was rented by several kids. I call them kids, but they were actually guys in their early to late twenties. I'm assuming they were trust-fund babies, because they were obviously having a lot more fun than I had when I was their age. They seemed to have a lot of functions at their home, and by functions I mean the alcohol-fueled, debauchery-laden parties that I might have enjoyed when I was their age if I hadn't been so worried about getting girls pregnant.

After Susan and I had been living in our house for a bit, we started to have some friends come over to drink wine and talk about non-gypsy-related subjects that mostly pertained to getting older and the fact that we were experiencing pain where there was no pain before. On one such evening, I was preparing for our friends to arrive when I realized that the youth-infused house across the street was also getting ready to host an event. As I returned from the store with three bottles of a nice Napa Valley pinot noir for our party, I noticed the guys across the street wheeling a keg of Miller into their house. Two other guys in UCLA T-shirts were inflating a small children's pool on the front lawn. From the recent cast of characters I had seen over there, I had a feeling that the pool would not be for children.

Once inside my house, I set the bottles down on the kitchen table, careful to move aside the latest *AARP Bulletin* first. God forbid that should get wet. We had all we needed now for our little blowout. Actually, "blowout" is slightly exaggerating. It's more like our little "gathering." We call our parties "gatherings" to avoid using the words and phrases that paint a more accurate picture of what it really is: a group of mostly forty and over adults standing around, huddled like penguins, discussing the relative merits of California vs. Australian shiraz.

One item that I've found to be a big hit at our gatherings is a little something called a digital blood pressure machine. Several years ago I bought one of these gadgets to keep an eye on my blood pressure. (Incidentally, I love gadgets—I even like the word *gadget*. The word *gadget* is almost like a gadget itself. I guess it's the official name for a "thingamajig.") When Susan and I started having people over, I quickly found that not only was this gadget a good way to assuage my neurosis about the possibility of having high blood pressure, but it made for an entertaining party game as well.

Here's how it worked: during the middle of the gathering I would proudly place the blood pressure machine on the ottoman and offer to take my guests' blood pressure. By their reaction, you'd think I just broke out the Hope Diamond. The process was very simple—I'd wrap the Velcro cuff around the guest's arm, then push the start button. The machine would then automatically take the reading. I knew that a normal blood pressure reading was 120 over 80, and I could then verify for people where their blood pressure was on the spectrum of things.

The guests on this particular night were quite interested in their results and couldn't wait to be next in line. "What did you get?" someone asked. "One-twenty-six over seventy-eight," replied our friend Rachael, whose arm was no thicker than a pencil. "What did you get?" someone else would ask. "One-sixty over ninety-five," they'd shout back, prompting an, "Awww, you are screwed!" from the others. It was a big hit.

As I was taking another guest's blood pressure (for the second time), I glanced out the window at our partying neighbors and had what can only be described as one of those moments when you realize that age has a lot to do with things. Their front lawn was full of inebriated young coeds, whooping and hollering, playing beer pong and jumping in the little inflated pool, halfnaked—and here we were, sipping our pinot noir and taking our blood pressure. With the cuff of the blood pressure machine tightening on me, I thought, When did this happen to me? When did I downshift into middle age? I didn't have an answer, but by my 152/91 reading, it obviously was bothering me. I guess if we really knew how to have fun, we would have made a drinking game out of taking our blood pressure. The person with the highest reading would have to guzzle his wine, then chase it with a shot of prune juice. We would then take everyone's blood pressure again, and the one with the highest readout would win.

As all good things come to an end, our gathering eventually wound down. Sadly, it was still light outside. Based on the blood pressure results, several of our concerned guests had already made doctor's appointments. Others tried to remain as calm as possible and even lay down on the couch with their feet raised,

trying to take advantage of the red wine's blood-thinning proper-
ties. When the final guest had gotten up the strength for his
return trip home, I stood on the porch waving good-bye and
couldn't help but notice, once again, the raging hormones from
our neighbors' festivities. It was like the party would not leave me
alone. It kept calling out to me, "Come and join us! This is where
you belong. Remember? Come!" I briefly entertained the idea of
bringing my blood pressure machine over there, ya know, just to
mix things up a little, but then thought, Nah, better not. It might
get wet. As people age, I've noticed an interesting concern arises.
We seem to be more and more alarmed with the possibility of
things getting wet. Potential wetness becomes a go-to excuse for
not doing things.

"Hey, Todd, you wanna go swimming?"

"Nah, we might get wet."

Soon thereafter, my wife and I locked all the doors, turned off
the lights, double-checked the lock on the back door, and went
to bed. As I reached for my dental guard on the nightstand, I
accidentally hit the remote for our Posturepedic bed. It immediately raised my back to a level where I couldn't help but see out
the window to even more young coeds dancing and splashing in
the little inflated pool. This party was not about to let me go. As
I settled back down and closed my eyes, I realized that our gatherings really weren't so different. They also had gadgets, but
instead of digital blood pressure devices they had bongs and
blaring ghetto blasters.

These ghetto blasters, as it turned out, made it difficult to
sleep. Susan and I lay in bed, unable to sleep for what seemed an
eternity due to the raucous laughter and shenanigans coming
from our insensitive, drunken, rowdy neighbors. Finally, my wife
blurted out, "This is ridiculous! Don't they realize it's almost nine
o'clock? Honey, would you please do something about this?"

Her request set off an alarm in me. Did I want to have this confrontation with a bunch of drunken kids? No, I hate confrontation; in fact I'm not even good at being direct. It's a family trait. Growing up, if we wanted the salt during dinner, we wouldn't directly ask for it. We would merely say, "Is that the salt over there?" Or if we wanted the rest of someone's dessert, instead of clearly asking, "May I have the rest of your dessert?" we would say something like, "Are you going to finish the rest of that?" This, we assumed, would imply that we would like it if you weren't going to finish it. This indirect approach would more often than not result in confusion and me not getting what I wanted. This type of behavior would affect me later in life. When I started dating, it became very difficult getting to second base. I would say, "Does your blouse open? It does? Are those breasts? Are you going to be using those breasts?"

But my wife was right. As much as I hated confrontation, I was the husband, and it was up to me to do something. I didn't want to be the bad guy in this scenario, but after all, weren't they disturbing our sleep? I swung my legs out of bed, slipped on my pants, zipping my fly up with extra determination and grit. I quickly pulled my sweatshirt on over my head. Since there was no zipper to pull up hard, instead I tugged the back of the shirt down to cover some of my butt. I think Susan knew that I meant business. There are some things in a marriage that the husband just has to do.

I marched downstairs to our front door and fumbled for the light switch to our porch. I braced myself, then firmly flipped the light switch on and off five solid times. If that wasn't a strong signal, I didn't know what was. I confidently returned to bed, informing my wife that I had taken care of our problem. After another half hour of drunken revelry, I informed my wife that maybe they hadn't gotten my message. I thought to myself, What part of the blinking of the porch lights did they not get? I knew I would have to take a more forceful measure now. I jumped out of bed again and marched over to our window. Determined to end this madness, I firmly grasped the bottom of the windowshade, then quickly raised and lowered it a solid six times. As I got back into bed, it dawned on me that I should have had the bedroom lights on so that they could see the contrast of the room going dark and light as the shade went up and down. Because of that, they once again didn't get the message that Mr. Nealon was disturbed.

The party got more and more raucous, and finally I realized there was no other way around it. Sometimes you just have to confront a situation and get it over with. I would have to be a man about this and take the most drastic measure. Once again I rolled out of bed. I stomped into the bathroom and removed eight Tylenol PMs from the bottle in the medicine cabinet. We each took two with room-temperature water from our preset bottles of Evian on our nightstand, and then stuffed the rest in out ears. Dude, we shut that party down.

In the days and weeks following our gathering and the party across the street, I looked back on my younger days, but as I reflected, I couldn't remember blowing it out as much as our neighbors were inclined to. I wasn't a prude, but I also wasn't a reckless, wild partyer like most of them across the street. I went to parties. I saw couples pair off and disappear into the rooms upstairs. Don't they worry about getting pregnant? I thought. What if someone got knocked up at that age? Wouldn't that put the kibosh on their partying? How would they deal with that? I could only imagine how high someone's blood pressure would spike if they were saddled with that situation.

The whole contrast of our party and our neighbors' had really put my age in a new perspective. This is not to say that I was having a midlife crisis, but I was becoming increasingly aware that I wasn't getting any younger (although I suppose that realization is what prompts most midlife crises). Since I had no kids that I knew of, I started to think that it might be nice to have one soon, seeing as how I had been putting it off for a while. I was at that age when not only was my hairline receding but so were my gums. It's like they're in a race to see which one can get behind me first. Between you and me, you really can't tell that my gums are receding because I comb them forward.

I was fifty-two, and for the first time, I started to feel the weight of my years. It's hard to tell the years and months in L.A. without the seasons. It is true, Los Angeles has television seasons, but it's just not the same. I mean, sometimes, just out of nostalgia, when the fall TV season begins I will wear my flannel shirts, but more often than not it is just too hot. Without the seasons to measure years, the only gauge that helped me recognize increments of time was how much my friends' kids had grown and changed since the last time I saw them. Children grow so fast, don't they? It seems like one minute the kid is in the maternity ward, and the next minute it's in rehab. Another alarming "lots of time has gone by" wake-up call to me is when someone in their mid-thirties approaches and tells me what a big fan they are and how they *grew up* watching me. When anyone, whether it's your kid or some guy on the street, comes up to you and says that they "grew up" doing anything with you, it's official that aging has come to your house.

Age creeps up on you and will frequently rear its head in different ways. I didn't think it would happen, but it did. It may sound cliché, but some younger people's music now seems like loud noise to me. Maybe some of it seems loud because it *is* loud. One of my pet peeves is when a car pulls up alongside me at a traffic light and the young driver has his windows down and is blasting rap music loud enough for the whole block to hear. The pounding bass notes register a 7.9 on the Richter scale, and I fear my windows are close to splintering into a thousand little shards. The audacity always amazes me. What makes him think I want to hear his music? Does he assume that I and everyone else within a square mile enjoy the service that he is providing? Does he just want everyone to know that he is party central? Well, guess what? Maybe today I am not a fan, and I don't appreciate it. My road rage begins to rear its ugly head, and I start thinking . . . How would he like it if I went and got my favorite book, highlighted several chapters, and held it out my car window right in front of him? "Here, read this!" I would yell, "Right here! See these paragraphs? Nora Roberts! It's okay, you don't have to thank me. It's a service I provide for everyone. Just wanted to let you know this is where the party is at!"

And what about having a baby at my age? Even if Susan got pregnant tomorrow, I would be fifty-three when the baby was born. I mean, it wasn't over for me yet, but I felt I was circling the drain. Incidentally, I love these phrases that signify someone is close to death. In fact, I've made up some of my own:

- He hasn't checked out yet, but they're bringing his luggage down.
- He hasn't bought the farm yet, but he's applying for a loan.
- The vultures aren't circling yet, but they're asking for permission to take off.
- She hasn't kicked the can yet, but she's taking one out of the pantry.

I felt as though the curtain hadn't dropped yet but I was somewhat into the third act. When I was sixty-three, the baby would be ten. When I was seventy-three, the baby would be twenty-five. I know, you're thinking my math isn't accurate. That's because my plan is to close the age gap over the years by using my wife's anti-aging moisturizing cream at night . . . and also by keeping it away from the baby. I figure I can shave off a few years with this strategy. My wife always uses moisturizing cream. It's amazing how many different types of moisturizers there are. They even have different moisturizers for different times of the day and different parts of your face. Occasionally I can tell what time it is by simply looking at my wife's face. There are also correct and incorrect techniques of applying these moisturizers—absolutely no rubbing under the eyes, just lightly dabbing. Apparently rubbing would only encourage wrinkles and crow's-feet. Once you are away from the eyes, you are free to rub—but ever so gently.

I've also noticed that a product always seem to sell better if there is a story about how the developer came up with it. For the price of some of these moisturizer creams, there had better be some very good stories behind them. There's one very expensive moisturizer I've noticed in our medicine cabinet that was apparently developed by an astronaut to treat his burns from an accident. I am guessing that this astronaut purposely tried to burn his wrinkles off. But nevertheless, if it's good enough for his burns, it will certainly take care of that slight wrinkle I have on my forehead.

More of a concern than the age difference for me was gas price differences. When he is ten, a gallon of gas will probably be $10.39%. When he is twenty, it will probably be $22.76%. In all honesty, I am confused about the rising price of oil. Something is not on the up-and-up, because I went into a pharmacy recently and noticed that the price of petroleum jelly has not gone up at all. Not one cent. I stocked up and got three cases because I know one of these days "the man" is going to realize that he hasn't hiked up the PJ, and then we're out of luck. Too bad our cars can't run on petroleum jelly. I guess it would be tough to get in the tank, though. You'd have to work it in and around with your two fingers. Could you imagine the people lined up at pharmacies to get petroleum jelly? Thankfully, there are no more lines at gas stations. In fact, gas stations have become the new pickup places—forget the club scene. Instead of sending a bottle of wine over to someone, you can send over some gas. "Excuse me," you would say to your service station attendant, "I would like to send four dollars thirty-nine and nine-tenths of a cent of your finest gas over to the young lady at pump five in the Honda Civic, please."

It's not just gas prices—everything seems to be going up. I don't like it when that woman comes through the restaurant with that basket of roses. They're like twenty dollars each—for a single-stem rose! I think that's pretty steep. I feel bad for the guy on his first date. He may not even like the girl he is with, but everyone is watching to see if he is going to buy a rose for her. It's awkward for him and for the date. That's all I'm saying. I mean, you don't see a guy coming through the restaurant with a bucket of tools, do you? "Buy a wrench for your date, ma'am? I have three-quarter-inch open end, I have ratchets, vise grips." Again, its always one sided.

It was not that I never wanted kids, I always did. It was just that I was never ready to have them. The more I thought about it, the more the timing seemed right for me now that I was "old." It must be the way I planned it subconsciously. I like planning things consciously and subconsciously. For example, there are a lot of DVDs that I purposely do not rent or want to watch now because I want to save them to watch when I am in a retirement home someday. The truth of the matter is, at that age, it probably won't make a difference whether I've already seen a certain movie or not—more than likely I won't remember seeing it anyway. I wish I knew how to plan unconsciously. That would be so much easier. Anything that happened in my favor, I could take credit for planning unconsciously. I also think it would make life a lot easier for me if I could get things done unconsciously.

I once worked with someone who desperately wanted kids. He was in his mid-forties, had been divorced several times, and had a successful career. I only learned of his yearning for a child after spotting an antique wooden cradle in the corner of his home office. At first it seemed sad to me. I thought, Poor guy, he really wants a child and this cradle reminds him every day that he doesn't have one. At the time I felt that, because he was in his forties already, he'd missed his opportunity. I soon realized that was probably *not* how he was looking at it. He was probably looking at the cradle as a reminder of what he really wants, instead of what he doesn't have. He saw the cradle as being half full instead of half empty. Of course, if the cradle were actually half full, then it probably would only have been a half of a baby. Today he is the proud father of two boys and a girl, and I am not sure if they are all sleeping in that cradle together.

Unlike my old coworker, I really wasn't taking any active measures to remind myself to have a baby. At the moment that I was contemplating all this, instead of an empty cradle in my office, I had an empty safe. One day, before too much time had passed and I was too old, I was intent on filling it up. I didn't have the same kind of daily reminder to have kids, and I came to realize that if I was going to have a child or children, it would have to be a conscious effort. If it didn't happen then, I wasn't meant to have one, and there would be no hard feelings with the universe. I guess I had always planned subconsciously to have a baby, but now I needed to transition into consciously planning and taking active measures. To create my own cradle, I cluttered my floors with toys, dirty diapers, and drool. I contemplated calling a company that baby-proofs homes and having them work their magic on my babyless home. I needed to think differently because up until now it had been me that was baby-proofed.

I thought back to Miss Edana and those three mysterious

children of mine who were supposedly floating around. I thought about the popes and their words of wisdom and how I had followed them so diligently for all my life—perhaps I'd been a little too diligent. I mean, after all, my wife was the one person that I was *supposed* to get pregnant. The more I thought about it, the more important the notion of having a child became. Even though I wasn't desperate to have a child, I also didn't want to regret never having one. I did not want to be rocking my frail body in a retirement home somewhere, someday, wondering what it would have been like to have one, kicking myself for never experiencing it. No kids visiting me . . . just a safe and lots of DVDs that I may or may not have seen. I made the conscious decision—I *want* to have a child. I may end up in an insane asylum, driven crazy by this kid and wondering what it would have been like if I never had him/her, but so be it.

Of course, all these aging baby thoughts were not taking place just in my mind. At some point, I looped Susan into what I was contemplating, since she would most likely be involved in the whole baby process. Susan also agreed that something was missing from our life, aside from a filled-up safe. She had always wanted to be a mother, so why wait any longer? It wasn't too late for me, but I was getting there. The fat lady hasn't sung yet, but she was doing her sound check. I was already receiving *AARP Bulletins*, but I didn't qualify yet for the discount at the movies or on public transportation. I was making more and more trips to the bathroom at night, and my joints were in the beginning stages of rigor mortis, but I could still lift weights in small increments. Heck, some of my friends were already becoming grandparents. Luckily, Susan was younger than me, and at thirty-four she was still "pregnantable."

Age is all relative. I really shouldn't be worried about mine. Since I come from good stock, I think I will live to be pretty old.

My grandmother lived to be a very, very old woman. She died when she was one hundred and one years old and was perfectly healthy most of her life. When she was one hundred, though, she had a near-death experience and her whole life flashed before her—and because she was so old, that flash took almost four weeks. I guess at that age anything you do could be considered a near-death experience. Her sister, Myrtle, died several years after her at the ripe old age of one hundred and two. Myrtle woke up one morning at her nursing home (which incidentally had an hourly rate) and confidently told the nurse, "Today is the day I am going to die." She had breakfast in the main dining room, then strolled back to her room, lay down, and passed away peacefully later that day. Now there was someone who could have considered a career as a psychic.

With age, hopefully, comes wisdom. With any luck, over the years you have gathered more information to exchange with your child, and hopefully you are more mature than a younger father would be. Tony Randall and Anthony Quinn had kids when they were in their seventies. (No, not with each other.) Some would say having a baby at that age is not fair to the child. Others, who had terrible fathers, would say the later the better. That way he won't be around too long, making your life miserable.

Yes, a baby would take up a lot of time and change my life, but hey, I'd had enough free time over the years to do what I wanted, or could have done if I wasn't so unmotivated. I'd been selfish long enough. It was time for me to grow up. Besides, how can you have a hot nanny if you don't have a kid?

TWO

Out of the Loop

What happened? What happened?" I screamed.

My five-year-old sister, Kim, had just run into our house crying uncontrollably with blood pouring from one of her tiny fingers, and I had responded by matching her hysteria level decibel for decibel. With my parents out, Kim had been under my watchful eye; unfortunately, my watchful eye had been on the television. I was too concerned with the trouble Barney Fife was in with the folks in Mayberry, and I had not seen whatever caused the small puddle of blood forming in Kim's palm. She seemed reticent about admitting to what had actually happened to her finger. I quickly bandaged it with about three feet of wet toilet paper and held it tight.

"What happened, Kim?" I asked again, this time in a more controlled panic. Through her tears she said she was bitten by Buffy, our neighbor's cute little miniature collie.

For eleven years I had been the youngest of three children, but then from seemingly out of nowhere, my parents decided to have another child and then another. It was almost as if my parents had two sets of children. (Clearly my father didn't take the pope's "don't get anyone pregnant" line as literally as I eventually would.) I was eleven years old when my sister Kim was born, and sixteen years old when my brother Chris was born. The rather large age gap almost gave me a sense of what it might feel like to one day be a dad, and frequently I was left "in charge" of my younger siblings when my parents went out. I was a parent with a shutoff time, and no matter what had happened, in the end they would return home from their outing and issue me a reprieve. In the meantime, I would rock Chris to sleep and help Kim color between the lines, all while figuring out how I might have to cheat to pass on my upcoming math test.

"Buffy bit you?" I asked in disbelief. Buffy had never bitten anyone before, and this would have been a first. Sure, she barked a lot, but the Buffy I knew was a coward who happened to have large incisors, and she would sooner turn tail and run than ever have to partake in mouth-to-hand combat. I would hate to wrongly accuse this dog if, in fact, she had nothing to do with this. At the same time, I didn't want to come right out and accuse my sweet little bleeding sister of being a liar. Why would she lie about Buffy? Did she have ulterior motives, a hidden agenda? Who was behind all this?

I unwrapped the toilet paper from her finger to take a better look. The bleeding had slowed now, and I could see the bite marks. They sure didn't look like dog teeth marks, I thought. They were small, almost pinlike, and close together. My forensic investigation continued. I was growing more and more suspicious of the origin of her wound.

"Where was Buffy when she bit you?" I asked.

Slightly confused, she said, "Buffy was in the garbage can."

"In the garbage can out by the garage?" I retorted, grilling her as though she were on the witness stand. Almost mocking her now, I followed up with "What was Buffy doing in the garbage can?"

Kim began crying again. "I don't know. She just jumped up and bit my finger and wouldn't let go. I finally shook her off back into the can," she said, reliving her ordeal. I gently probed some more, asking, "Is Buffy still in the garbage can, Kim?" She nodded her head yes. "I think so." I was trying to visualize Kim shaking Buffy off her finger. She's a small dog, but still too heavy to lift off the ground while dangling from a finger. She was also big enough to get out of the can if she wanted. At this point, I was wishing that it *was* Buffy that bit her, but deep down I feared it was something else. No further questions, I thought, and dismissed her from the stand. I hugged her and assured her that she would be okay. As the responsible adult, it was my duty now to visit the scene of the crime.

I slowly approached the garbage can with my baseball bat, afraid to confirm my deepest fear. My stomach was in knots as I cautiously peered over the rim, bat at the ready. As I gazed deep down to the bottom, the first thing I saw was a small, shredded bag of garbage and no Buffy. I recognized the crumpled Breyer's chocolate chip ice cream container that I had polished off several days earlier, and the wrappings from a Hostess cupcake I had inhaled a few nights earlier while watching *My Favorite Martian*. As I continued perusing the contents of the can, my heart suddenly sank when I saw, at the very bottom, a long, thick, grayish pink tail protruding from a box of Cheerios—the very box that I had been dipping into myself yesterday afternoon while lying in bed. My body weakened as my fears were confirmed. Unless Buffy had shaved her tail and gotten smaller, there was no mistaking this: it was a rat. A huge, beady eyed, Cheerio-pilfering rat. This is what Kim had dangling from her finger and could barely shake off.

We had occasionally seen rats around a nearby stream and in our backyard on the rare occasions that it flooded, but never this close to our house. I didn't know why Kim blamed it on Buffy—probably because she was playing with the rat and didn't want to get it into trouble. I didn't know what to do now. What if the rat had rabies? What if Kim started foaming from the mouth? What if Kim then bit me? The whole situation was too much for me to handle without parents. I was totally unprepared for these possible scenarios. When I signed on for being "in charge," the terms—at least the terms as I understood them—involved resolving disputes, making sandwiches, and possibly cleaning up a skinned knee. Disposing of potentially rabid, garbage-dwelling rats that bite people was not on that list. This would have to wait until my parents returned. The rat wasn't going anywhere, since it was trapped in the can, and it certainly wasn't going to starve to death. I kept an eye on Kim's finger and, most important, on the corners of her mouth.

When my parents returned home, my father made a few phone calls. We were all gathered in the living room when he emerged and promptly declared:

"The rat's head will have to be sent to a laboratory in New Haven." He said this in a very matter-of-fact way, almost as though we should have assumed this would be the answer. It turned out that he had been on the phone with Disease Control.

"They just want the rat's head?" I asked, disgusted.

"Yes," he said. "From that they can determine whether or not it has rabies."

"Well, who's gonna cut off the rat's head?" I asked nervously. Were there little rat guillotines somewhere, or a man in a hood with a tiny ax? Because I was certainly not holding any rat down so that someone could cut its head off. Aside from being disgusting and inhumane, there was no way my stomach could handle it. This is where my parents' skills as responsible overseers came into play. My father would off the rat in the most humane way that he knew: he would drown it by sliding the garbage can with rat together with another garbage can and then feeding a hose between the two. This would fill the chamber with water and drown Buffy the rat.

We all felt bad for the rat, and my mother, who could find the positive side to any situation, said, "Well, at least the garbage can got a good cleaning." My father then packed the lifeless rat, in its entirety, in dry ice and shipped it overnight to the lab. I was just grateful that it wasn't Buffy the dog that had to be drowned. Packing her in dry ice would have been a huge undertaking. A few days later, we were notified that the test results came back negative. Great news! We could finally stop treating Kim like a leper, untie her, and let her out of her room.

This episode with the rat was only one of the many reasons that I always felt fortunate having the parents that I had. I had complete confidence that whatever unpleasantness had occurred while they were out, they would always return and fix the problem. I looked up to them, trusted them, and learned so much about drowning rats from them. It was for all these reasons that during the weeks after Susan and I had officially decided to start thinking about trying to have a child, I was haunted by my own substantial fears of inadequacy. Could I live up to the example that my parents set? Could I be as good as a father as my father was to me? Would I have his patience and compassion? Would I have my mother's optimism? Did I have what it took to raise a child? Did I know how to drown a rat in a garbage can? These were the kinds of large, weighty questions I would have to answer if I was going to make becoming a parent a reality.

At the time I was born, my father, Emmett, was attending Saint Louis University during the day and working odd jobs at night. Like many other students, my parents lived in a low-income housing project on Seventh Street, with my brother Mike, my two-year-old sister Sharon, and me. Several months after I was born, my father graduated, and soon thereafter we moved to Bridgeport, Connecticut, with my mother, my siblings, and me taking the train and my father following behind with all of our possessions in his battered 1941 Chevrolet Fleetline sedan.

The youngest of ten children, my father's father came to America from Ireland, through Ellis Island, and soon thereafter met his wife, whose parents were also from Ireland. They married and settled in the Bronx. Like other people from the Bronx in his age group, he is extremely fond of and nostalgic about his hometown. To this day, if he meets someone who is also from the Bronx, he will invariably spend hours reminiscing with him or her about it. In fact, whenever he meets anyone, his first question is "Where are you from?"—always hoping they'll say "The Bronx." I remember we were in England once and he was talking to a bobby, which is a British policeman. I'm sure my father asked the man where he was from, hoping it was the Bronx, even though all signs, including his accent and British police uniform, indicated that he was originally from England.

With such a clear notion of what makes a good hometown, it's ironic that he decided to move us to Bridgeport, a place that was and still is the object of jokes and ridicule rather than nostalgia. There wasn't much about Bridgeport worth writing home about, especially if your home was Bridgeport. There was no shared camaraderie or sense of belonging with the other residents because you lived in the same place. I always dreamed of living somewhere out of a Frank Capra film—with maybe a gazebo in the little town square, bands playing on warm summer nights, cake sales, people necking in cars during Fourth of July fireworks and not getting anyone pregnant, families picnicking—perhaps somewhere in Minnesota or Michigan. In Bridgeport there was no gazebo and no town square, just a homeless shelter off the interstate.

Some people claim that there is nothing to do in Bridgeport, but that is not true. There are lots of things to do there: you can go to New York City, you can go to Boston, Providence—see, there's plenty to do in Bridgeport. In the years since I left, my hometown hasn't fared much better. A few years back the city nearly filed for bankruptcy, and at least one of its past mayors is currently serving time for corruption. My family and most of my friends have moved away from there, and it had nothing to do with a witness protection program. Until recently I hadn't been back. I returned to visit a few old friends and see if it really was true that you can't go home again. At JFK Airport, in New York, I rented a car that had a GPS navigational system in it. All I had to do was type in where I wanted to go, and a computer voice would tell me how to get there. I typed in *Bridgeport*, and the voice responded indignantly, "Why do you want to go to Bridgeport?" It was the first time I ever had to argue with a navigational system. We went back and forth for a bit, and finally it said, "I'll take you as far as Fairfield, but you're on your own after that."

Nevertheless, Bridgeport was where my father began his thirty-seven-year career as an aeronautical engineer at a helicopter company called Sikorsky Aircraft. We had left behind the Saint Louis arch, the gateway to the West, and replaced it with the golden arches of McDonald's, the gateway to obesity. It seemed like there was a McDonald's on every street corner in Connecticut. Within six years, my father had moved up the ladder at his company, and his job took us all to Germany. We lived in the suburbs of the beautiful, historical, and romantic town of Heidelberg, known for its large university and the remains of a castle perched high on the hillside above it. The only arches here were the ancient stone arches that held up the bridge over the Neckar River, which ran through the center of town.

My father worked as a consultant for our first year overseas. Sikorsky had a contract with what my father called a "German outfit"—and by a German outfit, he did not mean lederhosen. He was referring to a German helicopter company. By the way, my father still uses a lot of expressions from his generation, which certainly date him:

- "I have a bum leg." (My leg doesn't work.)
- "The stereo is on the fritz." (It's broken.)
- "Let me spell you." (Relieve you.)
- "Hold on . . ." (Wait a minute.)
- "Deep-six that!" (Get rid of it.)
- "On the lam." (Running from the police.)
- "Top drawer." (The best.)
- "Ham n' Egger." (Someone who is second rate.)
- "Out of the loop." (Clueless.)

A year later, under contract to the U.S. Department of Defense, my father became an aviation action officer and was assigned to the logistic division of the U.S. Army. He wasn't in the military, as most Americans that lived in Germany were, but he was "on loan" to the army and held the civilian rank of a colonel. The only difference was, he didn't get to wear a uniform with shiny, colorful medals, and nobody saluted him. It was like he was an undercover colonel. That was all fine and well, unless a war broke out. It would then be my father, the only one running around on the battlefield with a jacket and tie, shouting out commands.

Often there were evenings my father would bring non-English-speaking German coworkers over for dinner unannounced, which posed something of a problem to our non-German-speaking family. Most families would have just accepted the language barrier and moved on in silence. They would have chewed awkwardly and smiled; swallowing would have been the loudest noise in the room. But this was not how it was done at our house. Instead we relied on alternative means of communication, which usually involved sentences punctuated with trips to the English-Deutsch dictionary and elaborate games of charades complete with arm waving, walking around, and head bobbing. As a result, these dinners frequently spanned entire weekends, as each side attempted to act out a conversation. My mother would stand there in front of everyone, contorting herself and intricately miming out the plots to whatever book she was reading, while my father would try to avoid interrupting her with his own frantic movements. By the end, the coworkers would feel so comfortable around our family, they would occasionally even visit when my father wasn't there, although I never did understand why they started bringing their families, showing up with friends, and offering to pay to see my mom act out a bullfighting scene from *The Sun Also Rises*.

My father was and still is very bright. He has an amazing analytical mind. Growing up, I helped him repair and build projects around the house. As an aeronautical engineer, he taught me that if you're going to build or fix something, do it right; employ correct angles, work on level surfaces, and utilize glue and clamps to their fullest. Everything was absolutely level in our house. My father had perfect posture because one Christmas my mother gave him the ideal gift: a belt buckle that was also a level.

When my parents went to a swap meet, my mother would naturally be interested in the merchandise for sale in the booth, but my father would be interested in how the booth was constructed. He would analyze the material, the support beams, and the type of rope and knots used to tie it down. If one of us slipped on the pavement, he would console us, and then inspect the soles of our shoes. Running his fingers over the bottoms, he would make statements like, "Yeah, Kev—there's not much grip on these babies. These aren't really designed for this type of terrain."

Unfortunately, Dad seldom had the right tools to do the job around our house because my brothers and I would always forget to put them back where they belonged. More often than not we didn't forget, we just didn't feel like it. I watched as my father built or repaired projects by improvising tools and rigging. He taught me that you don't always need the *right* tools to get the *right* results. His philosophy was quite basic. For example:

1. The side of a plumber's wrench can be used as a hammer.

2. A yard is never too small to cut the grass with a sit-down tractor mower.

3. Fixing something "for now" means that it is as fixed as it's going to get with tape. There will be no more fixing until it falls apart again. At that time, its status can be reassessed and inevitably fixed "for now" again.

4. You don't really have to know how to whistle to get drivers to slow down as they speed past your house. Just put two fingers in your mouth and blow hard. It will have the intensity of a whistle except for the noise. Follow that immediately by yelling, "Hey, slow down!"

5. You should take your time in life, especially when photographing someone while the sun is glaring in their eyes.

6. A good nap in the afternoon gives you more energy for another nap later in the day.

7. If, during a slide show, a slide is in the projector sideways

or upside down, you can correct it by turning the entire projector on its side or upside down.

8. There is no limit to the amount of items that can be strapped to the roof of your car, providing you use the correct slipknots.

9. There is no food that doesn't taste better cooked in brown sugar.

10. Milk is always much more refreshing in a glass full of ice cubes with a large splash of root beer. Also, it's not a bad idea to keep the used glass in the freezer for future use.

11. A nice big bowl or two of ice cream at night, right before bed, just hits the spot.

My father knows how everything works, and why it works. He knows stuff like why the qualities of nitrogen make it capable of combusting. He knows how to cut wood molding at a 45-degree angle. He knows what fulcrums are and why they're important. He knows how to jack up the foundation of a house and how to repair a furnace. These are just the tip of the iceberg. Oh, and he knows how icebergs are formed.

Thinking about this list, I was consumed by the idea that I would never be able to be as good a model for my child as my dad was for me. I feared that I would never possess as many pockets of wisdom and mostly useful information. It wasn't that I didn't know anything. The problem was that I knew a lot of things . . . but nothing about them. Would our child grow up having no clue? I just didn't know how a lot of things worked. I asked myself questions like, How does a car engine work? How does the lightbulb work? Why does it take a different number of people to screw one in, depending on where they are from and what they do for a living? What will I tell my child when he or she asks?

Here are just a few other things I didn't have answers for:

1. Who invented the patent, and did he/she get credit for it?
2. Does a fishing village have to be near water to be successful?
3. If someone sneezes into my orange juice, does the vitamin C neutralize the germs, making it okay for me to drink?
4. If Batman becomes a victim of identity theft, does it screw up Bruce Wayne's credit?
5. How do we know Chinatown isn't developing a nuclear weapon?
6. Can you get a spray-on tan look from the sun?
7. Do you look like a cheapskate if you use leftover Christmas stamps on your summer mail?
8. Why do some people get their stomach stapled? What if you wanted to just lose a little weight? Could you paper-clip your stomach? And what if your eyes are bigger than your stomach? Would it be better to staple your eyes?
9. When a girl gives you her mobile phone number, does that mean she lives in a mobile home?
10. Do babies that are breast-feeding from anorexic mothers have to watch for bones?

As I discussed these fears with people, many told me that I would be a great father, and after hearing them out, I did come to believe that if paternal skill were judged solely on the basis of how well you could distract your baby and get it to stop crying, then I would be right up there with the best. Over the years, I have learned how to make lots of different noises using my mouth, and I know several silly magic tricks. But as I continued to think about it, my lack of paternal preparedness felt glaringly obvious. Being a good distraction is only one of the factors that people usually take into account when they think of what constitutes a "good" father, and I wasn't so sure that I had many of the others.

I lacked the ability to have the answer for every question possible, or in lieu of the actual answer, a very carefully worded disguise to hide my ignorance. Everyone knows that making up answers to hide ignorance is one of the essential tasks of fatherhood. You can never make it seem like your kids might know more than you do—at least until they're a bit older, like forty. A friend of mine was walking in the yard with his six-year-old child one night, and the child looked up to the moon and said, "Look, Daddy. The moon." His father quickly answered, "Yes, Jonas, I know." He was the father that had to always be right. One time, when we were all having dinner at a restaurant, his son told him he had a piece of food on his face. He said, "I know. It's there for a reason." His son didn't tell him the reason was that the piece of food came from another diner at a nearby table. I guess it's just important for some fathers to come across as know-it-alls.

As useful as my father's knowledge of obscure power tools was, my lack thereof was only responsible for half of my prepregnancy anxiety. The other half came from my mother, who remains to this day one of the most understanding and accommodating people that I have ever met. Unlike my father, she was an only child growing up, and because of this, you'd think that everything would have to be her way, but nothing could have been further from the truth. Her laid-back nature was one of her greatest traits, and no matter what happened, she was capable of dealing with change.

Somehow I think that this flexibility trait skipped a generation, because it did not find its way into my veins. I didn't mind change, and I was okay dealing with it as long as it wasn't long-lasting change or monumental. I was okay with, say, a season changing, but having a child seemed like it would be a little more permanent. The more I thought about it, the more I realized I was never going to be as easygoing with children as my mother was with all of us. I would probably always be running after my kid, trying to catch him/her from falling like a baseball catcher scrambling after a high foul ball.

In hindsight it amazes me that my mother stayed so flexible, with all the traveling and upheaval in our lives. After four years in Germany, my family returned to the United States and settled back into our life in Bridgeport. We were back on the mother ship now, but we were in a different house and in a different time. My father had actually designed our house himself, and had it built by moonlighting firemen. I've been through enough home renovations of my own now to doubt the ability of full-time workers to get the job done—forget about moonlighting anything. Though we lived in a pretty average middle-class neighborhood, our time in Europe had clearly influenced my father's architectural plans. Driving through the neighborhood, there was little doubt as to which house belonged to us—ranch house, ranch house, ranch house, Swiss chalet, ranch house, ranch house, and ranch house. Most people would have balked at living in a ski lodge, but my mother liked it. Nothing ever seemed to phase her. Moonlighting fireman? Living in Germany? Not a problem. Clearly she would have been a great First Lady.

My mother spent her childhood living in several small New England towns over a period of a dozen years, and all that moving probably contributed to her flexible character and prepared her for life with my father. She and her parents finally settled in Kittery, which is the oldest town in the state of Maine. In fact, the early pioneers had also actually settled there because of its proximity to the advantageous inlets and outlet stores. It also probably contributed to how my mother emerged from her youth with such an optimistic disposition—always able to look at the positive side. "Yes, she did get whiplash, but at least the neck brace makes her look taller," she'd say. "That was terrible about the fires in California, but at least the smoke will make the sunsets spectacular."

Up until a trip I took a few years ago, I knew very little about my mother's heritage. Though I knew quite a bit about my ancestors on my father's side of the family, my mother's side remained something of a mystery. Because she was such a good sport, she would always go along with celebrating my father's Irish heritage with the rest of us, but never promoted her own background in the same way (Irish families have a way of dominating a room like that). To pay respect to my mother's ancestors and hopefully collect a little information about them, I found myself traveling to Isleboro, a charming small island off the coast of Maine. Armed with some information my mother gave me, combined with some of my own superficial research, I discovered that my mother's great-great-great-great-grandfather, Elihu Hewes, had been killed in a shipwreck off the coast of New England, and he and the rest of his family had supposedly been buried on the island. During the ferry ride to the island, I spoke with the ferry master, who suggested I look up a minister who lived there who would probably know of any old Protestant graveyards on this end of the island.

Unannounced, I showed up on the minister's doorstep; since he still had a doorstep, I could only assume he was totally confident that he had no children. When he answered the front door, he had a white napkin tucked into his shirt, and was still chewing a mouthful of food from his interrupted dinner.

"Can I help you?" he asked in between swallows in his best Pepperidge Farm accent.

"We're sorry for interrupting your dinner," I said, and then told him, "I'm searching for my mother's relatives."

"Are they lost?" he asked, concerned.

"No," I said. "Worse. They're dead. Been dead for over two hundred years."

The minister thought for a few seconds and then told us he did, in fact, know of a very old Protestant cemetery on the island, and would be happy to drive us there. The minister drove about ten minutes down a paved road and then made a left onto a small two-lane dirt road. The farther we traveled on this road, the narrower and grassier it became, until finally it ended, and we were in the woods. The minister stopped the car and said, "Should be right around here." Surely he must be mistaken, I thought. All we could see were trees. As is often the case, we soon learned, cemeteries that are ignored and neglected for many years become overgrown with weeds and then eventually trees . . . and in some cases housing developments, where one of the houses becomes haunted because someone later learns it was built over an old cemetery.

If you didn't know there was a cemetery here, you would have walked right past it. As we pushed back some of the high grass and shrubs, we discovered a very few small, old, and weathered grave markers. Some were tilted at an angle, and others lay on their side, no longer able to withstand the harsh New England winters. The past three hundred years of wind, rain, and snow had eroded the tombstones, making it almost impossible to read any inscriptions. We shuffled through the leaves and bushes, uncovering several other fallen tombstones, still unable to find any Heweses.

Just as we thought we had exhausted our search, a loud crow, perched high above in the tree, crowed. As we looked up, we saw an eerie image; over the years, some of the tombstones had been picked up by the roots of the growing trees and were now embedded in the branches and trunks, fifty feet above us. Suffice it to say, we were not about to climb the trees looking for the Heweses; we were only grateful that the trees and roots had left their remains in the ground. We thanked the minister for his time and returned to catch the last ferry back to the mainland, deciding instead to wait until a house is inadvertently built on the cemetery and it becomes haunted by Captain Elihu Hewes, so that we can return to meet him personally.

On the ferry ride back to dry land, I thought that there were worse places to be buried than that cemetery. For some people, the thought of being stranded in a tree for all eternity with their family is pretty unappealing, but I kind of liked the concept. I'm sure a family of tree huggers especially wouldn't mind.

The more I thought about it, the more I realized that I really didn't like the thought of being buried alone. If I was going to have a family of my own, I'd want it to be the kind of family I wouldn't mind being forever buried next to—a family like mine. My family has always been incredibly close, but it wasn't until we returned from Germany that I realized we were unique in this regard. I always assumed that, like us, all American families enjoyed spending time with each other. Boy, was I wrong. That impression changed when we moved back, and I made some American friends. I would go over to a friend's house on the weekend, and after a day spent playing Mousetrap, I would get the chance to see how the family acted around one another. I was surprised to find that some parents had very little interest in their children and could go what seemed to be days without seeing them. It was like being part of a Charlie Brown television special where you never see the parents or other adults. I soon recognized that some parents got into actual yelling fights, not just charade fights. They screamed at each other and got into long, drawn-out arguments; most shocking was when some of them actually divorced.

Sometimes the parents would also scream at their kids, which was always an awkward moment to be your friend's guest. You'd be sitting there, huddled over a board game, when all of sudden your friend's parent would burst into the room to yell at him for some minuscule problem like mispairing his socks. After a few moments of protest from your friend, he would inevitably disappear into the other room to pair his socks correctly, while you would sit there playing with some plastic piece, feeling guilty because your punishments never seemed to come at such a loud volume. Then there were also the parents who I *thought* were yelling at their kids, but I later learned weren't. What appeared to be abrasive lashings merely turned out to be their normal Italian nature of expressing themselves, and there was no anger or disciplining attached to it at all.

"Billy? Where the hell were you?" my friend's father would yell.

"I was sittin' out in the car, Dad!" Billy would yell back.

"Well, get in the house before I smack you in the head," his father would yell.

"Yeah, yeah, okay, Dad!"

This was the way they always communicated.

Of course, I got in plenty of trouble growing up, but my parents always seemed to deal with my poor choices well. I can remember crossing the line at times and hearing my mother warn me, "Wait until your father gets home!" Saying that was basically like reading me my Miranda rights. I would then have to wait and worry all day about the punishment I would receive from my father when he got home from work. What would he say? What would I lose? There were so many things to take away, but ultimately, it was almost always the same thing: I would lose precious TV-watching time. Still, the uncertainty of the whole thing was enough to make me learn that I had done something wrong.

Would I be able to discipline my child as effectively? Would I be able to punish him with as much love and care as my parents? Would she still love being around me once I had taken away her chance to watch *Family Guy*? As my fears of parental inadequacy continued to stunt my thoughts on raising a child, I came to the conclusion that at a certain point, the drive to continue my bloodline would have to play a role. Several years ago my parents, my siblings, their spouses, and I went to Ireland to celebrate my parents' fiftieth wedding anniversary. Like many other Americans with primarily Irish roots, we searched for my father's ancestors' home. We eventually found it in an old farm town in county Clare called Feakle. The town name is pronounced the same as *fecal,* as in "fecal matter," but is spelled differently. Unfortunately, they both smell the same.

We weren't sure of the exact address, but after stopping in a pub and grilling some of the longtime locals, we gathered some useful information. They told us exactly where they thought it was. Our ancestors' home was situated on the edge of a field, they said, not more than three kilometers down the road from where we had stopped. We all suddenly became ecstatic at the prospect of knowing that we would soon be standing before our ancestors' home. After driving for another hour or so, following the directions the locals had written, we were still at a loss. We had passed old stone walls, an old dilapidated stable, a small stone church, and several small towns. We backtracked again, past the stone walls, the dilapidated stable, and the small stone church. But nothing seemed right.

After revisiting the locals at the pub, we realized that we had passed our ancestors' home several times, not knowing it. It was the old, dilapidated stable. I think we had something a bit grander in mind for our ancestors' home. We were thinking more along the lines of a traditional Irish thatched-roof cottage with flower boxes than the ramshackle ruins that we were now standing before. Seeing as how our ancestors hadn't lived there for quite some time, though, perhaps those expectations were a bit unreasonable. It had been painted white, and half of its rusty, corrugated tin roof was missing. Several cows wandered through it, while a goat stood on a nearby stone wall. At one end of the home, what once served as the living room was now filled with manure. Under the wild ivy that had engulfed half of the structure, my father surveyed the rotting beams and cross-joints, probably determining what would be needed to repair the roof. It didn't matter that no one would be living there; he just felt the need to fix it.

Somewhere over the years it had become a stable, and now it was an abandoned stable. I was thinking to myself, This is probably the structure they send all annoying American tourists to who are looking for their ancestors' home. If we looked inside, we probably would have found a guest book to sign. We were all a little disappointed, but still took pride in knowing that this was where our distant ancestors had once lived. Perhaps some of the animals wandering around the pasture were distant relatives of the pets or farm animals that our ancestors once had. As a souvenir, my brothers and I took a few small stones from the stable's foundation back to the States with us. The goat would have been more difficult, so we abandoned that idea. On the flight home I considered the idea of making Ireland an annual trip and each time bringing back more stones from the cottage, until eventually we transported and rebuilt the entire structure in our backyard. But that seemed like a lot of work.

Luckily, rebuilding my distant Irish ancestors' home stone by stone was not the only way to connect with my bloodline. Somehow through all of this debilitating insecurity, I began to recognize that the only way to guarantee my immortality would be for me to pass on my family's DNA to a child—preferably mine. The downside to passing on your DNA, though, is that it could one day be part of an embarrassing scandal or criminal case. With the way DNA technology is emerging, who knows what they'll be able to trace? People will be looking at their family trees and saying things like, "You know, I go all the way back to Brad Pitt and Angelina Jolie." Of course, if they stay on their present course, it seems like millions of people on several continents will be able to say that.

I was coming to see the reality: I was a person who was destined to have a child—it was just part of the big plan of the universe. Regardless of how nervous that fact made me feel, my Irish ancestors, who may or may not have lived in that stable, would have wanted me to reproduce—they would have mandated it, if for no other reason than the Catholic Church would have mandated it. This was how it had been for generations and generations leading up to me. It was up to me now, and I didn't want to drop the ball. How could I let down my distant could-have-been future ancestors? I pictured them running in front of me, reaching back for me to hand the bloodline baton to them. It was my responsibility to show up to that race with that baton, and I had been procrastinating for quite a while.

The bottom line was, I'm definitely no Einstein. I'm not even a baby Einstein. In fact, I have always felt intellectually inadequate. I accept that I was not born with my father's analytical mind. My mind can't even process the simplest of problems. I once called Apple tech support to ask how to open the box that my new computer came in. I actually had more fun playing in the box than with the computer. I may not be the brightest bulb in the box, but I know there are a few dimmer than me. Apparently, someone my wife once knew thought Mount Rushmore was created by a natural phenomenon of wind and rain. She honestly believed that over the years the wind and rain just happened to wear down this huge granite mountaintop to look exactly like the presidents. Across the country, however, there are many landmarks that are the results of natural circumstances. For example, in Phoenix, there is Camel Back Mountain, a mountain that, if you use your imagination, could resemble a camel lying down. Another was the Old Man in the Mountain rock formation in the White Mountains of New Hampshire. Looked at from a certain angle, this rock formation resembled an old man looking out across the valley. New Hampshire even has it on their license plates. Unfortunately the old man's face fell off the mountaintop recently, and that *was* the result of years of wind, snow, sleet, and rain. He probably wasn't using a good moisturizer.

In high school I was presumptuous enough to apply to Harvard, even though my combined SAT scores were equal to the fever I must have had when I thought Harvard might accept me. In fact, the morning I sent it off, I saw the mailman use it as a pooper-scooper. It's not that I wasn't smart. I was just more interested in hanging out with my buddies than studying. Why study when I could fake a good grade (i.e., cheat) or coax my genius sister, Sharon, into doing my homework? I even created absurd ways of cheating—like the time I glued two little pieces of mirror to the inside corners of my glasses so I could see behind me. Unfortunately it didn't work. I had to seriously strain my eyes, and even then, all I could see was the hair on the side of my head, which, of course, provided no answers.

For some reason, Harvard wasn't convinced I was smart. Instead I was accepted at a small college in Connecticut not far from where I grew up. Noted for their intramural sports and afternoon table tennis in the student lounge, this school at the time was a lot like a community college but without the academic pressure. In fact, it put about as much pressure on its students as the showerheads at a downtown YMCA. I was happy to hear recently that it has grown in leaps and bounds since I attended, and is now a very fine and respectable institution. I am proud to be an alumnus, but that still doesn't get me to the point where I can effectively raise a child and impart various wisdoms about the ineffective nature of wood glue or the proper way to retile a floor.

So I don't have my father's knowledge or my mother's flexibility. So what? Most people go to therapy because of bad parenting, while it seemed more and more that I would go because of good parenting. The whole thing was ludicrous, and Susan told me so. Just because I didn't have the knowledge of my father and the patience of my mother didn't mean that I would be a bad parent. I would be able to teach my future child a few other things that I'd picked up during the course of my fifty-three years—like how to attach a colostomy bag, how to build a wheelchair ramp, and how to get cheaper prescription medicine from Canada. At fifty-three, I'd be much older than my parents were when they first started having kids. I wasn't entirely sure what that would add to the situation, but it had to help on some level. Perhaps in those extra years I might have learned things subconsciously that I didn't even realize would be useful.

I didn't have all the answers, and I probably never would, but that didn't stop Britney Spears from procreating, so why should it stop me? I mean, seriously, how hard could it be? Besides, when anything else that I needed to know did come up, there was always Google. As it turns out, my father is still "out of the loop" when it comes to that.

THREE

Relationship Protection Program

Two years into my first marriage, my wife, decided that she didn't want children after all. With this announcement came a decorating change in our house. I had a sweet photo hanging in our hallway of a one-year-old boy at the beach, fast asleep on the back of his snoozing father. From the style of the father's bathing suit, it appeared to have been taken in the 1960s. It gave me such a feeling of contentment, reminding me of the closeness I shared with my father growing up and the possibility of being a father myself. One day, not wanting to promote or encourage this possibility, my then-wife asked if she could remove the photo. The photo was eventually replaced with a print by the talented artist Sue Coe. Miss Coe is known for her stark renditions of animal brutality, among other social commentary. This black-and-white print depicted farm animals running for their lives as nuclear explosions and human chaos erupted in the distance. The swap was a premonition of things to come.

Of course, I felt it was her right, as a woman, to change her mind and not have a baby. I didn't feel as though I should be trying to talk her into something that she really didn't want to do or might resent later. Since she knew that I had wanted children, respectfully, she gave me the option of leaving. Much to her relief, I didn't. I believed that I was with her out of love and not for the sole purpose of having a baby. Without kids she would have plenty of time to immerse herself in her real passion, animal rights activism. Fur was one of her biggest targets, for which she took up a practice that I called stickering.

Stickering took place in the winter, most frequently in New York City, since it rarely gets cold enough for people in L.A. to rationalize wearing fur (though, surprisingly, some still do). Here's how it worked: she would be walking down a busy street and would spot someone—usually a woman—wearing a fur coat. Picking up her pace until she was dangling on the woman's heels, she would furtively glance around before gingerly applying a harmless sticker to the back of the woman's fur that read in bold letters I'M AN ASSHOLE. I WEAR FUR. She would then turn to me with a devilish grin: mission accomplished. There was always the risk that the person in the coat would feel the passing brush and react, and her technique reflected this ever-present risk. In early December things might be a bit rough, coming off the fur off-season, but by Christmas she typically had her delivery down. A bug landing would have applied more pressure. It didn't matter if the person was in the middle of a pack and surrounded on all sides by pedestrians. These were more like challenges than actual impediments. She would expertly weave and maneuver her way through any crowd, evading steps and treading lightly on the balls of her feet—an elaborate ballet in the name of fur.

Each time a fur coat passed us or appeared in front of us, I cringed because I knew it was destined to be stickered. It wasn't that I didn't agree with the sticker's message, it was that I felt she was at times shoddy and hasty with her stickering. Oh, sure, her technique was fine from an application standpoint, and January to March she was lights-out, but her weakness was occasionally not doing the homework to figure out just how many people were in the fur wearer's group.

"Someone from that person's group could be behind us and witness you doing that. We could be caught! Then what?" I would say.

"Then," she said, "I would explain to them why they are insensitive and ignorant for wearing fur. I would tell them how, in order to make the coat she is wearing, little, innocent animals are caught in steel-jaw traps or anally electrocuted." How could I argue with that?

She kept a roll of stickers on her person at all times. One never knew when a fur encounter would occur, or how many of them would be out and about, so she was always prepared. As you can imagine, the tricky sticker application process and the sheer number of furs in New York made punctuality a thing of the past. We could be walking down the street with bags of groceries in our arms, but if she saw a rotund woman in ankle-length chinchilla, all bets were off. We lost many boxes of Tofutti Cuties that way. (Tofutti Cuties taste like ice cream sandwiches, only made with frozen soy instead of ice cream. Actually, they are quite delicious!)

Although I didn't always agree with her daring methods, I admired her passion and dedication in bringing about change and raising awareness in the animal rights movement—and still do. Over the years that we were married and even in recent years, she has changed many people's opinions on animal issues and has saved countless animals.

From the time that she made her decision not to have kids, I accepted that I would probably never be a father. When I was younger, I thought by the age of twenty-four I'd have the white-picket-fence thing and children, but instead I was now thirty-seven with a retaining-wall thing and four cats. Instead of pushing a stroller down the street, I was leading the Fur-Free Friday march on Sixth Avenue. Instead of extra pacifiers in my pocket, I had stickers that read I'M AN ASSHOLE. I WEAR FUR.

Needless to say, I didn't have much faith that my bloodlines would be carried on. Now this is fine for some people, but in my case, there was some crazy bug in my head that made me think I'd be a sizzling failure in the chain of life if I didn't procreate. This would be the last stop for my DNA unless you counted the minks we likely saved. I would not live on in this universe in whatever infinitesimal, biophysical way we do when we have off-spring. But still, there was always something inside me telling me that I would not leave this planet without having a child.

Sadly our marriage dissolved after eleven years. By the way, divorce is an incredibly excruciating experience. No, wait a minute, when you talk about divorce, it can't be a "by the way" or even "as an aside," or "as a footnote." It is a heart-wrenching, life-altering, torturous experience. I don't think people who haven't been through it can appreciate all of its grief and anguish. When I told people I was divorced, their reaction was always the same, "Oh, sorry to hear that." And the next question was always this: "Did you have any kids?" And I'd say, "No." And they'd say, "Oh, well, that's good. That makes it easier." Kids or no kids, divorce is still painful, and some people are just not as sensitive as others. Okay, here's an analogy. It's as if you got your legs blown off, and someone said, "Oh, sorry to hear that. Did you have any nice shoes? No? Oh, well, that's good. That makes it easier. You'll be okay. Walk it off."

Marriage is not easy. Sometimes it's just the little things. When I was growing up, my mother taught me to put the toilet seat up so I wouldn't pee on it. When I got married, my wife told me to put it down. Marriage is definitely work. In one of Johnny Carson's monologues, he said a study was done once that showed that married men live 3.7 years longer than single men, but the study also showed that the married men were much more willing to die. I had a friend who went to a marriage counselor with her husband of ten years. Their marriage had been rocky for some time, and the husband was going on and on to the counselor, complaining, "She's crazy! She's impossible to live with! It's all her fault! She's the one ruining this!" The counselor interrupted him and said, "Wait a minute. Listen, I've been in this business for twenty-five years, and it's never been just one person's fault." The husband quickly injected, "I know, it's just my luck, isn't it?" He went on to say that she was greedy and spoiled. He claimed that she would never give him a divorce because she knew if that happened, she would *only* get half of everything.

I always took breakups hard. Even if I had only been in the relationship for six months, when the girl dropped me, I would still be devastated. I would stay in bed and sob most of the day, lose my appetite, and eventually drop about twenty pounds. It would take some time before I got myself back together enough to find another girl who also wasn't right for me: maybe a wonderful woman who was insecure and needed me to rescue her, maybe a jealous one who needed to berate me and accuse me of infidelities every other hour of the day, or maybe just a serial killer who needed some laughs. I was open to any of these potential keepers. One time a girlfriend of mine had an affair during our relationship. I agreed to take her back, but only if she had another affair first with another person, because I didn't want to be the "rebound relationship." Here is another sure sign, aside from an affair, that a relationship is about to end: when you're visiting her family over the holidays, and during the group photo they make you sit at the end of the row. This seating arrangement makes it very easy for them to cut you out of the picture after the breakup. Another definite sign is if they don't let you get in the picture at all.

After my divorce, I had no desire to be involved with anyone. I moved into a beach house about twenty miles south of Los Angeles. My former wife and I had bought this property several years earlier, thinking that one day, after we retired, we would move into it. Well, since we'd retired our marriage, I thought now would be as good a time as any. I hoped that living at the beach would be uplifting and a nice distraction for me.

I soon realized that this beach community was a breeding ground. It seemed like the sidewalks were loaded with breeders or the breeders' nannies, pushing strollers. The bike paths had become stroller paths. Like the ancient grooves from chariot wheels in Rome, the strand's pavement was worn down from stroller wheels. I also noticed that for the most part the breeders were older, and most of them were pushing twins and even sometimes triplets. I can't be sure, but these might be the people that waited until they were in their forties and had solid careers going before deciding to have kids. When couples are in their forties, conceiving becomes more difficult, and some need help from science and technology. Simply put, the procedure often produces twins and sometimes triplets.

Having a recognizable face made it a challenge for me to be discreet. That's okay, though, I thought. I needed some time to "get my head together." There wasn't much privacy, and it would be difficult to go unnoticed, but within a short two months I fell in love with the beach lifestyle. I decided that, from now on, this is where my home would be. The house just needed a little TLC, which I figured wouldn't cost too much—just a few little improvements here and there; a fresh coat of paint, some better lighting, and maybe a new window or two. Within a week, I spotted a small pile of tiny, perfectly shaped granules on my windowsill and by the back door. I assumed they were sand particles blown in through the cracks. I tasted them. The granules had no taste at all, just crunchy, tasteless matter—sort of like Grape Nuts, only much tinier and not in a box. I got the DustBuster out and vacuumed them up. Every week they would reappear, and I would vacuum them up again. One day I felt the need to spend more money, so I called Enrico, the interior painter, to get an estimate for slapping on some paint in a few bedrooms. I asked him how he thought those granules of sand were getting into the house. "Through a termite's ass," he said. It was termite excrement. "That's how the termites do it," he told me. They eat through the wood and then poop out these granules—basically, wooden turds. So odd, I thought. It was like they were smuggling drugs into my house by eating them and then pooping them out, once inside. And to think that I actually tasted them! Not only tasted, but I was sprinkling them on my salads and cooking with them.

Something had to be done. If I didn't take action, the termites would eventually pass my entire house through their colons. It would just be a windowsill buried in a large mountain of termite turds. I was told that my house would have to be "tented." This involves fitting a big, unsightly orange-and-green-striped canvas snugly over the entire house. The exterminator then pumps gases in that kill all the insects. After three days, they take the tent off. I suggested that maybe we didn't need to tent the house, since that would draw a lot of attention. After all, I was trying to be discreet. "How do you suggest we do it, then?" he asked sarcastically. Not knowing the business, I suggested that perhaps they could tent each individual termite, so all you would see were a bunch of teeny-tiny tents running around and bumping into the walls. The people outside would never know we had termites. I had seen houses that were tented and always thought, How unfortunate for the owners, and what a spectacle. And then I started wondering, What if a circus tent has termites? Would they tent the tent? How would that work?

After the exterminator explained to me, as if I were a three-year-old, that there was no other way to get rid of the termites than to tent my house, I agreed, but insisted they paint the outside of the tent to look exactly like my house. No one would notice, that way. Then I thought, Better yet, maybe they can paint it to look like a mansion. People would walk by and think, Wow, that guy must be loaded! For an extra fee, the exterminators agreed and painted the canvas to look exactly like my house. The tent was off in three days, and nobody knew the difference.

Now the actual house would need a fresh coat of paint. I found a reputable painter by word of mouth. A local surfer dude who grew up in the area, Steve was in his midforties, had a long, graying ponytail, and still surfed bright and early every day. He came by to give me an estimate and said, "Dude, this is a bitchin' house!" He loved the old charm and said it reminded him of his youth. We settled on a price, and now we just had to settle on a color. "Let me get back to you," I told Steve. I looked through a collection of paint chips supplied by the Sherwin-Williams paint store, small sample squares of colors. I knew I wanted a red door, and for the house, I liked yellow because it was bright, fun, and uplifting—exactly what I needed. I just couldn't decide what shade of yellow. Sherwin-Williams had about a thousand different yellow blends—Break of Day, Decisive Yellow, Daisy, Glisten, Banana Cream, and so on. I guess there's a person whose job is to come up with these names. I would stand in front of the house for hours, holding up the various of yellow paint chips. It was difficult to get an accurate idea of what the entire house would look like in that color, so I had to stand farther back and close one eye as I held out the chip so it blocked out the whole house. This technique gave me an idea of how my house would look if it were just one big Banana Cream yellow chip with no windows or doors. I couldn't decide.

After a week or two of intense soul searching and polling, I made a decision. I ruled out Urine Sunshine, Jaundice Morning, and Toxic Sludge. I narrowed it down to Firefly Glow, Lemon Slice, and Chickadee. The first two yellows were very sedate, safe, and conservative. Chickadee was bolder and more daring. To make my decision easier, Steve painted three larger swatches of the colors, which I taped to the house and stared at for what seemed eternity. In that time babies were born, new homes were built, and wars were fought. On the morning of April 2nd, I made up my mind. It would be Firefly Glow. I had surrendered and would have no regrets. I excitedly called Steve to drive over and take a look. He stood next to me, sizing up the choices. He would close one eye then look back and forth between Firefly Glow and Chickadee.

"I don't know," he said. "That Firefly Glow is pretty soft. After a few years the sun is gonna fade it, and it won't look yellow at all. I like the Chickadee," he continued. "It's a bitchin' beach color. The Chickadee pops!"

"Yeah?" I asked, liking the idea that something about my home would "pop." "You like the Chickadee?" I remembered that Chickadee had not really scored high when I took my poll, but then again, Steve knows his paints, and he knows this town. I hemmed and hawed for a few minutes then agreed to go with the Chickadee. After all, I didn't want a color that didn't pop. Steve rolled up his sleeves and got to work—meaning he brought in his three Mexican painters and then flew off to Costa Rica to go surfing.

After all the prep work, I came home from work one day to

find the house already half painted. I was absolutely horrified at how bright the Chickadee was. It wasn't poppin'—it was exploding. That couldn't be the same paint chip I'd been looking at.

"Wow, that's really yellow, isn't it?" I said to Damian, the head painter. He stood back with me and said, with a combination of what I perceived as shame and empathy, "Si. Eee's jellow . . ." His eyes never met mine.

In a panic, I said, "I wonder if we can soften it up a little?"

"Well, we could," said Damian, "but it would cost a lot of money." His eyes were still averted.

"Okay, never mind," I said. Not wanting to hurt his feelings or my bank account, I smiled and said, "It looks . . . pretty good." In a few days the house was totally covered in bright yellow paint. So much for being discreet—with the house yellow and the door red, it now resembled a day care center or a McDonald's without the golden arches. All it was missing was red playground equipment out front. My discreet house was now a beacon.

One morning, after it was finished, I was standing near the front window when a surfer on his way to the beach ran up to the house with his fluorescent rock-and-roll yellow surfboard. He couldn't see me watching from inside as he leaned his board against the front of the house and stepped back. From the sidewalk, his buddy laughed and said, "Dude, I can't even see your board! It blends right in." The surfer chimed in, saying, "I can understand seven feet of yellow, but I don't know about a whole house!"

I didn't know what to do. Steve was surfing in Costa Rica and wouldn't be back for another two weeks. I started apologizing to my neighbors, assuring them that the yellow would fade in a few years. It was actually so bright that the side of my elderly neighbor's brown house looked yellow from the reflection. He said he didn't mind the color. In fact, he loved how bold it was and thought the neighborhood needed a little color. "The old fogies around here, including me, need some pizzazz. Besides," he said, "it will be much easier now to explain to everyone where I live." From inside I could see people stopping in front of the house, pointing and gawking. "Where's the drive-thru?" someone would usually comment. I couldn't hear most of them, but from their reaction it was easy for me to read their lips. "Oh, my God! That's awful! I can't believe it!" Then they would walk away, shaking their heads as if someone had just peed on the statue of David. So much for being discreet.

It was in this state—divorced and living alone in a bright yellow house—that I first started to revisit the idea of having children. The problem with meeting someone my age was that they are usually set in their ways. I needed to meet a woman that was set in *my* ways. If that meant going a little younger, then so be it. Nobody likes to get back into the dating scene again, and I was no exception. It's difficult meeting people. When I was working on the road quite a bit, doing stand-up comedy, I found it easy to start conversations with waitresses. It was easy because their job requires them to converse with you—even if it is only about food. I found it much more difficult to strike up a conversation with a woman who was not a waitress. The problem is, you can't just walk up to an attractive woman on the street and say, "Hi. What's your special today?" And if she answers you, then she's probably a prostitute.

I was never very good at approaching women, anyway. I was always so intimidated. It was especially difficult and torturous in high school. I was normally attracted to the classic bad girls—the girls who wore the black leather jackets and would hang out at the corner after school. They all smoked and wore heavy black eyeliner and the hem of their plaid dresses was an inch or two higher than what their Catholic high school deemed appropriate.

Nowadays, the bad girls would all probably have DUIs and be wearing those electronic ankle-monitoring devices. To me, these devices represent modern-day stockades; not only a form of public humiliation but also a way for the authorities to keep an eye on you. (Incidentally, at the rate people are getting these ankle monitors, I'm sure it won't be long before there are all types of accessories available to adorn them.) This was not, mind you, the type of girl that I eventually wanted to settle down with. These were just the girls, from a nearby school, that sparked my interest. But the girl that I wanted to spend the rest of my life with I did meet in high school.

St. Joseph's was an all-boys Catholic high school that I transferred to in my junior year. I couldn't have been more uninterested—that is, until I learned that it would soon be going co-ed. All of a sudden there were teenage girls everywhere, in knee-high plaid skirts and eye shadow; you can only imagine how this could renew my interest in learning.

Actually, the only thing I was interested in learning was the identity of this amazingly cute girl in Homeroom 208. Her name was Roxanne Bellwood, and she was the only reason I went to school. She was the only reason that I wanted to exist. She wasn't one of those bad girls, but the girl that I dreamed of settling down with one day. She was also a junior and absolutely, hands down, the most stunning girl I had ever seen. (At the time I didn't know that teachers were an option.) Every morning, on my way to my locker, I would purposely walk by her homeroom just to get a glimpse of her sitting in the last seat in row two. The standard-issue plaid dress with knee socks and saddle shoes was the perfect icing on the cake. On an occasional magical moment I might see her again during the day, walking past me in the hall or coming down the stairs the other way. I could never make eye contact with her—it was just too intimidating.

After school she was usually met by her older, out of high school mechanic boyfriend. Roxanne had a few different boyfriends over the next two years. They always had the hot, souped-up cars with loud mufflers. (I think they called it a "Hemi" or something.) I would attend our high school dances in the school gym just to catch another glance of her. I couldn't have been shyer. I would stand near the back of the gym pretending to listen to the live band playing Cream's "Sunshine of Your Love" or "White Room," but really I was watching Roxanne dance and mingle with her cheerleader girlfriends. I know it sounds like stalker material, but it was really just my falling head over heels for this stunning girl and being so unbelievably scared to talk to her that I hid in the corner instead. I looked forward to our school's basketball and football games, if only to have the opportunity to watch her from the stands, cheering along the sidelines. I don't know why I was so intimidated by her.

There was no way I could impress this girl. I didn't have a hot, souped-up car; in fact, most of the time my mother dropped me off right in front of the school in our 1967 Dodge with the automatic push-button transmission on the dashboard. Sadly, things didn't get any better after I bought my first car during my senior year of high school. It was a used '65 Chevelle Malibu, with the three-speed manual stick shift on the column. Occasionally the gears would jam, and I would have to drive for weeks in only second gear. Since I knew nothing about automotive mechanics, the most I could "soup it up" was by painting the gas tank white. I had seen white gas tanks on some of those cars that had been jacked up in the rear. I guess I hoped that Roxanne would see me pulling into the parking lot and notice the white gas tank. The truth is, since my car wasn't jacked up in the rear, the only way she would have seen it is if I had accidentally run her over. I imagined that she would be lying on the ground, faceup and in shock. As she watched the bottom of the car pass over her she would be going through the twelve stages before death—denial, sadness, disbelief, etc.—but then, just as she was about to enter the anger stage, the white gas tank would pass over her. It would snap her out of her shock. It would probably be the last thing she would remember: the cool white gas tank of Kevin Nealon's car. I imagined in her last breath she would say, "If only I had known."

I also tried to improve the interior of the car by painting the drab, faded metallic blue dashboard using a black paint that was supposed to simulate vinyl once it dried. Unfortunately, for me, that wasn't the end result. Instead of getting the vinyl appearance, it looked more like the dashboard had been through a three-alarm fire. It looked totally charred. It's better that she never saw the car. It was an old, rotting piece of metal in desperate need of a new engine. One time I parked in the high school lot and turned off the ignition, but the car's engine kept sputtering and rocking spastically. As I walked into the school, it was still choking out enough toxic exhaust to wipe out a small village. It was like something right out of a Stephen King novel—the eerie blue swamp fog slowly engulfing the entire parking lot. It sputtered long enough for me to walk past Roxanne's homeroom and witness her and several of her cheerleader girlfriends pointing and laughing at it. I prayed that under the cover of the exhaust smoke she hadn't seen me get out of the car.

• • •

After my divorce was finalized, I had a few rather interesting opportunities to have children. Because the Internet had made much of my personal information available, I began receiving fan mail at my home address. The eerie thing is that one of these letters came from a woman who was serving time in prison for throwing acid on her husband. She told me she was a huge fan, wanted to have my baby, and would love to spend the rest of her life with me. She said she would be out in a year. "This is crazy," I thought. "I can't wait a whole year for her!" That's wasted time. After all, I was on the wrong side of forty.

Tempting though it was, this was not the only child-based offer that I had received, so luckily I knew how to turn it down without hurting anyone's feelings. Much earlier in my career, I was approached by an old cigar-chomping character actor/comedian, who will remain unnamed even though he has a name but has since passed on. Here's a little hint that might help you identify him and, if not, will only make you more curious; a lot of baby boomers grew up watching him on a hit TV series. Okay, just for the sake of a name, I will call him Larry.

Back in Larry's heyday, there were no "comedy clubs." Comedians performed their routines on the strip-club circuit. Strippers and prostitutes were no stranger to Larry and his buddies. He befriended me when I was starting out as a stand-up at the Improvisation in Hollywood, and one night many years later he approached me with what he called a "job offer."

"What is it, Larry?" I asked.

He bit off the tip of his cigar and said, "I'll let you know. But just know it'll pay the same as you get for doing your stand-up routine in a club." At the time that was twenty-five dollars. I couldn't imagine what this "job" was. Again, I asked him, "What's the job, Larry?" He put his cigar in his mouth and held a match to the end of it . . . the end that was not in his mouth. As he sucked ferociously on the cigar, the end grew brighter and brighter.

"Ah, what the hell, I'll tell you now," he said. "You know, I married Trudy a few months ago, right?"

"Yeah," I said, and then, lying, I added, "She seems like a great girl, Larry."

It was common knowledge that Trudy was an ex-prostitute that Larry had known and found work for on numerous occasions. She reminded me of a poor man's version of the Mia Farrow character in Woody Allen's *Broadway Danny Rose*. She was probably about thirty-five but looked to be in her early sixties. She wore oversize rose-colored sunglasses to conceal her left eye—or where her eye should have been. Apparently, years earlier, a disgruntled pimp in Memphis had shot out it out, and shortly thereafter she was fitted with a glass eye. You actually couldn't tell it was a fake unless you took her sunglasses off and tapped the eye with the end of a pen. Her pale, pasty skin looked as though she had been floating in water for several days, and if you touched her, her skin would come off on your finger. Her shoulders were hunched over, and the ashen skin of her arms was filled with track marks.

Despite all of this, I guess you could say she looked at the world through rose-colored glasses—but then again, that was only because she was actually wearing rose-colored glasses, not to mention she was only seeing the world with one eye. Obviously, she had lived a difficult life, and now she was being rescued by a washed-up comic. I was happy for both of them. Larry nervously worked his now-soggy cigar to the other side of his mouth and said, "Let's sit down over there in a booth where we can talk more privately." I followed him to the corner booth, away from anyone who thought our business was his business. Larry removed his cigar from his mouth, and spit out a few tiny, wet specks of tobacco leaf.

"Look," he said, "you're a young strapping guy, good sense of humor, come from a good family . . ." He momentarily paused to spit out a few more pieces of tobacco leaf, then continued, "Trudy wants to have a baby, and well, quite frankly, I'm seventy-two years-old. . . . I got nothin." I am paraphrasing here now, but he said all I needed to do was "take a roll in the hay" with her. "You'll have a good time," he added. "She'll also throw in a few extras." By extras, I didn't know if he meant a free pair of sunglasses, a six-pack of Coke, or maybe extras as in "atmosphere people" for films. He said, "When you're finished, I'll give you the twenty-five bucks." He relit his cigar and stuck it back in his mouth, sucking on it like he was giving reverse mouth-to-mouth to a dying wad of cancer.

Naturally, I assumed that he was kidding. He was a comic, after all. I looked at him for a few seconds, waiting for him to laugh and say, "Nah, I'm only joking," but he didn't. He said, "You think about it and let me know." He quickly spat out another tiny speck of tobacco. When our food came, he changed the subject and started talking about the early days. He talked about everything from whores to cheap Scotch to the Jay Leno Reuben sandwich on the menu to how much he loved the coleslaw tonight. When it was time to go home, he slid out of the booth, stood up, and readjusted his pants to get rid of his wedgie.

He said good night and wandered off with what barely resembled a cigar, now held loosely in the center of his mouth. As I went to slide out, I casually looked down at the booth's vinyl bench and noticed the wet-tobacco-specks-and-coleslaw outline of his rear end. I carefully maneuvered myself over this carnage and left. I couldn't believe this proposition. Yes, she was a prostitute with a glass eye and an arm full of track marks, but—didn't I like the bad girls? Wasn't this my chance to be with the ultimate bad girl? The very next night Larry came back into the Improv and made a beeline for me. He bit off the tip of another fresh cigar and asked if I had made a decision about his proposition.

"After carefully weighing the pros and the cons, I have to decline." I said I was very flattered but would feel uncomfortable with it. He understood and once again quickly changed the subject to French whores. In a way I felt bad, because basically what I told him was "You couldn't pay me to have sex with your wife!" And it's not that he couldn't pay me, it's just that I wasn't about to whore myself around like that for only twenty-five bucks. Fifty bucks might have been a different story. I just have too much self-respect.

Larry died several years later from a massive heart attack while performing stand-up at the condominium complex where he lived. I attended his memorial service, and the pews were full of his friends—some young comics, some old comics, some older B-movie actors, and some sitcom actors I had watched on my favorite sitcoms while I was growing up. The last pew, though, was full of seventy-year-old-plus bleached blonde former strippers who probably had names like Bunny, Violet, Dolly, and Trixie. They dressed and carried themselves as if they were still in their twenties. Obviously, they hadn't gotten the memo. Larry seemed to lie peacefully inside the open coffin. I wondered if, when his body eventually decomposed, there would be specks of cigar tobacco and coleslaw outlining where his body had once rested. I felt bad that he had died, but also felt bad that he never had a child. As I returned to my seat, I walked past the rows of mourners. In the front pew, near the aisle, sat Larry's grieving wife, Trudy, a balled-up handkerchief clenched in her hand and a tear rolling from her eye down onto her cheek.

I thought about these offers from the safe confines of my bright yellow house during the months following my divorce. Wasn't there a middle ground that I was missing here?—the vague, gray area between husband-murdering ex-convict and one-eyed prostitute. I really didn't want to miss the boat like Larry had. I wanted a kid before I was dead and laid out in an open casket in front of a bunch of strippers. But the dating scene was incredibly daunting, unless I was willing to settle for someone with fewer than two eyes.

I was in this state of mind when I got a call from my friend John Henson, best known as one of the former hosts of the E! channel show *Talk Soup*. John was asking for a favor, but what I didn't know at the time was that this favor would put me on a path to meeting a beautiful woman who still had both her eyes, a fully operational biological clock, and a fondness for bright yellow houses.

FOUR

The Pumpkin Dance

As a comedian, I've always been asked to do random projects for friends here and there. These friends are usually shooting a short pitch for a network series, and they ask me if I will play a part—for free, of course. Sometimes it is a table read for their movie script, and they will ask if I will read a part—for free. I am always happy to help, since they are my friends and I want them to succeed. Of course I am always hopeful that they will succeed so they can employ me one day—not for free.

The phone call from John Henson was no different. He was putting together a new talk-show pilot, and he wanted to know if I would be a guest in the lineup. When I arrived in the makeup room to get ready for my appearance, I noticed a very cute girl sitting in one of the other makeup chairs. She had thick, curly golden hair, steel blue eyes, skin as smooth as a baby seal, and luscious, full lips, as full as they could be without the help of collagen. I plopped down in the empty makeup chair next to her and met my makeup artist. As I stole another look at the cute girl, she seemed to be miles away, daydreaming. I desperately wanted to know what she was dreaming about and how I could work myself into that dream. Loud enough for the cute girl to hear, I mentioned to my makeup artist that I was thinking loosely about the notion of adopting a child if I was single much longer. I added that you don't hear much about single men adopting, and wondered aloud what the deal was.

After a fair amount of internal debate and shyness on my part, I introduced myself. Her name was Susan Yeagley, and she was an actress, hired to be the comedic fashion correspondent for the pilot. She had already been waiting two hours to perform her segment and was bored to death. The show was running behind, and we both ended up waiting another hour or so before we would go on. In that short amount of time we laughed at each other's jokes, shared show-business nightmares, and generally just enjoyed each other's company. I detected a slight Southern drawl and asked where she was from. "Nashville," she said, with a nostalgic smile. Hoping to cinch the deal, I immediately told her I play the banjo. She laughed at what she perceived as a joke, but I was serious. To cut my losses, I dropped the banjo references right away. Soon after that show, we decided to see each other again. In the end, even though John's talk-show pilot didn't get picked up, she certainly did.

When Susan and I had been dating for a few months, we decided to take our first vacation together. I never had a huge desire to go to Mexico, and I wouldn't have ever suggested that we go there, but I was offered a free trip to Puerto Vallarta. Since I was in a new relationship and I wanted to impress this woman, I jumped at the opportunity. Although I was perfectly healthy, I had long been plagued by the fear that if I went to Mexico, I would somehow have a medical situation and end up in a Mexican hospital emergency room. I had heard plenty of nightmares over the years about Mexican hospitals and how risky they were. I did not want to be that guy on the gurney lying in a dismal, dank emergency room chock-full of flies, mosquitoes, malaria, and malpractice. I didn't want to come back with some exotic form of parasite that baffled American doctors and required me to move a bed into my bathroom. Oh, sure, I had ventured into Mexico before, but never so deep that I couldn't get back to an American hospital if something happened.

Though Susan is somewhat younger than I, I was of the opinion that when you reach a certain age, that gap doesn't matter so much. We left on our trip in . . . I think it was March. Yes, that's right. It was definitely March, because I remember she was on spring break. In all honesty, she was thirty and I was forty-seven, but I still felt the need to prove myself. As I look back, I think I might have overdone it on the trip. I wanted to show Susan that, although I was a little older than her, I was still fit and youthful. So during our week in Mexico, I was running around, playing volleyball, Jet Skiing—took only *short* naps, and did every other activity under the sun, and I do mean under the sun. It was at least one hundred and ten humid degrees, day in and day out. On the next to the last day, I had just completed a round of volleyball and then jumped into the pool with her. I couldn't believe how well suited we were to each other. It was one of those rare relationships where we just connected on both the emotional and intellectual level. I would yell out "Marco!" and without missing a beat she would answer with, "Polo!" I didn't even have to explain the rules to her. She knew the game! God, was I crazy about her. Her timing was impeccable. We hurtled down the water slide, time and time again, laughing and screaming as we wound and turned, finally being projectiled out of Montezuma's mouth like tequila-induced vomit. In the pool, out of the pool—"Let me ride on your back," Susan yelled. I yelled back, "Okay but you have to catch me first!"

After frolicking in the pool for an hour or so, it was time to get out. I have a thing about getting out of a public pool if there's no ladder. You do not want to get out of a public pool flailing around like a sick sea lion trying to get to higher ground. It must be done gracefully, in one fell swoop. The movement goes like this: you propel yourself up from the bottom, grabbing the edge of the pool as you break through the water's surface, using this momentum along with your arms to get your leg up on the deck, which in turn lifts the rest of your carcass out of the water—all the while, keeping your jelly-belly sucked in. And that is exactly what I did. After eight attempts and with the help of the life-guard, I was finally out of the pool.

As I strutted back to my chaise longue with my chest puffed out and my tummy still sucked in, I suddenly felt my heart kick into overdrive. It was beating at least two hundred beats per min-ute. It felt like it was a distant Mexican marching band drum section resonating through my chest. There was no pain, no fatigue, and no shortness of breath. From behind me, I heard Susan yell, "Marco!" I answered immediately with a faint "Polo." She sensed my heart wasn't into it—and that's because my heart was into doing the tango and the rumba and firing off more beats per minute than a fully automatic, military-style M-16 rifle. I guess my pool antics, combined with my physical exertion over the week, had taken its toll. My walk to the chaise longue became as clumsy as a baby colt taking its first steps.

I sat down, took a deep breath, and looked toward Susan. She was walking over to me now, taking big awkward steps to accom-modate her flippers. I didn't know exactly what was going on inside my chest, and I didn't want to panic her. I calmly called to her, "Hey, Suz?" And right then, three gardeners named Jesus (pronounced "Hey-suz") turned to me. I waved them off, saying, "No, not you guys—I'm talking to the girl with the floaties." I calmly told Susan that my heart was beating very rapidly and that maybe I should get some attention just, ya know, out of curiosity, and just to maybe be on the safe side. We immediately went to the hotel doctor, walking softly and slowly as to not have my heart beat any faster and explode like a can of paint left out in the hot sun.

The doctor's office was on the first floor next to the hotel's live animal exhibit. When I entered, he was just finishing up a Big Mac with extra onions. I sat down, and he pulled up his chair in front of me, listening to my heart race through his stethoscope. I started to feel faint, but only from smelling the odd combination of onion breath and nearby llama dung.

"Have you ever experienced this condition before?" he asked with a mouth full.

"No!" I said indignantly.

"You should go lie down somewhere cool," he instructed me. "And if it continues like this, you should go get an EKG." An EKG?

I shuffled back to my hotel room and lay in the cool, dark room for several hours, checking my pulse every twenty seconds. All I could do was just sit back and wait. Susan stood by closely, looking down at me as if I was in a coffin, already dead. Eventually, my rapid heart rate slowed down, but it slowed to an irregular heartbeat: "Bump, bump-bump . . . bump—bumpity, bump—bump." I couldn't tell which was my heartbeat and which were the steel drums down by the pool.

It was not long before we found the hotel doctor again and piled into his little Hugo, which had no air-conditioning and no automatic windows. It did, however, have very warm sheepskin seat covers. Somehow, it felt that nighttime was hotter in Mexico than daytime. He strained to remove the Club from his steering wheel as I struggled to get my long legs into the car. In order to fit in the front seat, I had to assume the cannonball position, as I had done several times earlier that day at the pool. In this particular case, though, it was not as much of a crowd-pleaser. The thirty-minute drive to the emergency room was hell. I felt like we were in a rolling oven. Once again, all I could do was sit back and wait. Susan sat behind me, snorkel and mask in hand, gazing ahead, as if comatose. She was probably thinking, What have I gotten myself into? She stared at the back of my head as if I were now sitting up in a coffin.

We finally pulled up to the emergency room and, surprisingly, it didn't look so bad. It looked like a sterile, small office building that maybe once housed a Gold's Gym. The hotel doctor said that the cardiologist would be waiting for us. He continued by saying that this cardiologist was the number-one heart doctor in the village. For some reason, being the best cardiologist in a village wasn't that reassuring. We walked into the small lobby and were then led to one of the hospital rooms down the hall. Oddly enough, there was a cuckoo clock on the wall. The entrance to the small private room was arch-shaped, and the air-conditioning was humming at a cool 65 degrees. What a pleasant surprise.

Jokingly, I said to the cardiologist, "Are you gonna use those electric shock paddles on me and yell 'stand back' to everyone?" He smiled, slightly. (Perhaps if I'd acted it out in charades I would have gotten a better response.) He then proceeded to hook me up to the EKG machine and stick an IV into my arm. He told me that I would have to stay on both of them overnight so that he might convert my heart back to its normal, stressed rhythm. Susan stayed with me overnight . . . FINALLY! She slept on a mattress on the floor next to my bed all night. Little did I know that I would have to have a medical emergency for her to spend the night.

The next morning, the cardiologist came back to my room,

just as the cuckoo clock went off. He stood in front of the EKG
and assessed the readout.

"How does it look?" I asked optimistically

He turned to me and said halfheartedly, "It deed not work."

"What do we do now?" I fired back.

"Well, you know, you were joking about the electric shock
paddles last night, but ninety percent of the time eet works."

So there I was, with my worst fears being realized. A Mexican
hospital, a village doctor, EKG, electro shock paddles, all great
tools, by the way, to impress a woman seventeen years my junior.
I could imagine her calling her girlfriends back home, "The
old man had a heart attack. Can you believe it? " I hemmed and
hawed over the electro shock paddle treatment and finally called
my doctor back in the United States of America, thinking he was
going to tell me to get out of there as quickly as possible. Instead,
he said, "Well, you might as well do eet down there, because if
you don't you will just have to do eet up here." Obviously, he was
Mexican, too. I couldn't believe it—my nightmare had come true.
I had a medical situation and was stuck in a Mexican hospital.
Meanwhile, Susan sat nervously in the waiting room, distracting
herself by reading the most current *Redbook* magazine that the
hospital had to offer. The issue was from December of 1992, and
she was riveted to the article about Madonna dating Warren
Beatty.

I, reluctantly, agreed to the shock paddles, and for a split
second I could have sworn I saw a look of surprise on the doctor's
face. He promptly called in an anesthesiologist. Within minutes
a small Mexican man in a flannel shirt arrived with what looked
like a tackle box. I wasn't sure if he was going to take me fishing
or hit me over the head with a bottle of tequila. Before I knew
it, I was out like a light. While I was floating in that unconscious,
never-never-land state, I remember feeling two blasts to my chest,

the second one stronger than the first—both separated by the faint echo of a cuckoo clock. When I came to, ten minutes later, the cardiologist was standing over me. By his expression, I ever so slightly detected that he was, once again, astonished that I actually came to. He then studied the EKG readout. I asked again, "How does it look?" He frowned and said, "It deed not work." I said, "What do we do now?" As he packed up his little kit, he said that they would hook me back up to the IV for another ten minutes, and then I should go and catch my plane back to L.A. and have some "history" done there. Unfortunately, American insurance is not accepted in Mexico, so I had to pay for my unsuccessful shock treatment with my credit card. And by the way, it's not a good sign when the cardiologist himself rings up your bill.

On the way to the airport, Susan told me that Warren Beatty and Madonna's age difference was twenty-one years. Upon hearing this news, my erratic steel-drum, mumbo-jumbo heartbeat finally kicked back into its natural rhythm. Susan was seventeen years younger, and I was coming to realize that although she wasn't "set in my ways," I recognized the potential. As with Warren and Madonna, the age difference meant nothing. I don't know if it was the IV drip or the shock paddles, but soon after we got back to the States, we fell in love. I knew this was the woman that I wanted to spend the rest of my time on prescription refills with.

We had dated for almost three years before I realized it was time to propose. I went to a jewelry store and got an education on diamonds. I couldn't believe how much there was to learn. My former wife had picked out her own ring, so I was not too knowledgeable about diamonds. There was a lot to know about them: their cuts, their ratings, their flaws, and their colors. Does it have fire? What about the relationship of the diameter to the depth? Pear-shaped? Marquis? Step-cut? Does it dance? How much should you spend on an engagement ring? It was so overwhelming that I had to run out to my car and breathe into a paper bag. (After my divorce, I was prone to panic attacks, and as a result I always kept paper bags in my car.)

Once I picked out the ring, I had to decide how I was going to do it. I had heard all of these romantic stories about how guys proposed to their future brides: on a hot-air balloon, on a gondola in Venice, at a Lakers game, the ring in the soup, in front of a fireplace in a chalet in Vermont—the list is endless. I felt the pressure to come up with a fun and surprising way to propose. I also needed to give myself a deadline. Since Halloween was right around the corner, I thought it would be unique and fun to pre-place the ring in a pumpkin. I found myself shopping for just the right pumpkin. I didn't know how much I should spend on a pumpkin for this purpose. I had so many questions for the farmer working the pumpkin patch. What was the rating of the pumpkin? Are there any flaws in this one, any inclusions, do you have any pumpkins that dance? I finally decided on just the right one.

This was my plan; I would cut the bottom out, remove the guts, position the ring inside, and then replace the bottom of the pumpkin. I would invite Susan to my house, where we would have some mulled apple cider in front of the fireplace, and then I would bring in the pumpkin. I would say, "Shall we carve a pumpkin?" When she removed the top of the pumpkin, she would find the ring inside and I would propose. She would be shocked, then cry, then kiss and hug me, cry, laugh a little, and then nostalgically relive the discovery of the ring. I didn't know exactly when I would do it, but I knew I only had two weeks before Halloween. If I were going to her house, I would gingerly load the pumpkin into my car trunk just in case the moment struck when I was with her. There were several trips when I put the pumpkin in the trunk, only to have to retrieve it and bring it back into my house later that night when I got home. The moment never seemed to be right. One time, after losing courage for the umpteenth time, I took the ring out and threw the pumpkin away. The next morning I regretted it, retrieved the pumpkin from the garbage can, and replaced the ring for a possible future opportunity.

I came up with an idea. I thought a pumpkin-carving party could be fun, and the perfect place to do it. We could invite a lot of our friends so they would be there when she found the ring inside the pumpkin. Everyone would be surprised at the same time. Great plan—but I was terrified, still unsure about getting back into another marriage. I chickened out during the party and set the pumpkin outside on the front porch. I didn't want anyone accidentally cutting it open and finding the engagement ring. Then I would feel obliged to propose to whomever found it. Everyone still had a good time, and I still had a few days before Halloween to follow through.

The next morning, when I went to retrieve the loaded pumpkin from my front porch, it was gone. I was horrified. How would I replace this beautiful, could-have-been-a-down-payment-on-a-house ring? I entertained a quick wave of panic, then saw the pumpkin. Halloween pranksters had smashed it on the street in front of my house! My trees had been toilet-papered as well. In a way, I suspected that Cupid, or Fate, or God, or whoever decides who we marry in this world, was fed up with my indecisiveness and did this to me. I couldn't believe my pumpkin, my buddy, so instrumental to my future happiness, was crushed on the street. It reminded me of when Tom Hanks, in *Cast Away*, lost his volleyball friend, Wilson. That pumpkin had become my Wilson. I sifted through the carnage and was relieved to find the ring—still intact. I quickly bought another pumpkin, reloaded it, and put it in the trunk of my car. Sadly, Halloween came and went, and there was no proposal.

Thanksgiving was right around the corner, I realized. This would give me time to get over my jitters. I could get a tofurkey (a vegetarian turkey made and shaped like a turkey, with wooden dowels as the leg bones) and plan a big dinner with everyone. Susan would reach into the tofurkey and find the ring mixed in with the stuffing. But I couldn't go through all that anxiety again, and I was running out of paper bags in my car. Besides, there were too many other holidays to fall back on if I chickened out again. It would then be Christmas or Martin Luther King Day—I would propose to her in an empty classroom. Or Columbus Day—we could rent a boat in Spain, and I could tie the ring to the end of a fishing line.

Why was I so hesitant to propose? Was I still wounded from my last marriage? Did I not trust it? Was I afraid of being too happy? This was ridiculous. Life is short. Susan was a wonderful woman, and I would be a fool not to settle down with her. A holiday or two later, knees knocking, I showed up at her apartment. This was it, and there would be no backing out. I was about to ask Susan for her hand in marriage. If the hand worked out, I would eventually ask for the rest of the body.

She let me in, and I immediately sat her down on the couch. I was totally focused and on a mission. In my peripheral vision I saw a small pumpkin sitting on one of her antique end tables. My heart skipped a beat. Had there been another proposal? Was there someone else in her life? I wasn't about to find out. I told her how much she meant to me and how much I loved her, then handed her the ring. As I held it out to her, I was hoping that my shaking would not loosen the stone from its setting. "Will you marry me, Susan?" I asked. With wide eyes she gazed at the ring, then at me. Through tears, she said, "Yes, I would love to marry you." That was basically it in a nutshell. Hmm, a nutshell could have been a good place to hide the ring. Too late.

A few months later we ran off to Lake Como, Italy, to tie the knot in the romantic town of Bellagio. Unlike the last time I tied the knot, I made sure that this one was not a slip knot. This was Susan's dream—to run off to Italy to get married. We planned the small ceremony through a wedding planner out of Colorado who also booked white-water rafting trips. It would just be the two of us, in a civil ceremony, with the town mayor. Having played a bride six times on various television sitcoms and commercials, Susan was tired of big weddings. I didn't care about having a big wedding, either. I had one once before, and felt it was more for our guests than for us. This would be perfect. No fanfare and no guests to worry about. It would be a beautiful, quiet, romantic wedding. More importantly, we both knew that if either one of us had a panic attack and wanted to back out, we could do so without disappointing a lot of family and friends.

After we returned from Italy, I helped Susan move into my yellow beach house. It had still not faded one bit. Some of the furniture from her apartment we used, some we gave away, and some we put into my storage unit. While I was making room for her boxes, I came across one of mine, tucked way in the back. It was not labeled and was sealed tight with packing tape. Curious, I ripped one of the ends open and reached inside to find a framed picture. As I pulled it out, I couldn't help smiling. It was the photo of the little boy on his father's back. My cradle—my reminder.

FIVE

I'm Not Ready, It's Just Time

Be careful not to throw the hot tea bag into the garbage. It could start a fire," my friend Elisa said. To say Elisa is a big worrier is an understatement. She worries way too much about everything. It's probably good that she doesn't have kids, because they would worry her to death. She is always on red alert and feels as though she is life's security guard. If you tell her what you are thinking about doing, she will find every possible thing that could go wrong and why you shouldn't do it. She is vigilant about protecting her family and friends from any possible far-fetched, potentially dangerous situation that could harm them. "Be careful when you eat those potato chips—they have sharp edges and could cut your mouth." "Don't lean too far back into that chair, the back doesn't seem too sturdy."

I have to think that, as a child, Elisa read too many children's rhymes and stories with careless characters or played too much Chutes and Ladders. Had she been policing those rhymes and fairy tales, no one would have gotten into trouble. Humpty Dumpty never would have had that great fall off that wall. Goldilocks never would have cut through the woods, and all Three Little Pigs would have built their houses out of brick, complete with a top-notch alarm system. Had she been a member of the CIA or FBI, the Twin Towers would probably still be standing today. Of course, she would have insisted they be reduced to one story for safety's sake. There is no doubt in my mind that she could easily work for Homeland Security, as long as they promised not to stray too far from home.

If we ever wanted to be talked out of having a baby, all we needed to do was run the idea past Elisa. Susan and I chuckled, thinking how it would almost be cruel to suggest this incredibly risky notion to her. The blood in her face would probably rush to her knees, and her internal caution circuit board would overload, opening a floodgate of potential doom-and-gloom scenarios. Upon hearing this, we imagined her eyes would roll back in her head and smoke would shoot from her ears. We decided to spare Elisa from our plan for now. We didn't need to hear what a sorry state this world was in and all the reasons why we shouldn't bring a baby into it. We already knew.

Aren't there too many people on this planet already? Weren't there obvious signs? Aside from long lines at the women's restrooms, telephone numbers are getting longer and longer. Whenever I watch an old show or movie, I marvel at the fact that people back then only had to dial a few numbers. Now you have to dial ten numbers just to make a call across the street (don't even talk to me about international dialing). Not only that, but here in Los Angeles they continuously seem to be adding more and more area codes. And what about those four extra numbers they added after our zip codes? The newer hotels being built are much larger now, with more and more rooms, so many rooms, in fact, that the room numbers, on the doors are longer than your checking account's routing number. Soon they'll have to install the doors sideways to fit all the numbers and only really short people will be booking rooms. It seems like, if people were really intent on making the world a better place, they would be searching for a way to minimize the numbers we have to remember rather than making new ones.

The same thing goes for the increasing amount of traffic. Whenever I am in a traffic jam, I curse everyone for procreating and proliferating this planet with children who grow up to learn how to drive. On the whole, traffic is a colossal worry for me. Here is my concern: I suspect that more and more double-decker freeways will be built in order to accommodate the growing population of drivers and their cars. At some point, the double-decker freeways won't be enough to handle that traffic, and then a third level will be added to accommodate everyone. I am not a scientist or an engineer, but my fear is that at some point the earth will be totally covered with these double- and triple-level freeways, blocking the sun from reaching the ground. If you ever wanted to get a tan, you'd have to drive a convertible, naked, on the top level of the freeway and hope for a traffic jam. Plants will no longer grow, and our food supply will dwindle. Also, wouldn't all of these added levels of freeways increase the circumference of our planet and possibly throw it off its axis? Look at me, I'm talking like Elisa now. But planets are probably meant to be a certain size, no? I have not researched this thoroughly, but I plan to.

But then again, there is "beauty in numbers"—or maybe the saying is "strength in numbers"? At any rate, I don't know if I believe in either. A few years ago I was taking the ferry out to Catalina Island from Los Angeles. It was a beautiful day, and I was really looking forward to it. About halfway there, our ferry was suddenly surrounded by hundreds and hundreds of dolphins.

I had never seen so many dolphins at one time. I thought, "Wow! This is really awesome!" They were jumping out of the water, splashing and shooting water out of their blowholes. And then I started thinking, "Ya know what, this is almost *too many* dolphins." It was actually making me a little uncomfortable. Seeing that many dolphins at once is really not as magical as seeing just two or three swimming around the boat. It was kind of overkill. It's like seeing a thousand breasts at once. It's just not as sexy as, say, seeing just three breasts . . . swimming around a boat. I'm just glad that dolphins don't drive.

Life is so fragile. It always amazes me that most of us can get through it, for the most part, unscathed. Our physical bodies, alone, are just so vulnerable. We are a collection of tissues, cells, bones, blood, and nerves, all coated in an epidermis. If the universe had a menu, we would be listed as a California Flesh Wrap. We are all so susceptible to injury and even death from our environment. To survive we are expected to navigate our delicate wrap through a world of fast-moving metal objects, diseases, freak accidents, fierce winds, snow, fire, and paparazzi. I'm lucky in that I have never known anyone personally who has been hit by a car or bus, or who has been seriously burned—in fact, I never knew anyone who was even slightly burned except for Bill Toonik. Bill is a friend who has the capacity for exaggerating and being melodramatic. He claims he was "severely burned" on his rear end last year when he spilled a hot bowl of Campbell's alphabet soup on his couch and then accidentally fell onto it. He immediately went to the doctor, who said that a portion of his rear end had received first-degree burns. I still don't know which *degree* of burn is the worst, but I think a first-degree burn is along the lines of a bad sunburn. In Bill's case, since it was alphabet soup, he probably had the outline of a few vowels temporarily branded onto his butt. I'm not sure there is a burn category for that, but being prone to exaggeration, Bill's always been interested in discovering new territory.

Being an overly dramatic type, Bill was quick to draw parallels between his burns and those that Ralph Fiennes's character suffers in the movie *The English Patient*. In case you haven't seen the movie, Fiennes's character is covered head to toe in white gauze to cover the severe and life-threatening burns that he received during a plane crash. He spends much of the movie in agonizing pain, barely able to speak. Nevertheless, Bill persisted with his analogy, saying:

- Ralph Fiennes's character crashed in his plane in the desert; I *live* in the desert climate of southern California.
- Ralph Fiennes's plane is a metal, cylindrical object. The can holding my soup was *also* metal and cylindrical.
- Ralph's plane had identification *letters* on the tail. My *soup* contained noodles in the shape of letters.

"The only difference between us," Bill said, "was, I survived; Ralph didn't." I don't know what he was trying to prove except that maybe there should be a movie made about him. At the end of the day, I suppose the full extent of Bill's tragedy lies in the eye of the beholder, but honestly, I don't really know how some people cope with their very real tragedies. I guess some reach to their faith to get them through, and for others it's just human resilience. Sometimes you just have to pull yourself up by your bootstraps and get on with life. Nevertheless, much of it is heartbreaking. Of course, first and foremost, I'm talking about Britney Spears losing custody of her kids. I mean, that came out of nowhere for me. I didn't know how to handle it. I couldn't get out of bed, stopped eating, and dropped about ten pounds. I guess she won't be writing that parenting guide after all.

Face it: life is just not fair sometimes. I remember when Hurricane Katrina hit New Orleans. I was actually supposed to be there a week after that happened. I had that vacation planned for eight months, and then the hurricane hit, wiping out the entire city, and obviously, I had to cancel my plans. I thought to myself, Why me? Why do these things happen to me? But you know what? I got through it. I dealt with it. I accepted it. I realized God must have other vacation plans for me. I pulled myself together and booked another vacation.

Natural disasters help put everything into perspective, because the bottom line is that some people just don't realize how lucky they are. They just don't appreciate what they have, and they take everything for granted. It's really quite sad, not to mention frustrating to watch. I remember, a couple years ago, hearing about the riots in Paris, and I thought to myself, What are they complaining about? At least they're in Europe! Some people have never even been to Europe!

Much to my dismay, it's getting harder and harder to travel to Europe, or anywhere else for that matter. Travel becomes just one more thing to worry about. Terrorism has been on the rise, and most of us, particularly those of us who travel frequently, deal with those concerns on a daily basis. It seems the lines going through security at the airports are getting longer and longer. People are required to take their shoes off now because of the Shoe Bomber. It's really quite amusing. People are standing around in their socks and bare feet, which started me thinking, Why couldn't it have been the Bra Bomber, or the Thong Bomber?

Shortly after September 11, Susan and I were going through security at LAX. She went ahead of me, sliding her carry-on bag onto the conveyor belt. I came through behind her. As I arrived at the other side, I saw a TSA agent at the end of the conveyor belt, holding a steak knife. I remember thinking, Who would be foolish enough to try to sneak a steak knife through security? That's some pretty serious stuff. It soon dawned on me that it belonged to Susan. Some weeks earlier, she had brought some cheese, crackers, wine, and that steak knife to my house in that very same bag. I was in the middle of moving, and she knew that all of my cutlery was packed away. We had a very romantic wine-and-cheese break in the middle of a crazy day of moving. When she got home, she threw that bag in the closet, forgetting to remove the steak knife from the side pocket. A few months later she packed her travel clothes in that very bag for our trip, completely unaware that the knife was still in the side pocket. She was desperately trying to explain this scenario to the TSA agent. "Look," she said, "you can still see the cheese on the side of the blade!" They sat her down in one of those plastic seats they use for interrogation, while another agent "wanded" her and began asking questions.

I was shaking my head the whole time, thinking, "How could she be so negligent?" Just then I heard another TSA agent call out from over my shoulder.

"Who owns this bag?" he asked.

I turned around and saw that it was mine. He was holding a Swiss Army knife up as if it were a dead mouse. It turns out that I, too, didn't realize that I had a knife in my bag. This didn't look good, since we were traveling together. Luckily for me, the length of the blade on my knife didn't qualify me to be a possible terrorist suspect. I think the blade has to be over six inches or so. The TSA agent broke off the blade and handed the rest of the knife back to me. My Swiss Army knife had suddenly become a Swiss Army spoon.

An L.A. policewoman was now interrogating Susan. I stood behind the red line and tried to keep Susan relaxed by putting a goofy grin on my face. My grin was supposed to convey, "Isn't this all wacky?" I knew that this whole process was making her scared and vulnerable. Susan has never broken any law and didn't want to become a criminal now—especially when she wasn't even wearing any shoes. They kept her until they could check her police record and verify that she wasn't a hijacker. The officer eventually came back and told Susan that she had a clean record—not even an outstanding parking ticket. She was concerned that they might have discovered a late American Express payment from the month before, but in the end, the female officer admonished her and then let her off with a stern warning.

Maybe all this will change when we get Osama bin Laden, but somehow I doubt it. By the way, I found out recently that there is a fifty-million-dollar reward if you have information on Osama bin Laden's whereabouts. You know what I am doing? I'm guessing. Why not? I call the Department of Homeland Security every day and say, "Osama bin Laden is—in a cave, one hundred miles north of Pakistan; thirty degrees latitude; one hundred twenty-five degrees longitude," then I hang up and wait. I take a guess every day—seriously, every day. Because you can't win if you don't play. You gotta be in it to win it, and I certainly am.

One recent video of bin Laden showed that he has dyed his beard and hair black. I was looking at it thinking, Great. That's all we need. A terrorist going through a midlife crisis. Saddam Hussein used to dye his hair black, too. But of course, he no longer has to worry about that. We got Saddam Hussein, and that chapter is over. I say "we," but I really had nothing to do with it, except for maybe the taxes that were taken from my recent purchase of a plasma-screen television. That morning, I didn't even know "we" got him. I was walking by a newsstand and on the front page of the paper was a picture of this disheveled, angry-looking guy with a scraggly beard and bloodshot eyes, and for a minute I thought, Oh no, Nick Nolte got another DUI! But, no, we got Saddam Hussein. We haven't gotten Nick Nolte yet, but we'll get him.

About five years ago I drove to the Breckenridge area of Colorado to go skiing. I had never skied there before, so I pulled into a convenience store and asked the man behind the counter, who happened to be white, for suggestions. Since there were a few different ski resorts within a few square miles, I asked which one he preferred. He told me he liked a place called Copper Mountain. He says a lot of people avoid it because there are too many blacks there. He continued, "I don't mind the blacks. I can handle them. I have a lot of fun with 'em."

I couldn't believe what I was hearing. I thought, Oh, my God. This guy is a racist. He went on to say, "Oh, they can beat ya up pretty bad." It wasn't until later that I realized that he was referring to the black diamond trails on the mountain, not "black" as in "African American." Ski resorts list the difficulty of their trails with signs on the slope and trail maps, black diamonds being difficult, blue squares intermediate, and green circles easiest. I found out later, he was right. The blacks over at Copper Mountain are pretty tough.

Then of course there's one thing that knows no boundaries and doesn't care about the color of your skin. I'm talking of course about disease. Is an outbreak of avian flu in the not-too-distant future actually possible? Incidentally, don't you find people who pose and answer their own questions annoying? "Do I like living in California? Yes, I do. Would I recommend it to someone else? Sure, probably." Did you ever notice they never ask themselves hard questions? "How do I overhaul a car engine?" Naturally, they only ask easy questions to make them look smart. Anyway, to answer my own question: No, I am not too worried about avian flu, but perhaps that's because I really don't know that much about it. I was wondering if you could catch it by someone flipping you the bird? If so, I am in big trouble, because today I got flipped off about three times on the freeway.

If it's not the avian flu, there are a slew of other flus you could catch. I have put together some measures you can take to avoid them:

* Do not shake someone else's hand and then lick your palm.
* Do not make out with someone with runny snot on their upper lip.
* Do not chew on the Kleenex that someone just sneezed into.

Now, I know what you're thinking: if I was this overwrought with worry, maybe I should have just gotten a pet instead of having a kid. While some people claim that having a pet is like having a child, I don't know if I quite agree with that. I once rescued two homeless cats, and I couldn't believe how much cats throw up. All night long, all I heard was, "Arrrrggggg! Gaggurrrrougk!" I woke up the next morning, and there was puke everywhere. It was like living in a frat house. It wasn't even puke, they were hairballs. You have to get them off the carpet quick, too, otherwise they will stain. You have to make a conscious decision about what to do with these hairballs. You have two options: pick them up and clean the carpet, or just leave them there and let them accumulate over time so you eventually have a sticky shag carpet. If you have to get a new carpet, bring one of the hairballs with you and use it as a color swatch—that way you'll know that future hairballs blend in better with the carpet.

Some people actively prefer having a pet to having a child, and that's fine. A pet comes with features you won't find in a child. When that tsunami hit Sri Lanka several years ago and killed hundreds and thousands of people, the animals somehow knew it was coming—the day before, they all headed for the hills. They didn't tell anybody else either. It was like their big selfish secret. After learning about that, I started giving animals a lot more credit, and today I have much more respect for them. In fact, now, when I see a dog chasing a car, I, too, will chase that car. I figure something is up, and I might as well tag along. I'll ask questions later. "What was up with that car?" I'd ask, but then quickly add, "It doesn't matter. I trust you. I'm sure something was up, and we'll probably read about it in the newspaper tomorrow, right?"

A part of me wonders if there's something going on with cows, too. Whenever the Weather Channel is covering floods in the Midwest, they always show a cow up on the roof of a barn somewhere. She is up there to get out of the water, not worried and in no rush. She's just calmly standing up there, checking the rising water every now and then. The funny thing is that the cameras never show how the cow got up on the roof. If I had to guess, I'd say she probably climbs up the stairs, crawls out one of the windows, and then grapples her way up to the peak of the roof. Apparently she just waits it out until the water subsides.

I only wish our pets would give us a little more time. Therein lies the reason that children eventually become more useful than pets. Unlike animals, they learn to communicate at a higher level, albeit mostly so that they can make parents worry more about how many inappropriate words they know. Though this child communication can occasionally be useful, it's mostly just disconcerting and not nearly as helpful as, say, a dog telling you when an earthquake is going to strike. Just think of the actuarial implications—no kid can compete with that. Until scientists invent a talking dog, though, you just have to know what warning signals to look for with animals. Like if you are living in the Midwest and you are coming down the stairs and there is a cow coming up the other way—get the boots.

You can't let the possibility of a tragedy stop you from enjoying life. When it gets down to it, everything carries a risk. Sometimes if you don't take these risks, you miss out on so much that life has to offer. I would have missed out on an opportunity to have John Travolta fly me halfway across the country in his private jet had I been worried about the risk. During the summer of 1987, Dana Carvey, Dennis Miller, and I went on a thirty-two-city stand-up comedy tour. At our last gig in Denver, Colorado, John Travolta showed up with mutual friends of mine, Anson and Linda. John had gotten his pilot's license years ago and had been an avid pilot ever since. They stayed for the show and then John offered Dana, Dennis, and me a ride back to L.A. in his Learjet. Dana and Dennis, who are not good fliers, politely declined, but I agreed. Hey, how often do you get a chance to fly with John Travolta at the controls? I thought. I tried to convince Dana and Dennis to join us. "Come on, just think of all the material this will inspire!" I said enthusiastically. "Even if we go down," I continued, "just think of all the laughs we'll have!" No use. They wouldn't have any part of it.

Several hours later I was strapped into my seat as we proceeded to barrel down the runway. Anson and Linda were used to flying with John but were still nervous fliers. Shortly after we got altitude and the landing gear retracted into the belly of the jet, we hit some pretty severe turbulence. The jet was being rocked pretty hard, and had we not been strapped in, we all would have been bouncing around the cabin like popcorn in a microwave. Linda and Anson abruptly turned a whiter shade of pale, which was not saying much since Anson, a redhead, was naturally pale white. If he had gotten any paler, I would have been able to see right through him. I was doing pretty well compared to them until suddenly we hit another violent air pocket and the cockpit doors flew open. I'll never forget the image as I peered into the cockpit: to me it was no longer Travolta but Vinnie Barbarino wrestling the controls. I say "wrestling," but that is just for effect. He and his silver-haired copilot might have been holding on a little tighter than normal, but they were hardly "wrestling." Nonetheless, I scolded myself for recklessly jumping at this chance. How could I risk my life just to experience a ride in a private jet with Vinnie Barbarino at the controls? Why couldn't it have been Thomas Magnum from *Magnum, P.I.* or Jack Bauer from *24* instead?

Eventually, Johnny calmly turned back to us with a reassuring smile and said, "Sorry folks, just a little bit of turbulence. It's not unusual when you are flying over the Rockies." Bam! We immediately hit another big air pocket, and the jet jolted to the right and suddenly sank one hundred feet. Johnny stumbled out of the cockpit, leaving the flying duties to the copilot. I say "stumbled," but once again that is just for effect. It was closer to his strut in *Saturday Night Fever.* The only nuance missing was the Bee Gees singing "Stayin' Alive," which is what we were all hoping we would do. Johnny sat calmly in the back with us for a few minutes, explaining our route and the dynamics and specs of this particular jet. It was obvious that this was his passion, and he loved every minute of it. The flight soon smoothed out, and Johnny and his copilot got us back safely to Los Angeles. Although there was no material to be had from this experience, I was glad I took the risk and would not hesitate to fly anywhere with Mr. Barbarino again. I say "would not hesitate," but again, that is just for effect. I might hesitate a little, but only to figure out how much I would be saving by not flying commercial.

Whether it's flying with John Travolta or walking down the

street, there's risk in everything. So what was the point then of getting all worked up and anxious, rather than just committing in my head to having a kid? Life is a dangerous obstacle course—whether you're talking about flying, driving, walking, or even sleeping. (I hear the number of people who die in their sleep increases every year. The three major causes of deaths while asleep are cardiac arrest, stroke, and having a wooden stake hammered through your heart.) But I guess the point behind all this worry is that life is an incredible gift, and you can't wait for the world to be a better place before you have a baby. You can't let the events of today deter you from having a baby tomorrow, or nine months from tomorrow, if you're going to be a stickler for numbers. It's like getting into the real estate market. Yes, the market is high now but you still have to get into it. It will only go up . . . eventually. It's the same with having a baby. Yes, the world is a crazy place to live right now, but think of how crazy it will be in five or ten years. It's only getting worse out there, but you have to get it into it at some point, so it might as well be now.

When I spoke to my parents about what I was going through, they were pretty dismissive about the whole thing, and they didn't hesitate to tell me so. Couples didn't used to put as much thought into parenthood as they do now. Back in our parents' day, they didn't analyze it or hem and haw over it. They didn't scrutinize the moon phase or the star alignment. They didn't analyze bank accounts or the futures market in the hope that some major convergence of events would make it clear that it was now time to procreate. They didn't consider the notion that the eventual added levels of freeways might throw our planet off its axis, or that we were running out of phone numbers. They weren't concerned that iPhones would take over their lives, not allowing for the added distraction of children. People usually just got married and had children. That was it. That's what you did.

Today it's different. Many people consider their career first, their financial situation, tax write-offs, whether they will have clothes that will match the baby's, and what schools will accept their precious child. Not to mention the host of other real-world concerns that I've mentioned above.

The more I thought about it, the more I realized that no one is probably ever completely confident about the decision to have a child. After all, it is a scary, life-altering experience. Things will never be the same, but I guess you have to feel that that in itself is inherently a good thing. As Lorne Michaels, my former boss and producer of *SNL*, used to say, "*Saturday Night Live* is never ready to go on, it's just time."

SIX

The Old College Try

When Susan and I got married, she had never been married before and had no children. This is not to say that she had a problem with kids; on the contrary, she adores them. Susan is one of those women who releases maternal instinct from her sweat glands; people can sense it about her from several blocks away. When we are out walking, she stops at every passing stroller and makes sure that I see how cute each baby is.

"Look, Kevin!" she says. "Awww, look how cute he is! Look! Have you ever seen anything so cute? Loooook!"

"Yes, I see," I reply. "I am looking. I can't look any harder. My eyes are taking him all in—yes, very cute. Adorable!" Actually, all babies look the same, if you ask me. I don't even know why people think they're so cute. Rolls of fat, bald, crap in their pants—just like an old man. In fact, I can guarantee that if a very old man in a nursing home walked into a room with rolls of fat, bald, and a load in his pants, not one person would go, "Ohhh, look how cute! Can I hold him?"

From the day we met, Susan was positive that she wanted a child. Call it maternal instincts or her biological clock, but she was definitely mother material. The only time she had second thoughts was when she would return from visiting with her friend and her unruly daughter. Never underestimate the power of a two-year-old as ultimate birth control.

"It was hell," she said, totally straight-faced. "I really don't think I want a kid after that." During those times I knew her biological clock was still ticking, but probably just needed some new batteries. I told her it would be different when it was her own baby. She wouldn't mind the screaming and carrying on, the dirty diapers, my staying out later, my taking more trips away from home.

But as I thought over her hesitancy, it suddenly dawned on me; what if I was not capable of getting her pregnant? What if she had something going on where *she* couldn't reproduce? There was, of course, the option of adopting. Did we want to take that route? Surely there are plenty of children in this world that need a loving home. And if we did adopt, and discovered we didn't like the whole idea of it, we could probably give it back. Right? I suggested that maybe we should ease into it by adopting a highway, perhaps an adorable Chinese highway—a cute little five-mile stretch? Ya know, just to see if it's something we really want to get into. And if that worked out, we would try the baby thing. We had to make a decision, one way or the other. There was no more sitting on the fence about this—no more procrastinating. We discussed it, thought about it, and weighed the pros and cons and then both agreed, we wanted children—at least one child, anyway.

Not wanting to waste any more time, we added another fun gadget to our collection. It's a device called an ovulation kit. This handy little gadget helps a woman determine the day of the month she's most fertile. From the instructions that came with the kit, I was surprised to learn that a woman is most likely to conceive during a twelve-hour window each month, and that was when I would need to be there.

We now had a blood pressure machine and an ovulation kit, and as unfortunately I found out recently, you're only supposed to pee on one of them for results. However, and I explained this to my wife, when I don't like the readout on *my* blood pressure machine, it is my right to pee on it. It did not take long for the ovulation kit to enter regular rotation at our parties. On the down side, it created long lines outside our bathroom, and between taking friends' blood pressure and assessing their most fertile days, I didn't have much time to party myself. The good news was, our parties started getting much more out of control, as guests would frequently disappear upstairs after learning it was their fertile period. It was like the best and worst parts of college all rolled into one, and the strange thing was that people actually wanted to have unprotected sex. While our gatherings with the ovulation kit never quite got to the level of the parties across the street, the frequent traffic up and down our stairs made for some odd parallels with our neighbors. Maybe midlife wasn't so different after all. The end result of all this was that two of our regular party guests are now pregnant, and four others are on beta-blockers for their high blood pressure.

Susan and I had decided on giving it the old college try for six months. If she were not pregnant by then, she suggested that I visit a fertility specialist. I didn't worry about that. I believed that my equipment and ammunition were in excellent working order. I was confident she would get pregnant immediately. There is a simple pregnancy test that you can take at home to see if your old college try is working. It is called the e.p.t—early pregnancy test—another gadget for our growing collection and also another possible game for our parties. It looks sort of like a big plastic thermometer. To get a reading, the woman is required to urinate on the end of it. (Thankfully there are not a lot of products that you have to pee on to get them to work. Can you imagine if your car required that? Your cell phone?) If you have a "pregnancy hormone active" result—meaning you are pregnant—two pink lines will appear in its little window. These two stripes make people either very happy or very upset, and they are quite accurate, too. Much more accurate than, say, one of those Magic 8-Balls that you ask a question and shake for your answer. Incidentally, we used that method the first month and weren't satisfied with its answers. "Am I pregnant?" we would ask. After we shook it, the answer would roll into view: "Ask again later," or "My sources say no." Eventually we realized it was just teasing us, so we gave it the deep-six.

After trying again and again for a total of . . . eight weeks, it was clear that for some reason Susan just wasn't getting pregnant. There were no pink lines. Cycle after cycle, she would disappear into the bathroom only to come back out, minutes later, holding the stick, with a dark cloud over her. At the ripe old age of thirty-five, she was pissed. After getting yet another visit from her "menstrual friend," she no longer considered it her friend anymore. In fact, her friend was no longer welcome in our house. It was showing up uninvited, and we were taking initiatives to ban it from the premises. "Maybe we should get a restraining order," I suggested.

All my life I'd been so worried about getting someone pregnant. If I'd realized it was this difficult, maybe I wouldn't have been so concerned or well-behaved. I must have gotten some misinformation in my high school sex education class, which would probably make sense, since it was a Catholic high school. I suppose if they told us it was really difficult to get someone pregnant, more students would be promiscuous.

Susan was having her doubts, and once again she suggested I go to a fertility specialist to see if I had what it takes to fertilize her eggs—or as I saw it, to see if I was a real man. I reminded her that it had only been two months of trying. We still had the original batteries in the ovulation kit, for God's sake. "Besides," I said, "some people try for years to conceive."

Susan agreed, and that afternoon, she found a fertility specialist for me. No recommendations, no references; she discovered Dr. Arjahani's ad in the yellow pages. Now I really have nothing against tradition, but considering how much information there is online these days, there was something off-putting about going to a place from the yellow pages. I think the last time I used the yellow pages was in 1989 to order pizza from Domino's. Nevertheless, Dr. Arjahani's big selling point was that he was Beverly Hills "adjacent." His ad boasted more about the benefits of being close to Beverly Hills than his expertise in fertility.

"Close to Beverly Hills downtown shopping!" the ad read. "Close to very good plastic surgeons!" "Close to expensive real estate!" I guess being adjacent is almost as good as having your office in Beverly Hills. Probably better than Beverly Hills "juxtaposition" or Beverly Hills "parallel." Not altogether comfortable going to a fertility clinic, I reminded Susan again that we had only been trying for two months, and I still had another four months before our self-imposed deadline. But Susan was determined. Two days later, I arrived for my appointment with Dr. Arjahani. My sole mission was to leave a specimen sample, and they would run tests on it and then contact me a few days later with the results.

Dr. Arjahani's office was like a brothel on a day none of the girls showed up. The waiting room was full of mostly middle-aged men, none making eye contact with each other. We all knew what we were there for; it was like pregnancy detention. I filled out a few forms, which assured Dr. Arjahani that either my insurance company or I would pay him for his services. As I waited self-consciously for my name to be called, I spotted an overflowing magazine rack: the *Atlantic Monthly, Newsweek*, the *Economist* magazine, and several other lackluster periodicals. I flipped through a medical science magazine that had all types of articles in it referring to infertility. One article claimed that they had found a cure for erectile dysfunction that only requires one needle injection into the penis. They also claimed they had found the cause of erectile dysfunction, hearing the phrase, "One needle injection into the penis."

The receptionist finally called out my name, loudly, and a nurse, whom I pretended was the madam of the brothel, waited for me at the door. Everyone seemed to be studying me as I crossed the room. This guy can't get his wife pregnant, they were probably thinking. I wonder if he has an erectile dysfunction problem? This guy is probably gay and is living in denial. This guy will be a hundred before his kid is out of diapers. The nurse led me into a tiny room that was only slightly smaller than my wife's walk-in closet, which, incidentally, occasionally served the same purpose. There was an old, worn vinyl chair directly in front of a TV and VCR. The nurse reached up into the cupboard and nonchalantly pulled out several old adult videos and a few well-worn girlie magazines. She placed a Dixie cup next to them on the counter, and I immediately thought, "Great, we're gonna be doing tequila shots together." Not so. Apparently the Dixie cup would be for my sample. As she was leaving, she told me to take my time and not to worry, no one would be coming in.

She really went overboard to make me feel comfortable. She continued by telling me that no one would be in the office when I was finished, and I could just drop the Dixie cup off on the counter. She ended by saying that "everyone would be at lunch (even though it was only 10:30 in the morning). "There will be jackhammers pounding away on the street outside, and no one will hear you," she said. As she headed out, she turned back and said, "And incidentally, I loved your work on *Saturday Night Live.*" She closed the door and was gone.

I wasn't worried about anyone coming in. What I was worried about was the state of the room. This room had clearly seen a tremendous amount of traffic over the years. Everything seemed so filthy. The magazines, the videos, the cracked vinyl of the chair. If ever there was a need for one of those toilet-seat paper gaskets, it would be here. I can only imagine all the germs one of those black lights would detect in this room. I'm not typically a germ-o-phobe, but I didn't want to touch anything. Just for kicks I put in one of the videos. I randomly picked one up with my elbows and slid it into the VCR. (This was as hard as, if not harder than, it sounds.) I then pressed the play button with my knuckle. From the content, I assumed that Dr. Arjahani picked out the porno selection. For the most part they were Iranian women with huge breasts that were covered with scars and lop-sided nipples. Some even had C-section scars. There was also one scene with a woman bodybuilder in a bikini, standing on a couch, flexing and posing. I wasn't totally sure if this was what Dr. Arjahani thought was sexy, but there was something unsettling about the idea that I was relying on a doctor whose turn-ons included oversize biceps and bad plastic surgery. Repulsed, I turned my head away and spotted a sign by the door that read, "Do not take videos!" The mere fact that Dr. Arjahani needed that sign said something about the clientele.

Clearly I had missed the boat for materials when I was in the waiting room. Even the *Economist* would have been more tantalizing than this. I cracked open the door slightly to see if there was a better visual aid in the hallway. I could partially see the receptionist, but she was busy shaving her back. Then there was the other dilemma: how long should I be in here for? I didn't want to come out too soon, but I also didn't want to stay in too long. That would be weird. Would I feel pressured to do this? Maybe I could also negotiate a six-month deadline with this doctor's office. I wondered what the average time was that people took to leave a sample?

I was beginning to experience performance anxiety. The videos and magazines she left weren't helping. If anything, they were making me nauseated. I tried everything. I even tried to visualize how sexy it was being Beverly Hills Adjacent. "Oh, yeah, 90211," I'd taunt. "I'm so adjacent to Beverly Hills. I'm right outside of you, 90210. I can see you from here, you dirty Rodeo Drive, with all your naughty Eurotrash. Oh, yeah, shake your booty, Little Santa Monica Blvd."

Eventually, when all was said and done, I did the walk of shame with my Dixie cup to the designated drop-off area. No one was there. Had it been so long that everyone *was* out to lunch? Without stopping, I set the cup on the counter and continued walking right out the door, like a spy discreetly dropping off a briefcase in a train station.

A few days later, my test results were in: I was totally capable of conceiving. I briefly wondered if perhaps I had gotten the Dixie cup pregnant. Once again, I reminded Susan that we had initially agreed to give it six months of trying naturally, and that's the path we should continue on. "You're right," she said, and then added, "We'll give it one more month, and if it doesn't happen then, we'll turn it over to the pros." One more month! That's all I needed—a shorter deadline. Okay, no big deal. I work well with deadlines. I was going to give it one more college try. Maybe *college try* wasn't the right term, since I hadn't tried in college. We'd give it one more shot, and if we had no luck, then we would just have to let science have a crack at it.

Susan was also doing her part. She had visited an acupuncturist and was given a blend of Chinese herbal tea to drink. She would empty little plastic bags full of what appeared to be twigs, dried mushrooms, and brittle brown leaves into a pot of boiling water. It made the whole house smell horrendous. This, the acupuncturist said, would make her more fertile.

A week or two after the terrible-smelling tea entered our life, Susan set up an appointment with the "pros" at the fertility clinic for us. "We could always cancel it," she said. It was just a backup, we told ourselves, but I don't think that either of us was really convinced that the pungent aroma and effects of the tea were actually going to help make her pregnant. If anything, it would make it harder for her to get pregnant, since it made practically everything harder. One morning, as we were packing for a trip, Susan plopped down on the bed and said she was feeling exhausted. After taking a two-hour nap, she decided that she was still too exhausted to travel, so we canceled our Memorial Day weekend trip to Lake Tahoe. Susan thinks she's psychic, but she's usually wrong about her predictions. The occasional times she is right, she is convinced that she has special powers. The next morning, she sensed something good was going to happen. Later that day she came out of the bathroom with the e.p.t. stick in her hand. She set it on the counter and asked, "Does that look like two pink lines to you?" I was in the middle of reading an interesting article in my *AARP Bulletin* about the joys of your children finally moving out of the house and all the benefits of having this free time with each other again.

"What do you think?" Susan asked again. "Does that look like two lines?" I casually peered over my *Bulletin* to look at the stick.

Initially, from my angle, it sort of looked like two pink lines. One was a little fainter than the other but, yeah, technically, there were two pink lines.

We looked at it again and then at each other. We kept trying to clarify that the lines were there. I would say, "Looks like two lines to me." She would agree and say, "And they are pink, right?" I'd look at it from several different angles, then hold it up to the light, hold it in the darkness of the cupboard, and then even sneak up on it to see if I could catch it off guard. Yep. Looked pink to me. "Let me see those instructions on the box again," I told Susan. Yeah, according to the instructions, we were doing it right. I would then do a recount of the lines: "One, two . . . Yep, two lines." We set it down, slowly walked away, and then would look back at it again, still a little unsure. It was that same sort of look you give an ATM machine after you complete your transaction. You're not quite sure everything is done. You look at it like, Did I do everything I was supposed to do? We set the e.p.t. stick down and returned to look at it at least ten more times over a period of fifteen minutes. Our reaction: disbelief, it can't be true. It must be a defective stick.

"Maybe you should pee on it some more," I suggested. We must be reading it wrong, or we'd suddenly become color-blind. We did a recount. "One line, two lines." Yep, two lines. Before long our kitchen was full of pregnancy sticks, all with two pink lines showing.

We started treating the original tester stick as if it were already our child. We swaddled it in blankets, carried it around, and set up three interviews with local preschools. Susan wanted to keep the stick for nostalgic purposes; she talked about putting it in a scrapbook. "Shoot, why not?" I said. "While you're at it, why not put some of your pee in the book, too." My wife tends to keep a lot of unusual things from her life that hold special meaning. She doesn't save things that people typically save, though, like napkins from a wedding or postcards from family members. During a tour of the White House, she took a tampon from the women's room. She said it was just like the presidents, tall and white.

When she was a younger girl she had two goldfish, Natalie and Constance. One ate the other and she found them both dead one morning. She kept Natalie in a plastic bag in her underwear drawer for many years after that. Natalie eventually dried up, which of course happens if you're not applying antiaging moisturizer cream every night. Natalie became fish jerky. Susan thinks she got this odd passion of nostalgia from her mom, who, in high school, once saved a French fry in a ziplock bag from a dinner date with Walt Odelson. She still has the fry today, although she claims that today it looks more like a green Tic Tac than a French fry.

Once we decided that there were indeed two pink lines, we started sharing this exciting news. Because it's not uncommon to lose the baby in the first trimester, many parents only tell family and close friends about the pregnancy until the first trimester is over—you don't want to have to call back tons of people to let them know your baby died. The sad fact is that during the first trimester of your partner's pregnancy, you are on "death watch." For this reason, we decided to only tell our immediate family.

Relaying the news to my parents was something I had been waiting to do for the last thirty years. Though they had five healthy, well-educated children, not a single one had produced an offspring to this point. What are the odds? Five grown kids, and not one grandchild to carry on the family name. My older brother has a stepdaughter, and even though she is adored and loved as their granddaughter, she is not biological. I will never forget my parents' reaction upon hearing the news. "Mom and Dad," I said with the excitement of a Megabucks Lottery winner, "you're going to be grandparents!" I'm sure that was a phrase they thought they would never hear. Needless to say, they were both ecstatic and overcome with joy.

It reminded me of the call my father made to us from the hospital, when I was sixteen, telling us we had a baby brother. Upon hearing this news, my sisters, brother, and I all danced excitedly in a circle, chanting, "We have a baby brother! We have a baby brother!" In a similar fashion, I imagined my mother and father now dancing and chanting, "We finally have a grandson! We finally have a grandson!" Had I known this is all it took to make my parents this proud, I could have saved myself years of hard work trying to become a successful comedian. When I initially told them I was moving to Hollywood to become a comedian, I hardly think they danced excitedly in a circle and chanted, "Our son is going to throw away his college education and become a comedian!" In reality, though, they would have been proud of me no matter what I did.

For the first two weeks, each morning, I would wake up and suddenly remember that I was going to be a father. All of my fears from high school would come rushing in again, along with the realization that now I had baggage. Although I hadn't been single in years, I suddenly felt like I would not have the life of a free young man anymore. I would be tied down with child, no longer free to meet the perfect bride. Then I'd realize that I already met the perfect bride, and none of that mattered. This irrational behavior was of course the result of having pregnancy brain. I became absentminded and started forgetting things. Susan knew me well, though, and humorously kept me on track. If I had to go to an event or something, she would tell me, "Give yourself enough time so you can still rush." Or, when pulling the car into the garage at night, she would remind me, "Better bring in your cell phone so you have something to look for in the morning."

Even though we had seen the two pink lines with our own eyes, we knew that we needed to confirm their existence with a professional, and so after a few days had passed, we made our first official trip to the ob-gyn. To this day, I don't know exactly what ob-gyn stands for, and for some reason I don't feel like finding out. We had no idea of how to go about selecting an ob-gyn, but after talking to a few people, we determined that word of mouth, not the yellow pages, was the best way. Some of our friends referred us to a Dr. Sarah Glass in Santa Monica, claiming that she was "the best" and that they had been very happy with their experience. I've noticed that whenever someone has surgery or some special procedure performed on them, they always claim that their doctor is "the best," or the premier physician in that particular field, having, allegedly, either trailblazed in that area or invented the latest medical equipment for that procedure.

"He's the Guy." It's always "guy," even if it's a woman. "Oh, you want my guy!"

"Yeah, I'm getting my varicose veins removed. Dr. Feingold is doing it. He is the leading doctor in varicose-vein research. He invented the Varicose Plucking Retractor."

You never hear anyone say, "Yeah, I'm going to Dr. Matthews. He just got out of prison for malpractice. He doesn't use anesthesia. He just distracts you with cat toys. You might have seen him last week on CBS's *60 Minutes*. Let me give you his number."

Anyway, Dr. Glass was our guy, even though she was a woman. We like to think she invented the vaginal birthing process. From this point on we would be relying on her to get us through the next nine months. During Susan's visit to the "best doctor around," she had some blood drawn to officially verify the pregnancy. Susan requested the "butterfly" needle that they use on kids because she read somewhere that it's less painful. Here she was, worried about the pain of the needle while preparing for one of the most painful experiences of a woman's life. I didn't have the heart to tell her that there would be no butterfly needles when it came time to deliver the baby. This is where the kiddy-friendly devices would end.

Susan does not have a high threshold for pain and is not good with seeing blood. Welcome to my world. I don't like the sight of blood either. I'm not good with blood, and I'm not good with placentas, and I am terrible with the combination of blood and placentas. That would be like a tornado and a hurricane hitting at the same time. I remember going to a nutritionist once where they formatted your diet based on your blood type. They took a little of my blood and put it under a microscope. The image was projected on a monitor where I could see the red and white blood cells dancing around. I kid you not, the sight of watching my own blood cells made me nauseated, mostly because they were not good dancers.

The very next day we got a call from Dr. Glass. I watched Susan pick up the phone. She just stood there and listened. Her jaw dropped. The blood work results were in, and Susan was definitely pregnant. We were officially breeders and active participants in the breeding ground. Susan hung up the phone and shared the news with me. We then both looked back at the phone to make sure that it was actually a phone and that we were using it right.

If everything went according to plan, I was going to be a father. I decided that I would need to make some changes in my life. First and foremost, I planned to stop making my regular visits to Dr. Arjahani's brothel. There would be no more Iranian woman bodybuilders or Dixie cups.

SEVEN

Brand Names

"How about Rosebud?" Susan suggested.

"Rosebud?" I asked, wondering if I had heard her right.

"Yes, I think Rosebud is a wonderful name for our baby," she said, smiling fondly.

I placated her and said, "Not bad," hoping that she would eventually forget that contribution to our name search and suggest others. I wasn't always on the same page with her on names, but I had to be diplomatic. I thought Rosebud was a great name for a sled, but not necessarily right for a child. One of the challenges that comes with having a baby is coming up with a great name—one that both parents can agree on and one that people won't make fun of.

I like to think that I am pretty good at coming up with names. After all, I came up with several names for the garage bands I was in, in our neighborhood, names like Stained Glass and the Hallucinations. This was during the psychedelic sixties, when my friends and I were in our early teens and pretended to be part of the hippie movement sweeping the nation. The real hippies were older than us, didn't bathe much, wore lots of tie-dye T-shirts, sported long hair and beards, smoked pot, and burned tons of incense. We burned some incense, but that was pretty much the extent of our hippidom. Stylewise, we did our best to emulate the Beatles, who at this time wore Nehru jackets but did not still live at home. The Nehru style was something they had brought back from India during their repeated trips to visit the Maharishi in their search for inner peace and LSD. While saving up to buy my very own Nehru jacket, I spent some time sick in bed with the flu. During this time, I was so excited about that jacket, it's all I thought about. To pacify me for the time being, I actually cut out a small piece of cloth and sewed together a doll-sized Nehru jacket. My parents were impressed with my handiwork but also probably concerned that I'd grow up to be a fashion designer for Mattel. Medallions were also popular at that time. Had I been sick much longer, I would have asked my father for a welding set to make a groovy medallion, which, coming on the heels of my sewing exploits, would have surely confounded them.

I eventually got my very own green Nehru jacket and a medallion, both of which I wore proudly. I was the rhythm guitar player in a band, and I played a wonderful Sears Kimberly guitar that my parents had given me for Christmas. The better bands around town had large amplifiers for their guitars and microphones, which cost tons of money. We would buy the small amps and then build large, casket-sized boxes that we would fill with several ten-inch speakers and a woofer. We would then staple mesh on the front of the box, glue vinyl around the sides, and then screw in a few coaster wheels on the bottom. Once that was done, we would spray paint the front with fluorescent paints, creating a very psychedelic mood.

Several years later, a few buddies and I started a new band we called the Soulful Six, aptly titled because there were six of us, our lead singer was Puerto Rican, and we played one James Brown song. The rest of the songs in our repertoire were wimpy ones like "Windy," by the Associations, and "This Magic Moment," by Jay and the Americans. We knew about twelve songs and then would start repeating the set, hoping that by that point a new audience would have wandered in. It didn't really matter because we mostly played gigs in our neighborhood, usually at my house or our drummer's. The base of our brick fireplace at my house served as our stage; unfortunately, only one of us could stand on it at a time. In retrospect, I think we only had this band as an excuse to have parties and invite the cute girls from down the street.

Names for bands are fun, fickle, and fleeting. They come and go and are as interchangeable as the drummers in *Spinal Tap*. Names for kids, however, are somewhat trickier. It seems there is always a reason why a particular name won't work. We didn't want a name that people might shorten or turn into an embarrassing nickname. After you find a good name, it's important to keep it a secret. Don't tell anyone, not even family or close friends. They will invariably give you a reason why you shouldn't go with that name. In fact, don't ever tell anyone the name, even after your child is born. Even if you think you've found the perfect name, you will probably change your mind several times over the period of nine months.

Due to an emergency landing on a commercial airline a few years back, Susan is a nervous flier. After she became pregnant, the only thing that would calm her when we hit turbulence was if I started suggesting possible names for our future baby. The captain would announce, "Folks, fasten your seat belts, we are hitting a little turbulence." That was my cue to start rattling off names: "Jerome? Matilda? Luke? Chelsea? Trixie? Chickadee?

Butter Cream?" She would smile and forget everything else. I would write the names on an airsickness bag. This way, if she started hurling, I would conveniently have the bag handy. The only problem would be that if one of those names turned out to be the one, it would then be immortalized on the side of a bag designed to hold vomit, which didn't seem like the right way to get this name thing started.

Once you have narrowed down the possible name options, start using them in a sentence. Practice saying them to see how they sound:

"Gracie, stop that!"

"Stella, don't put that in your mouth!"

"Peter! Why were you out so late?"

"Who was it that dropped you off, Latrice?"

"How much is the bail, Travis?"

I knew that some parents name their kids after characters in literature or names in famous poems, which I think is very urbane and sophisticated. For that reason I suggested we name our child Nantucket—"There once was a man from Nantucket, who went to the moon in a bucket . . . " This way, I figured, people would think I was sophisticated and into poetry or literature. We also picked up several different baby books just on names. I don't know why we got more than one. It's the same names in all the books, just different covers. After perusing thousands of names in all three books, we considered naming our child Book. The whole name thing is just so difficult and frustrating. We wanted a name that was somewhat interesting and unique, but not too Apple-ish, if you know what I mean. We looked everywhere for inspiration. We found ourselves looking at street signs, bill-boards—even menus. For a while we considered the name Maple but then thought better of it.

"When you have to go to IHOP to get permission to use a name, that is not a good sign," I said.

"Hey, how 'bout the name IHOP?" my wife joked.

"Not bad," I replied politely, "but let's keep thinking. Wait a minute. You just gave me an idea." Maybe we could approach a large corporation for sponsorship? Raising a child is not inexpensive these days. Good schools cost money. I wasn't unfamous, and as such my child would surely attract some form of attention during his or her life. Why not one-up all those other celebrities competing with each other for the most exotic name in Hollywood? Not only would our name be exotic, it would be subsidized.

I started drafting a corporate pitch that sounded something like this: We will name our kid after your company and/or new product if you agree to pay for college tuition at a four-year accredited institution in eighteen years. Should the company desire the child's name to be more than one word, the price of tuition would extend to include either the cost of a master's degree or the first two years of a doctorate, as this second word will be considered the child's middle name. For example, the name Verizon Nealon would only cost college tuition, but Taco Bell Nealon would incur the added tuition charge, it being understood that "Bell" would be considered his middle name.

At this point, pretty much everything was on the table. Best Buy Nealon? Google Nealon? Velveeta Nealon? Red Lobster Nealon? How about Welbutrin or Zoloft? "Zoloft! Settle down! Get off the couch, Zoloft!" We were even considering the name Keys, Keys, Keys of Van Nuys, which was a car dealership in the valley.

I had taken to reading *Forbes*, and I was contemplating setting up meetings with some Fortune 500 marketing departments, when I became distracted by the possibility that we could use the name of a European port city instead. Unfortunately, as I scoured an out-of-date atlas (the Soviet Union was one big blob on the page), none of these sparked any ideas.

The whole thing seemed to be spiraling out of control. We couldn't make up our minds, but we didn't want to go to outside sources out of a fear that we might taint the results. This paradoxical situation brought us to the one unexplored possibility: hire an ad agency to come up with one based on think-tank market research and focus groups. But when confronted with the prospects of what that might cost, we decided instead to collect a bunch of names from our friends and families and see if we liked any of them. Here are some of the more interesting ones, most of which sound like old blues musicians:

Prayin' Wyle Nealon
Nellie Nealon
Ricky Bobby Nealon
Conan Meconium Nealon
Kneeling Nealon
Firecracker Nealon
Garry Emanual Shandling
The Honorable D'Brickashaw "Little Peetey" Nealon
Bundt Cake Nealon
Kumquat Nealon
Glorious Jesus Explosion Yeagley Nealon
Nuggets Nealon
Florida Coastal Waterway Nealon
"No" Nealon
"Don't Touch That" Nealon
Big Balls Nealon

Here are some names we were definitely ruling out:

Trump
Baked Beans
Valium
Vente
Kato
Latte
Ambien
Poop Head
Britney
Lindsay
Paris

Since I would be an older father, I liked the idea of something easy to pronounce for when I am on my deathbed and exhaling my last weak breath. Something that will be able to just roll off my tongue with no effort like Al or Shar, but not Hal, because that could be confused with "Help."

I thought about the whole situation, and I couldn't even decide why a name was so important anyway. Most people would inevitably take the name, truncate it, and mold it into whatever nickname they wanted to say. Some people wouldn't know the name to begin with and would call my child a generic name, like Chief, Sport, or Boss. "Hey, Boss!" they'd say. "Can I pull your car around, Boss?" It confuses me when someone calls me Boss because then I start thinking, Do I own a company? Is this guy my employee? If he is my employee, why is he standing around chatting and not working? Then I start thinking that I might have to fire this guy, and I don't even know what he does, which would make it difficult to replace him.

It would have been easier to come up with a name if we knew what the sex of the baby was. I still think it's amazing that, through ultrasounds, they can tell what the sex of the baby is going to be before it's even born. That's modern technology for you. The only challenge now is finding out what the sex of the baby is going to be later on in life. Talk about your life changing! I liked the idea of not knowing the sex until the baby is born. It's like going to pick up your dry cleaning after a month. You really don't know what garments you dropped off, and it's kind of a nice surprise when you get certain clothes back you forgot you had. Some friends were adamant about not knowing the sex before it's born. They say it was the last great surprise in life. I would actually say the *last great surprise* in your life is how you die. The only problem with that surprise is after it happens you're not around to appreciate it and say, "Wow! I'm shocked! I never saw that truck coming!" It's just lights-out. It might even be fun not knowing when the baby is due, I thought. Can you imagine how exciting that would be? It would be like musical chairs except instead of the music stopping it would be her water breaking. "Is it now?" I would ask, excitedly. "Honey? Are you okay? What's going on? Is it now? Is it now?" We would then scramble to the nearest available hospital. I guess you can make a game out of almost any situation in life.

Sometimes surprises aren't all they're cracked up to be. I have mixed feelings about the whole surprise-birthday-party thing. I suppose it's nice to surprise someone with a party where lots of their friends are waiting to celebrate their big day. I can't help thinking that it's more fun for the people that lie in wait. Everyone gets a thrill from jumping out and yelling "Surprise!" as the startled guest of honor arrives. It's like a big practical joke played out by an entire group. How often do you get to do that? Everyone is giddy as they are relayed the information that the subject is on the way.

A surprise birthday party doesn't always happen without its snags, though. Sometimes it's too difficult to protect your secret planning from the party girl or boy. Guests may not arrive early enough, and show up at the same time as the subject. And what if some guests are inadvertently invited that the subject disapproves of? What if the subject is not having a good hair day? Most worrisome, the subject may be so shocked by the surprise that he experiences a heart attack. The entire planning/strategy/deceit to get him there is proudly discussed later that evening. It is soon thereafter that the subject realizes that he has actually been lied to, usually by someone that he really loves and trusts. This could be the biggest snag. It starts to set in—"How could someone I love and trust so much lie to me? Not only did he lie to me, but he also did it so well. He was really good at it. Where did he learn how to do that?"

And usually it is not just the person you love and trust that has lied to you, but also more than likely a few other close friends or family members that served as accomplices, or to corroborate a fictitious meeting place or excuse. The postparty planning discussion reveals just how much work went into misleading you. Again, the troubling thought is just how easily they were able to deceive you. Then you start thinking, has he done this before? Now that he knows how easy it is, will he do it again for something other than a surprise birthday party? Will you ever be able to trust him again? So the next time you walk into a room and a bunch of people jump out and yell, "SURPRISE!"–just know what they are really saying is, "SURPRISE! THE PERSON YOU TRUSTED MOST IN LIFE IS A BIG LIAR!"

Trust is especially important when it comes to selecting godparents. While it may have been a little premature to be thinking about godparents at such an early stage, nowhere is it more appropriate to put the cart before the horse than when you learn you are pregnant. Even though there is the possibility that the baby will not survive the first three months, you have to start planning because it is an all-consuming distraction. Picking suitable godparents is almost as hard as picking a name. It is really the only thing you can do at this point to protect your child's future.

"Who, of our friends, would be suitable enough to take on this role?" I asked Susan. None had the ideal lifestyle situations. One might be traveling too much for her career, another was a potential alcoholic, one was too famous, others were too old, another couple looked liked they were going to split up, others were single, and some, we suspected, were dabbling in occult activities—it seemed that virtually everyone had some kind of situational problem that eliminated them from the running. After careful consideration, we came to the conclusion that if anything ever happened to us, we couldn't trust our children with any of our friends. We needed to find someone who could look after our child and set a good example if anything ever happened to us.

I myself am a godfather, so I think I have a pretty good sense of what the job entails. When my godson's mother initially extended this flattering offer, she sat me down, stared at me, and said that under no uncertain terms, if I accepted this, I would have to live up to the requirements of being a good godfather—remembering his birthdays and being there for him if he needed me would be standard for this type of commitment. Several times she clarified the duties that would be involved with this position and wanted to hear if I was physically and mentally willing and able to perform them. I felt as though I was sitting in the emergency exit row on a commercial airplane, and the flight attendant was addressing me before takeoff. I got the impression that she didn't have a lot of faith in me. I assured her that I would perform my duties, and since then I have not missed a birthday card in twenty-three years.

As the date for our first ultrasound loomed, we were nowhere near finding a suitable name or a suitable set of godparents. When we arrived at the doctor's office, the technician, or ultrasoundist as I called her, led us into a small room equipped with an ultrasound machine and an examining table with stirrups. Handing Susan a hospital gown, the technician instructed her to put it on and climb up onto the table. Susan completed every step just as she was told, and lay there with her feet resting on the cold metal of the stirrups, waiting to see what her child looked like. The ultrasoundist flipped on the machine and removed the connected wand that resembled . . . well, a wand. To get a picture of the baby, she slid the wand under Susan's gown with one hand and adjusted some knobs on the machine with the other, all the while watching the images on the screen. Judging from how little attention she paid to the wand, it was clear she had been doing this job for many years. Meanwhile it occurred to me that this was probably the closest I would ever come to having a threesome.

We reminded the ultrasoundist not to reveal the sex of the baby to us. As I fixated on the monitor, it suddenly dawned on me that I was about to meet my kid for the first time, and in one fleeting moment, I became paralyzed by anxiety. What if the monitor revealed an image of just baggage? What if the fetus saw us looking at him/her and shook its head no? What if the fetus was dancing around and chanting, "You're gonna be a father! You're gonna be a father!"

I awoke seconds later to find the ultrasoundist holding smelling salt under my nose. I guess this experience was all too overwhelming for me. I got my head together and refocused on the monitor. The monitor suddenly revealed a grainy black-and-white image. I examined what looked like a large black lima bean (the uterus) with just a little nugget (the baby) clinging to the side. The ultrasoundist moved the wand around a little, trying for the best picture, before she casually tossed out that Susan's uterus is inverted. My blood pressure immediately shot up to 195 over 98. Concerned, I asked if that was a problem.

"No, no problem," she replied. "Everyone is different, and an inverted uterus is no big deal." My blood pressure came down a little. She was very nonchalant about this information. With her matter-of-fact way of speaking, I would have believed her if she had said that it was also perfectly normal for Susan's vagina to be located on her knee. It's amazing how much trust a white coat on a person will instill.

She maneuvered the wand around a little more to get a better shot. By the way, at this stage we had begun calling our child everything from Peanut to Raspberry. As I stared blankly at the screen, the ultrasoundist told us that if we were very quiet, we might hear Peanut's heartbeat. We listened, and sure enough, its little heart was racing faster than mine the last time I was in Mexico. The baby's heart rate was one hundred and sixty-seven beats per minute. To give you an idea of how fast that is, sneak onto a roller-coaster track and try to outrun the cars for two minutes. Once again, all perfectly normal, she assured us.

Like a photo booth at a carnival, the ultrasound machine spat out a column of pictures for us to take home as a memento, photos that, upon closer inspection, kind of resembled a satellite photo of a hurricane tearing through the Caribbean. Each photo had only a few slight differences, but it seemed to me that if I let my eyes move across them in quick succession, it looked as though they had the potential to destroy our personal property and wreak havoc on our life. As with an impending hurricane, we were determined to keep an eye on the development of our baby, and provide evacuation warnings should wind gusts get above sixty miles an hour.

Since I now had something substantial to show in the form of pictures that looked more like satellite imaging than a baby, I decided I could officially consider myself a proud father. I took a snapshot of the best ultrasound picture with my cell phone camera and started to use it as my phone's background. Having the photo on my phone, I reasoned, could only help my marketing pitch to cell phone companies interested in sponsoring our child's name. It also gave me the chance to get used to the idea of a brand name contrasted against an image of my child. That way, if I looked at the background enough, it might come to make sense that my baby would be named T-Mobile. A great name if he/she were to become a rapper.

When I showed the photo to people, they were amazed that I was able to get it on my cell phone. They asked me how I got it on there, and I would tell them that I just put a little gel on it and rubbed it over Susan's lower stomach. When I felt it was the right spot, I snapped the picture. T-Mobile, it turns out, has a great family plan and only charges a nominal fee for each ultrasound picture. Of course, now, all my calls go through the baby.

On our way home we stopped at Kinko's to make copies of the ultrasound picture to send to friends and relatives. This would be the beginning of the onslaught of baby-related photos sent from us. The photocopies of the already grainy ultrasound pictures slid out of the copier and landed in the bin. Since they were third generation copies now, the ultrasound was beginning to resemble a Rorschach inkblot test. I knew our family would love it anyway. My parents got the ultrasound picture in the mail two days later. My father looked at it and saw a butterfly dancing on a stovetop. He said it was the cutest butterfly he had ever seen. My mother said it looked like an Indian with a big headdress scalping a pioneer, but the cutest Indian she'd ever seen.

We were still on cloud nine as we continued home. Everything was right with the world. As we pulled into the rush-hour traffic on the freeway, my wife turned to me with a sweet smile and asked, "How 'bout the name Kinko?"

EIGHT

Tightly Wrapped

I came home one evening to discover that a couple of pages had been ripped from the latest issue of a women's magazine that Susan likes to read. I liked this particular magazine because some of its articles gave me some insight as to why some women behave the way they do. My wife had subscriptions to several magazines, of which a few I found to be quite informative. *O Magazine* was one of these. Since my wife had been buying this magazine over the past year, I've noticed that Oprah puts only herself on the cover, wearing one fabulous outfit or another each month. And why not, I say? It's her magazine.

If I had a magazine, I would do things my way, too. Each month I would put a different celebrity or notable person on the cover, but I would stock each magazine with lots of those annoying inserts that always fall out—and I would have *my* picture on each and every one. Whenever I had an ad that used a picture of an attractive model in my magazine, I would print her name and how she could be reached. I think all magazines should consider this, even the Sears catalog. I can't tell you how many times, while growing up, I saw a hot model in an ad and wanted to know more about her—like, who was she, and was she available? What restaurants did she frequent, and where did she live? Basically, all the information necessary to stalk her. (Hey, it's my magazine, and I can do what I want.)

Puzzled by the missing pages in the magazine, I asked Susan if she was responsible. I assumed it was a recipe, maybe, or something baby-related. At first she didn't answer, just stared off. Finally, after some more prodding, she admitted that it was an article she had read about how pregnant women are the number one most murdered demographic. Apparently, she said, some husbands freak out, like the infamous Scott Peterson, and kill their pregnant wives.

"But, sweetheart, why did you rip it out of the magazine?" I asked. She confessed that she had torn the article out so I wouldn't see it. She didn't want me getting any ideas, she said. Not only had she ripped the pages out, she also admitted that she'd put them through the paper shredder and personally hand-delivered them to the outside garbage cans.

"Honey," I said, "I can't believe you actually got rid of the article because you thought it might give me an idea." It was insulting. She was giving me no credit, assuming that I would have to get the idea from an article instead of coming up with it on my own. Seriously, though, it's hard to not be offended when someone you love makes it clear that they think a magazine article could cause you to go on a murderous rampage. I guess I'm being a bit hypocritical, because I do shred a lot of her catalogs that come in the mail before she ever sees them. I really do believe they might give her some crazy ideas to *kill* time at Neiman Marcus.

This magazine incident was not her normal behavior. As I soon discovered, her pregnancy hormones were starting to awaken, and take her hostage and me along with her. It was the beginning of her temporary transition; the pods were beginning to open up in the *Invasion of the Body Snatchers*. I learned, as a husband, you have to be extremely aware and sensitive to this condition, and for this reason going through a pregnancy can be very challenging. As your partner experiences hormonal upheaval, you, in return, will be experiencing stress. Unfortunately, you will have to deal with both. I was told that the situation I was going through is not uncommon. Neither stress nor hormones are something to take lightly. As we all know, stress is the silent killer—unless, of course, you're one of those people who sighs often and says, "Oh, I am so stressed." Then you are ruining the concept that stress is the silent killer for the rest of us. It's never said that women's hormones are the silent killer, but they do bring you close to the brink. In fact, they couldn't be further from being silent; they scream as loudly as possible all the time.

On at least one occasion, I carelessly let my guard down. It was a stupid mistake that occurred early on in the pregnancy, and I was probably not as sensitive as I should have been. I had been invited to play three glorious days of golf in an exciting golf tournament in Lake Tahoe. There would be lots of fun people and an incredible gift bag. Susan could come with me, all expenses paid. When I presented this opportunity to her, she just frowned. She had read somewhere that in the first trimester it's not healthy for a pregnant woman to go to altitudes over five thousand feet above sea level. A wave of disappointment rushed over me as I remembered hearing that Lake Tahoe was just at a little over five thousand feet. I didn't want to abandon her, but I also didn't want to miss out on this incredible opportunity. You can imagine my frustration. I believe that old adage that there are no problems, there are only solutions, and this is where I think I might have been a little callous.

"Sweetie, couldn't you go on the trip and just crouch the whole time, keeping yourself just under five thousand feet? I mean, just don't stand up straight."

It was at that moment that my battles with the hormones officially began, and sadly, the common man is no match. This chemical imbalance can play strange games where there are no rules or boundaries. During these times of confusing behavior, I quickly learned to never try to reason with a woman experiencing hormonal mood swings. Do not try to defend yourself; it does no good. Just surrender and go along on her hormonal trip with her. I know your instinct will be to try to explain reality but, once again, you must just surrender. A pregnant woman will cry at any given moment for absolutely no reason, and you must remind yourself that it is most likely nothing you have said or done—it's simply the hormones.

This being so, it was not much of a surprise that the hormones prevented Susan from hearing out my perfectly rational solution to this Lake Tahoe altitude problem. It was as though the hormones threw all logic out the window. Here I was, trying to come up with a solution to keep our unborn child healthy and my chip shot in its best form, and all she could do was scoff. "Just remember," I said to myself for the first of many times, "it's not me that is acting crazy."

If the golf course fiasco wasn't enough, there was also the night that Susan couldn't bear my smell. When I come home from the gym or a walk, sometimes she'll jokingly hold her nose to emphasize how much I really smell. We'll have a laugh about it, I'll shower, and that's that. But on this particular night, I hadn't just returned from the gym, and there was absolutely no reason for this behavior. Nevertheless, she insisted that my bad smell was too overpowering. I told her I had never heard this complaint from her or anyone else before, but she insisted that the smell was awful. I proceeded to change my shirt and add a ton of powder and cologne, but when I got back in bed, she smelled the cologne on me and wanted to know if I'd been with another man. I just surrendered and said, Yes. Sometimes that's all you can do.

Ultimately, if this is all the man has to put up with, it's not that bad. Let's face it; we don't have that much to do during the pregnancy except endure the temporary madness. There are no major demands on us. It's not like *The March of the Penguins*. We don't have to balance an egg on our feet in the freezing cold for a month—although some of us might prefer that option if we had it. The most important thing for the husband/partner to do is to be one hundred percent supportive. It doesn't matter what it is. If she wants to yell at the mailman about something, you had better be right behind her, saying, "Yeah. You heard her! Bring more catalogs and water the grass!"

Still, there are other side effects beyond hormones that husbands must navigate successfully—especially during the early stages of the pregnancy. Nausea, fatigue, and impatience were also very common, but all that subsided once I cut back on my partying. My wife, on the other hand, quickly became susceptible to these conditions. Unlike many other "women with child," she managed to avoid the morning sickness. They call it morning sickness, but it can last throughout the day or come at different intervals. My friend's wife was vomiting so much and so spontaneously that, as to not mess up the house, she spent a lot of her day standing outside on the patio. My friend, her loving husband, would stand nearby with a garden hose, spraying the puke off the patio each time. That's one of the great things about going through a pregnancy together; there are just so many loving memories to create.

I don't have any idea how working women tolerate this phase of pregnancy. Simply put, it is no fun going to work when you are ill. One time I flew up to Rochester, New York, to do a show with Tommy Davidson and Bill Maher, and by the time I arrived at this beautiful outdoor amphitheater, I was experiencing terrible flu symptoms. I felt absolutely horrible, and the last thing I wanted to do was stand-up comedy. I didn't want to cancel, though, because, quite frankly, I had flown all the way up there and didn't want to go home empty-handed. While Tommy was performing, I was able to find a cot to lie on backstage. I was lightheaded and on the verge of throwing up, but I felt better as long as I was lying down. Eventually, Tommy finished his act, and I could hear them introducing Bill. I tried getting up off the cot, but each time I did, I felt dizzy and nauseated again. I was hoping that Bill's act would never end, and if it did, that he would get extended encores.

As my turn onstage drew closer, I came up with an idea. Why not perform my act from the cot onstage? I would weave my jokes around the premise of being depressed and tell the audience that I couldn't even get out of bed. Just before I was introduced, I had the stage manager bring the cot out. It worked like a charm. I came out and told the audience I had been really down lately, explaining that it was all too overwhelming, and I would need to lie down. I brought the microphone as I lay down on the cot. The audience loved it. Occasionally, during my act, I would try to get up from the cot, but the light-headedness would return, and I would tell the audience that I needed to lie down again. The bit worked so well I incorporated it into my act on several occasions after that.

Unfortunately, most jobs are not open to the idea of lying

down on a cot whenever nausea occurs, which can be incredibly tough on pregnant women who are working, because the frustrating truth is that you just never know what is going to trigger the nausea. One morning, I was lying in bed with Susan and telling her a joke that I was working on and had tried at a comedy club the night before. Even though I didn't have the exact wording of the joke down, I knew it had a lot of potential and I couldn't wait for her feedback on it. It had been extremely hot in Los Angeles this particular month, and the joke involved repeating a lot of temperatures and rising gas prices in the surrounding areas. In other words, the joke was rather long and tedious, and it came off sounding a bit like the local news. In the middle of the joke she began to look pasty and white. She signaled me to be quiet by putting her finger to my mouth, explaining that the very sound of my voice was making her nauseated. She began to gag, then quickly got out of bed and ran to the bathroom. As I lay in bed staring at the wall, I could hear the echoes of her gagging as she tried to throw up. The sound of my voice had never made anyone vomit before, and that's saying something, because there are a lot of people who have heard my voice. I wasn't feeling very good about myself, or about that particular joke. While the audience's response had been less harsh and noticeably cleaner than Susan's, I ended up dropping the joke.

At times I became so overwhelmed with all of these side effects of pregnancy that I just had to lie down on my cot. When Susan asked, "What's wrong?" I would then be forced to lie and simply tell her, "Nothing. I'm just a little tired."

Men's difficulties during pregnancy are usually brushed aside, but their stress can show itself in different ways. Apparently, grinding your teeth at night is a sure sign. It's really something that should be avoided because it wears your teeth down. I have put in far too much time in the dentist's chair over the years trying to preserve my natural teeth to fall victim to that. Besides, I would imagine that the sparks coming from your mouth at night could present a fire hazard. My dentist recommended a night guard. I don't know if you're familiar with a night guard, but I wasn't. At first I thought it was a guy who stands by your bed all night and watches your teeth; probably very professional with a nice uniform. When he sees you grinding your teeth, he simply wedges his finger between them, and that will pretty much stop it. In actuality it's a fitted piece of rubber that you put in your mouth at night. All in all it's less obtrusive than an actual human guard would be, although there's something to be said for that kind of one-on-one attention.

Another sign of stress was my noticeably tighter grip on the television's remote control. Not only a tighter grip, but the constant switching of channels, flipping quickly through all one hundred channels over and over until eventually the buttons had worn off. The channel numbers from the remote control were permanently embedded on my thumbtip. Perhaps someone needs to come up with a night guard for the remote? It seems that stress manifests itself in our squeezing harder on things; that is to say, more force per square inch applied by the stressee. Road rage is a result of stress. A stressed person has the need to squeeze the gas pedal to the metal, and when the car in front of him doesn't allow for this because it is not going fast enough, well, that's when heated words are exchanged.

There are certainly many ways of relieving stress. Some people meditate; some exercise, golf, or get a massage. I happen to enjoy a good massage, which is why I occasionally pay for a professional masseuse to come in. Susan will offer to give me a massage, but it's usually not very relaxing because I need to constantly encourage her to keep on massaging. Her mind quickly wanders; she doesn't focus, and the next thing you know the massage has stopped and she's reading a magazine or watching CNN. The nice thing about paying for a massage is that you don't have to continuously encourage the masseuse by saying, "Oh, that's nice! That's great! Where did you learn how to do that?" You just pay, and you will get a massage for an hour.

Do you know what I really like to do to relieve stress? I feel awkward talking about this, but it's pretty obvious—yes, that's right, I like to hike. I love being out in nature. I leave my cell phone home so I am not disturbed. Who's kidding whom—I'm not going to miss it for five or ten minutes. Last month I was hiking through some of the small hills just outside of Los Angeles. It was so serene and relaxing: no cell phone and no traffic. I walked up the long, winding trail and along the ridge, where I took in some stunning views of the Pacific coastline. It was so calm and peaceful. I eventually came upon some deer droppings. I used to be a Boy Scout, so I found a little stick and sifted through the droppings to see what the deer had eaten most recently. I found that the deer had eaten a couple of berries, but mostly . . . turds; little round deer turds. Not a very good diet if you ask me. Where's your fiber?

It always amazed me how deer and coyote can live within the Los Angeles city limits. Most people get really excited when they see one, too. I was golfing once at a public course, and a coyote scurried across several of the fairways. Someone from the group in front of us spotted it and yelled, "Look! A deer!" Once the coyote had reached another fairway, I heard another golfer on that hole excitedly yell, "Look! A fox!"

If you should choose to hike as relaxation, find a trail that matches your comfort level. For years, a couple of writer friends of mine would talk about how much they loved hiking. It seemed like they were always hiking. I eventually went with them on one of their hikes. It's funny what some people consider hiking. Their so-called hike consisted of walking through a neighborhood on a hillside and looking at open houses. This was their comfort level.

During my repeated showers to get rid of my supposed nauseating odor, frequent trips to the kitchen at 3:00 A.M., hiking trips to relieve my stress, and various other responses to Susan's pregnancy side effects, I found myself thinking of something that had happened to me not long after Susan and I started dating. It was the morning after Christmas, when, following a bowl of cereal and a large cup of coffee, I excused myself to the bathroom. As I prepared to do my business, I could hear my housekeeper's seven-year-old daughter, Angela, playing in the next room with the baby Jesus from the manger. She had him driving a toy Hummer through the stable. At one point she had two of the Wise Men carjack the Hummer. They dragged the baby Jesus out from the front seat, kicking and screaming, and sped away into the surrounding fields. The third Wise Man lived up to his name and wanted no part of this. One of the shepherds tried to intervene but was beaten mercilessly about the head and body . . . all, incidentally, caught on videotape. I don't know where Angela's rage was coming from, but within two weeks she was on Zoloft.

After no success for at least ten minutes in the bathroom, I finally diagnosed myself with acute constipation. I knew what lay ahead of me from experiencing this once before about fifteen years ago. I also knew the only thing to relieve this incredible pain and break up the "gridlock" was a product called Fleet. Fleet is an over-the-counter enema that comes in a squeeze bottle, available at your local pharmacy for about $13.75. (*Checkwithyourdoctorormedicalpractitionerifyouarepregnant.*) You simply unwrap it, insert the nozzle, and squeeze. In a few minutes or so traffic should be moving again. This was exactly what I needed, but I was in no position to be walking, not to mention driving.

Further complicating things was the fact that I had no one to get it for me. Lupé, my housekeeper, who spoke no English, was downstairs scrubbing the counters. I could only imagine miming to her what an enema was—it would consist of me straining until my face was red and then squeezing an imaginary bottle into my behind while in the prone position. Not even my mom could pull that one off.

Somewhere off in the other room I heard Angela pistol-whipping Mary and Joseph. I briefly considered asking Angela for help, but she was too young to drive and would only complicate matters. With both Lupé and Angela out of the question, there was only one other person who I could call: Susan.

Something worth noting here is that at this point, Susan and I had only been dating for two weeks. Some would say, "Hey, isn't that a little early into the relationship to be asking for your girl to pick you up an over-the-counter enema to deal with your acute constipation?" I know that there are tons of dating rules and relationship faux pas that cover all aspects of dating etiquette: when to call and when not to call, how long to wait before you get frisky, when to tell the other person that you love them. I'm sure there are some manuals or experts that would say that this was a little too early into a burgeoning relationship to be asking for this type of favor. But I'm sure the experts who would say that have never been seriously constipated before. Let me tell you something—when you are constipated, or, in fact, "impacted," you are absolutely desperate, delirious, and not thinking straight. All you want is immediate relief and to survive. You are just looking for anybody to latch on to and you would promise them the world if they would just help you.

Another sharp pain, and I was on the phone to Susan. I could not afford the luxury of considering the repercussions this call would have on our relationship. Thank God she was home. I explained my dilemma and begged her to go to a pharmacy as fast as she could, but still be careful, pick up an enema called Fleet, and rush it up here to me as fast as possible . . . but still be careful. She must have sensed the desperation in my voice, because she was out the door before she hung up.

By now the pain was so intense I could only splash water on my face to keep my mind off it. I could now hear Angela in the other room singing "The Twelve Days of Christmas," except she didn't know the words. Everything was "five turtle doves." "On the tenth day of Christmas my true love gave to me . . . five turtle doves, five turtle doves, fii-ive turtle doves, five tur-tle doves . . . five turtle doves," and so on and so forth. It was more of an annoyance than a distraction. I wished that she had gone back to her manger scene with maybe a domestic dispute between Mary and Joseph.

I called Susan every five minutes, frantically asking, "Where are you now?" "I'm just turning on Highland Avenue," she'd reply. "Okay, please hurry . . . but be careful!" I'd shout back into the phone. While I was waiting for her to arrive, I decided to call my doctor. He was a big help. He calmly said to go ahead with the Fleet enema when it got there. I hung up and immediately called Susan back. "Where are you now?" I demanded. "I am just coming up Outpost Road, and I have your Fleet!" she replied, overwhelmed with the urgency of my condition. I splashed more water on my face.

Finally I heard her car stop outside, the door slam, and then her racing up the stairs. She entered the bedroom cautiously, not certain what she would find. "Here!" she said, out of breath. "Here it is!" I was so happy to see that bag. She reached in and pulled out a package of Fleet suppositories and some type of Fleet cream. I guess Fleet makes all kinds of anal products. I couldn't believe it—there was no Fleet enema.

"Where's the enema?" I snapped. "That's NOT an enema, that's a suppository!"

I was even more desperate now, and taking it out on an innocent woman I barely knew, who was only trying to help. It was total displaced anger. "I told you . . . Fleet enema!! It's a bottle with a nozzle and you squeeze stuff out of it!" She was horrified that she had the wrong Fleet, and also probably horrified that she was going out with a guy that was so impacted he needed her to pick up an over-the-counter enema.

She ran out of the room, yelling, "Oh, my God, I am so sorry! I'll go to the pharmacy down the hill and see if they have it!"

"Please, please hurry," I pleaded, bracing myself for another twenty minutes of sheer pain.

I picked up the phone and called her immediately. "Where are you now?"

"I'm running to my car through your kitchen," she replied.

"How 'bout now? And now?"

This went on for the next twenty minutes as I squirmed and "Kegeled," which I think is a Pilates term that means "to squeeze your sphincter." (More on this later.) Nothing was happening. This would be the time where if I were lost in the wilderness I would write a note to my loved ones. I finally put down the phone to die.

In my daze I heard more "five turtle doves" coming from the other room. As I lay on the floor, writhing in pain, I decided, as a last resort, to take one of the suppositories. I tried to insert it, but I was not having much luck. It was like trying to pound a tent pole into a block of cement. The only way this would work is if I had a pile driver.

I weakly grabbed my cell phone for another "Where are you now?" conversation with Susan. There was no answer because she was now running full speed through the downstairs living room. Lupé saw the concerned determination on her face and asked, "Is Mr. Kevin okay?" Susan said "Si" and charged up the staircase as if returning from a scavenger hunt. Even the two Wise Men stepped out of the way.

She triumphantly entered the bathroom to find my face dripping in what appeared to be sweat. I was now lying in the prone position on the bathroom floor, on two large, clean white towels that I had laid out. I was like a dog preparing to give birth to a litter of puppies in a garage. I had even considered lining up a midwife to help. She quickly emptied the CVS pharmacy bag in front of me. Not one bottle of Fleet, but *three* bottles with big block letters reading ENEMA. My Fleet had come in.

I frantically grappled with the secured plastic wrapping, noticing the holiday mistletoe decorations on the discarded box. Susan watched me pathetically fumble with the plastic for what seemed like eternity. It was harder than opening a CD! Ironically the Fleet itself was impacted in its own plastic wrapping. Why do they make it so hard to open packages? If they don't want us to open them, why do they make them available? Why do they tease us? It's like when they put the go-go dancer inside the cage at some of these clubs. Trying to open a CD package is the worst. Once you manage to break through the plastic shrink-wrap, then you still have two or three more strips of tape to get through to open the box. By the time you get this thing open, the songs on the CD could very well be golden oldies. An enema should be the easiest product to get out of its box. It should jump out like a jack-in-the-box. Susan asked if I wanted her to help or wait outside? To save any shred of dignity that I might salvage from this, I opted for her to wait outside the bedroom.

I finally ripped the bottle from the package, grabbed it like an alcoholic falling off the wagon, and applied the medication. I had been saved, and it was truly a miracle. When the dust settled, ever so faintly I heard, from the other room, Angela reading the two Wise Men their Miranda rights.

As my adrenaline levels came down, and my blood pressure receded, I lingered on the toilet seat—grateful for Susan's help, but horrified that she had witnessed this. My dark side was hoping that maybe she would fall down the stairs, hit her head, and forget all of this. Then I started thinking, Maybe I could *push* her down the stairs. I stared at the phone that I had used to call her so many times, and the full weight of my decision became apparent. It would never be the same between us. No matter what happened, no matter where we went, she would have seen me at my most vulnerable. Some husbands go a whole lifetime without displaying this level of vulnerability; I was barely two weeks in, and she had already witnessed me backed up like a porta-potty at a Stones concert.

People say that really intense events that occur early on in a relationship can make the romance that much stronger. Now, I'm not going to say that I was sitting on the toilet and thinking that this was the woman I would marry, but the thought wasn't that far from my mind. There's something uncommon about a woman who, on the day after Christmas when you've only been dating her for two weeks, is willing to drop everything and go to two pharmacies for you because, as you've so delicately explained, it feels as though your sphincter is about to rupture. There are plenty of intelligent, funny, attractive women in the world, but if you asked them to go through this ordeal when you'd only been dating for two weeks, most would just let your repeated calls go straight to voice mail. Then they would play your messages back to their friends and cackle nonstop. But not Susan. Apparently she had been to lots of Stones concerts.

As I thought back to this story during the pregnancy, it seemed a bit unfair that this was my benchmark for side effects and

vulnerability in this relationship. After all, this had only happened to me that one time. But I also knew that when a woman
goes through a pregnancy, there will be many such days of
humiliation and necessary immediate attention, and I was
more than willing to step up to the plate. After all, she had saved
my ass.

NINE

Out of the Woods, but Still in the Dark

You're not fat. You're pregnant," I remind Susan as she steps off the doctor's scale. This official doctor's scale has been a fixture in my garage for the past several years. I bought it because not only is it extremely accurate, but it's also fun. To determine how much you weigh, you get to slide the little weights across the horizontal bar until it levels off. Whatever number the weights are on equals your pounds. Even before Susan got pregnant, we had a routine of weighing ourselves. About every other day we anxiously tiptoe through the morning dew to the garage, strip down, and gingerly step on the scale, naked. The person not on the scale keeps watch by the door to make sure a neighbor or a worker isn't walking by. Some might say we have become quite obsessive about our weight, but I say your weight is just as important as your blood pressure. Incidentally, I've added this scale to my blood-pressure-machine-and-ovulation-test-kit collection. At this rate, I may soon have enough medical equipment to open up my own practice.

That morning, Susan's weight had gone up slightly, and my weight had gone up significantly. During pregnancy, this is what they call "sympathy weight." I call it "significant weight." In my case, this significant weight gain came from sampling. If it was a protein shake, I'd sample it. If she didn't finish it, I would. I'd say to myself, "Ya know, that's not so bad. Maybe I'll make one for myself." This type of behavior might explain why I couldn't fit into most of the pants in my closet. For that matter, I almost couldn't even fit into my closet. I'd walk by the mirror in the bathroom and would be repulsed by my larger-than-ever image. In this very short time I had gained nineteen pounds, and it showed.

People would tell me, "Don't worry, you're tall. You can carry it."

"Well, tell that to my pants!" I replied.

I found myself avoiding the bathroom during the day so I didn't have to see myself in the mirror in this out-of-control state. Typically I didn't look at myself in the mirror anyway. When I turned forty, I didn't like what I was seeing. My face was beginning to sag, and I was losing hair. From that point on, whenever I used the bathroom, I made it a practice to leave the lights off. I didn't want to see or accept the beginning stages of my body decomposing, even though most people would probably never have noticed. Even though I would occasionally end up missing the toilet at night, it was worth not seeing my love handles.

I had never weighed this much before, and I immediately went into damage control. First, I joined a gym. Like most other people, I go regularly for the first two weeks, and then I start making excuses not to go. During my first two weeks I would, occasionally, notice the same few pregnant women exercising. I came to call it the "chat to lose fat" program. The two women will basically stand in front of, say, the leg-press machine, where they will have a few minutes of conversation about a sale at Macy's or some latest celebrity gossip. Then, without ever using the machine, they will say, "Okay, let's go do our back now." They will then stand by the back machine and talk about something else for a few minutes, until it's time to move to the lat machine. This intensified program usually lasts around thirty minutes and, depending on how much gossip there is, can burn off up to five hundred calories.

My backup plan to counter my weight gain was simple: aside from joining Weight Watchers, I called my publicist and told them to announce that I was doing a movie that requires me to gain weight. By the way, becoming an actor is worth it for this reason alone. I find this to be a great explanation for any shortcomings. If I accidentally knock out a tooth, I tell people it's for a boxing movie I am doing. If I appear to be losing hair, I tell everyone it's for a movie about aging. If someone flips me the bird for driving poorly, I yell out the window, "It's for a movie I'm doing!" It reminds me of the excuse that most people use when they get a nose job. They always blame it on a deviated septum, which is yet another excuse you can run with. "I just had a sex change—had to—deviated septum."

With such a terrific excuse for things, you might be surprised to learn that I was on the lookout for more excuses, but as I quickly discovered, Susan's pregnancy could be used as an excuse for almost anything:

- "Sorry, we can't go. My wife is having morning sickness."
- "Sorry, wish we could have been there. My wife had no energy."
- "Sorry I was speeding, Officer. My wife has to throw up."
- "Sorry for shoplifting. My pregnant wife is home waiting for me."

What are they going to say? And can you imagine the myriad excuses for getting out of things once the kid is born? I've seen this before with friends who became parents.

- "Sorry, I can't stay. My son is homesick."
- "We would love to go, but we can't find a babysitter."
- "I really want to donate money to your organization, but my kid is in rehab."
- "Sorry for the illegal turn, Officer, but my kid grabbed the wheel."

Unfortunately, I fear I haven't hit rock bottom yet, which means I may be using these excuses for some time to come. I find that I have developed a constant craving not only for food, but specifically for sweets. I admit that I have a real sugar problem. I'm not diabetic, but at this rate I will be if I don't stop consuming these large quantities of sweets. I know for a fact that other people battle these same problems, too. I believe this ugly addiction is just as prevalent and serious in our country as an addiction to alcohol. If there were support groups to help you stop eating sugar, I would be at every one of them. When I go grocery shopping, the first thing I do is head right for the cookie aisle. I will open a bag of Pepperidge Farm Double Chocolate Milano cookies and eat them while I shop for the rest of the groceries. The bag is always empty by the time I check out, and I always deliver my standard, corny, smart-aleck line to the cashier: "Whoops, looks like someone got into these already!" I tend to do the same thing when I'm shopping for shoes. When I find a pair that I like, I will wear them around the store, then put my old pair in the new shoe box before I check out. While paying, I'll open up the box to reveal my old, worn shoes and deliver the zinger, "Are you sure these are new?" I imagine most stores would prefer for you to pay for your stuff before you indulge in it—probably the very reason drive-thrus were created.

I wish I could just eat a few cookies and be satisfied, but I never am until the whole bag is gone. Sometimes I eat so much sugar I crash by mid-afternoon and literally can't get off the couch. I call various friends, desperately asking if they know how I can get the sugar out of my system. I wonder if there is a clinic somewhere, or a sugar-free rehab where I can do a stint—a place where they can flush the sugar out of me like a full-body colonic. Once I can get the sweets consumption under control, then I have to figure out how to stop from shoveling every scrap of food I see into my mouth. I keep reminding myself, I am not pregnant; I am fat.

Three months into the pregnancy Susan got up on the examining table and put her feet in the stirrups. I stood alongside her head, assuming my position, which was the position of *not* watching what Dr. Glass was doing as she examined Susan's reproductive organs. I didn't need to see that. As always, I tried to reduce the stress of the situation with a stab at being funny. I said, "I'm sorry, I'm new to all this, but are you actually delivering the baby now?" She popped her head up and said with one of those sarcastic smiles, "No, not yet." I believe the smile was accompanied with the rolling of the eyes. It was probably at this point that she knew what she would be in for during the next six months. Yes, I was trying to reduce my stress level, but I think I was also checking to see if she had a sense of humor. The answer was yes.

Much to my wife's dismay, my behavior in Dr. Glass's office was not a new development. My father, brothers, and I have always been corny smart alecks when it comes to people helping us in the professional field. By professional field I mean anything from a waitress to a doctor. Like, let's say we have just arrived at our table, and the waitress asks us if we are ready to order. One of us will say something like, "We are actually in a hurry—can we just have our check?" Or one of us might ask the waitress what she likes on the menu. When she points out what she likes, one of us might say to her, "Okay, then, why don't you get that, and I'll have the soup." We all get a little chuckle out of it and then wonder why it takes so long for our food to come out. These corny smart-aleck remarks usually only occur when we are together, but apparently they also happen in obstetrician's offices.

Dr. Glass continued with the exam, looked at the blood test results, and said everything looked fine. With that pronouncement, it was official: we could now tell the world, or at least our friends and coworkers, that we were going to have a baby. We could finally spill the beans. It was okay to leave the stadium, since our team was far enough ahead.

Despite the fact that we could officially tell people, I still found myself apprehensive, mostly due to the fact that although Susan was not showing yet, I certainly was. I kept envisioning the awkward conversations that we would have with friends we hadn't seen in a while. They would marvel at what great shape she was in, how healthy she looked, and then they would move on to me and say something like, "Wow . . . Kevin . . . you look . . . well." This would then be followed an awkward pause, after which I would be forced to respond with something like, "Yeah, well, I'm eating for two now," and we would all have a good laugh, but deep down there would be noticeable anxiety for everyone, since we would all recognize that basically they were calling me fat.

When it finally came around to making the announcement, we decided that instead of a mass e-mailing, we agreed on a time and place to share our news in person. That weekend we were invited to fly on a chartered plane to Las Vegas with a bunch of friends for a birthday, and we thought this would be a good time to make our announcement. Before our trip, Susan and I discussed exactly how we were going to tell everyone. Would it be just before takeoff? Would it be once we leveled off? Before the snacks were served? This was all fun planning for us.

"Above all else," Susan instructed me, "don't turn it into a joke. Don't be a smart aleck." She knew me too well. What she meant was not to follow up our announcement on the plane with any version of the following:

- "We don't know who the father is, yet."
- "Not so fast—we're putting it up for adoption."
- "We're currently negotiating with Angelina Jolie."
- "It was a mistake, but what the hell."

I followed Susan's warning and kept it sincere. Since there were others on the plane, I gathered our friends together next to our row. They were mostly overjoyed and supportive when they got the news. The hilarious British comedian Eric Idle noted that we are the only friends he has left that can still conceive. We were honored to be part of that group, even though we were its only members.

I also reminded everyone that we weren't out of the woods yet. It was still early in the pregnancy and anything could happen, but we just had to tell them. I don't know why the expression "We're not out of the woods yet" has such a negative connotation; to me there is nothing wrong with not being out of the woods. The woods provide shelter, shade, and food. It's when you are out of the woods that you are vulnerable and a sitting duck. It's the same with the phrase "I'm in the dark." I see nothing wrong with being in the dark. Dark is good. People can't see you, you're safe—and also, it's easier to catch a nap.

Our news affected people in so many different ways. As we told more and more people, it was interesting to see how they reacted. "I'm so glad!" a friend would say. Others would say, "You are going to make a great father!" They were so happy about it. Women, especially those with children, usually become ebullient, teary-eyed, and loving, whereas men might force a smile, say, "Congratulations," and then change the subject. I think it's safe to say that men as a whole don't react nearly as enthusiastically as women when it comes to children. Single men especially are much more unpredictable. Privately they would say, "Aren't you rushing this pregnancy thing a little? Don't you want to get your career going first? Why not wait until you're sixty? Why don't ya wait for a younger wife?" I'm guessing they were merely acting out their own fears. For God's sake, Susan was already seventeen years younger than me. It already struck me as bizarre that we were receiving the *AARP Bulletin* and *Pregnancy* magazine at the same time.

I quickly learned that there are two types of guys on this planet: the ones that have gone through pregnancy with their partners, and the guys that haven't. It's like the soldiers just completing an active combat tour passing the new recruits on their way to the battlefield. The veterans have a look in their eyes that says, "We've seen it all. We've been there." There's no way that a guy can know what the whole process is like unless he's experienced it. It's nothing you can learn from a book. The guys that have been through it totally get it. There is a depth to these guys. They know everything—the terminology, the buzzwords, the jargon, and most important, the hormonal mood swings. No one else could know that unless they have been through it. They immediately sympathize with the pregnant woman. They ask things like, "Have you packed your bag for the hospital?" "Have you tried Colace?" "Have you been experiencing any Braxton Hicks contractions?" (I call them Toni Braxtons.) It's like a club. You don't have to explain things to them, like why you want to go home to bed at seven, or why you are reaching for the fourth doughnut.

There were quite a few parents, too, who, when they heard we were pregnant, looked at us intensely and said, "Your life is going to change." They would then pause, forming what I believe is what's known as a pregnant pause, and halfheartedly add, "but good changes, though." Somehow I always felt the pause was too long and that they were hiding something from me. I would try to get them to expand on their meaning, but somehow they all knew how to be equally elusive. I had friends who had never kept a secret in all their lives who would suddenly become so tight-lipped you'd think they'd received security clearance. "What?" I would ask. "Is there something I should know?" They would then back away nervously, as if a mountain lion had just crossed their path. Since I heard this forewarning many times, I started trying to cherish every free moment I had until the delivery. I began living every day to the fullest because soon, apparently, my life would change drastically, and possibly for the worse.

Sometimes when you make an announcement like this, to some people, it triggers an alarm. Some couples were older, and maybe this reminded them that they'd missed the opportunity to have children. Some perhaps wanted children but were biologically incapable of it. One or two others were possibly considering it, and maybe another was frustrated that she hadn't met that special person yet, and her forty-year-old biological clock was ticking down.

My accountant was extremely happy for us, but only wished the baby would be born before the end of the year so we could get some tax benefits. This was something I had never even considered. I really wish I were savvy enough to do my own tax returns each year. Couldn't they have, like, a really easy form to fill out? Maybe a coloring book, where they would draw a stack of money, and all we would have to do is color in about how much we think we should be getting back. And I don't know, maybe there could be a penalty if you went outside the lines—maybe in that case you wouldn't get any money back? We don't care about the tax breaks on the baby. The bottom line is, giving life is such a gift in so many ways. And if I remember correctly, you can write off a small percentage of a gift on your taxes.

We also told our contractor, since he was working around the house and had probably already seen all the baby books lying around. In fact he actually built a deck for us out of the used e.p.t. sticks. We also told our housekeeper for the same reason, though she spoke very little English and probably thought we'd told her to clean the windows that week. She smiled and said, "Si."

It did not take long for me to notice that everyone—man, woman, old, young—has their own special advice on the proper raising of a child. Even during pregnancy, they say the baby can hear everything that is going on outside the womb. They suggest talking or singing to the womb, and your baby will hear it and get accustomed to it. In reality, though, all he hears is his mother's superloud heartbeat and the rushing of her blood through the veins. It actually sounds like a plunger trying to unclog a toilet. Others insisted, "Once he's born, don't talk to him like a baby. Always, even when he's a month old, talk to him as an adult." Did that mean that right off the bat, I was supposed to start talking about stock options and the crisis in the Middle East? It was hard to see how that wouldn't be a one-sided conversation. Still more people said, "Let him see that you and your mother love each other. Show affection but don't show him weakness." As I was listening to this it reminded me of the instructions that special agent Clarice (played by Jodie Foster) in *The Silence of the Lambs* got before meeting with Hannibal Lecter in his cell: "Don't show fear. Don't look him directly in the eyes. Don't trust him."

As we checked names off our list of people we thought we'd told, it suddenly dawned on us that we'd been putting off one of the most important and most readily impacted people. Perhaps it was our subconscious trying to avoid the conscious reality. Either way, we both knew that it was time to tell Justin, the wonderful, sweet tenant who rented our guesthouse. This had been his home for five years, but now we would need that space for future visits from relatives and in-laws. More important, I would need that space for an office and a personal panic room.

My overwhelming fear of confrontation dictated that telling Justin was going to be a difficult thing to do. No one likes to be uprooted, and I didn't want to be the bearer of bad news. Justin was the one nonfamily friend that we probably should have told before the first trimester ended, but I still put it off. Now that we were telling everyone, the new officialness of the situation did not make it any easier. Not only would we be losing someone fun to hang with, someone amazingly accommodating and responsible, but Justin was also really helpful. He was always willing to get our mail when we were away on trips, water our plants, and keep an eye on our place when we were gone. There were also several other reasons I dreaded telling him:

- He might not like us anymore.
- If the baby didn't survive, then we would have lost the best tenant in the world. We would have to find a new tenant, and no one would be as good as Justin.
- We didn't want to inconvenience him.
- He might not like us anymore.
- He was always around to keep an eye on our house when we were out of town.
- He might not like us anymore.

It dawned on me that these were also the same concerns people have when they are considering breaking up with someone.

In fairness, so that he would have plenty of time to find a new place to live, we needed to tell him soon. We also would need the time to do renovations on the guesthouse before family arrived. I was the one who needed to tell him. It was one of those responsible, mature, adult things I just had to do—unless, of course, I could find someone else to do it. I suppose I could flip the back porch light switch on and off several times, but somehow this message seemed too complicated for that.

I never like having to break bad news to someone. I remember the one time I broke up with a girlfriend. I felt terrible to be on that side. In a nutshell, we had been dating for six months when I went out of town for a week and fell in love with someone else. When I came back to town, I met up with my soon-to-be ex in the park and was totally up front and honest with her. I knew this would not be welcome news, but I prided myself at least on being truthful with her. Some guys will beat around the bush. They'll reassure the girl, telling her, "It's not about you. It's about me." But what they are really saying is, "It's not about you. It's about me . . . and that blonde I met at Starbucks." Being honest, though, didn't make it any easier. You would think I was the one who was getting dumped. I was devastated to have to share this information with her, but I knew it was the proper thing to do. She was a wonderful, beautiful girl, and even though I was being honest with her, I felt like a huge cad. As I was trying to get it out, I started sobbing.

"What?" she said compassionately as she rubbed my back. "Did someone in your family die?"

"No," I said through tears. "Worse," I said for effect. I finally got it out, and she was floored. This news came out of nowhere. I was now sniffling and sobbing like a little baby who just had his pacifier yanked from his mouth. I was pathetic. I think she was more confused about my breakdown than she was about me meeting someone else.

She eventually said, "Pull yourself together, for God's sake, and go home." Looking back, I guess it's somewhat narcissistic to fall apart when breaking up with someone, because what you are really expressing are tears for this person because they won't get to hang out with you for the rest of their life.

I needed to tell Justin about his ticking clock. One evening I saw him coming back from a workout. It seemed that he was always coming back from a workout. He was always tanned, shirtless, and sweating, and never without his Bluetooth cell phone earpiece. Justin had a job that allowed him to work from home, so he was almost always there. Most of Susan's girlfriends exclaimed how good-looking he was when they first caught a glimpse of him.

"He lives in your guesthouse?" they would say, astonished. "He is Brad Pitt hot!"

Susan would always downplay it for me, telling her friends, "Really? I don't see it. My type is more of the tall, rounded-shoulders, bad-posture, love-handle type guy with a sense of humor."

On this particular day Justin seemed to have an extra bounce in his step. I thought this would be a good time to break the news to him in an indirect, nonconfrontational way. I promised myself I wouldn't cry. I braced myself and yelled, "Hey Justin, you got a minute? I want to show you something." He happily pranced over to our back door, sweat glistening in the afternoon sun from his rock-hard chiseled chest. I showed him the ever-so-slight pooch in Susan's stomach and told him she was pregnant. He smiled and congratulated us.

Then I said, "That's the good news. The bad news is . . . that we will need to be taking over the guesthouse eventually." I couldn't even bring myself to say, "October fifteenth," the date that Susan and I had decided on. As he stood there taking this all in, I felt bad and thought maybe I should soften the blow by telling him Susan and I had decided to name our child after him—whether it was a boy or a girl. Before I could get to that, Susan immediately chimed in, "We would need you out by October fifteenth." Justin hid his disappointment well and said, "Really? Oh, okay. I understand."

The reality was, he had been seeing the writing on the wall ever since Susan and I got married. He knew we were trying for a kid and realized that eventually he would have to relocate. I guess that's just an instinct you have when you've rented enough apartments over the years. Even though Justin's occupation was finding housing for college students, we all thought he'd have difficulty finding a deal like the one he had with us. The beach area was slim on rentals, but about a month later a great opportunity presented itself—the garage apartment just next door to us opened up, and Justin moved into the newly vacated unit for less than half the rent we were charging him. I was happy for him, but also disappointed that I hadn't heard about this deal first.

"That unit would have made a very nice guesthouse," I said to Susan. I now found myself angry with Justin, and avoided eye contact with him whenever possible. "How could he do that to us?" I would lament, just before I opened the cupboard and tore open a family-size package of Chips Ahoy cookies.

TEN

My Child, the Loser

Y our child is going to be a total, irresponsible idiot—a complete loser," the lawyer told us. "This is what you have to assume when you're planning for its future. That's what the entire trust-fund philosophy is based on."

If we had any money left after this lawyer billed us, our goal was to work out a plan to eventually leave it to our child. I was told that a trust fund is a must. You never know when you might buy the farm, so it's a good idea to have a plan that will financially protect your surviving family members and your estate.

"A loser?" my wife asked.

"I guess you have a point," I said to the lawyer, trying to sound interested. "I mean, even when the baby is inside the mother, it's being a total parasite. It might as well be sitting on the couch and not paying any rent."

I glanced over to Susan and couldn't help notice her dismay at the hypothetical assumption that our baby would be subpar in some fashion. Now *I* was jumping on the bandwagon.

"It's sponging off of her every day," I said, "absorbing nutrients and minerals, right?"

"Absolutely," replied the lawyer. "And why do you think that is going to change once the baby is born?"

We had decided to draw up a trust that would include a list of demands our child must meet before he or she got the money we would eventually be leaving. This trust, of course, is all predicated on the notion that you and your wife have died—and your child hasn't killed you. We would also have to decide how we wanted our child to receive our assets. First and foremost, we don't want it to be known as a "trust-fund baby." They're considered spoiled, rich kids, getting through life with Mommy and Daddy's money. Most counselors and attorneys suggest some type of plan where they don't get all the money at once in their teen years, since they will probably squander it away on stupid stuff like parties, cars, eBay junk, and friends.

"Having lots of money available at an early age, with no restrictions, is a recipe for disaster," the lawyer added as he glanced at his ringing cell phone. "They won't have the desire to actually go out in the world to work and make something of themselves."

With these words, the lawyer had gotten me all fired up. "I am not about to let this punk kid piss away our life savings!" I said to Susan.

Noting the ridiculousness of this conversation, Susan cynically injected, "Well, we might as well put our loser kid into rehab as soon as it's delivered, or send it to a reform school—maybe hire a parole officer and set aside some bail money."

"Absolutely," the lawyer chimed in, not getting her cynicism. "That's the supposition you have to make when planning a trust fund for your baby."

You and your partner also have to decide who is going to take care of your child if anything ever happens to both of you, e.g., you die in a horrible fiery car accident. This person will be known as your child's guardian. As with the godparent situation, we had a difficult time coming up with someone suitable. We also needed a trustee. This was someone who would oversee how the money was distributed to the guardian. Everything had to be spelled out to a T, since once again, you have to assume that your appointed guardian and trustee are complete imbeciles.

As our meeting progressed, we found ourselves coming up with many unrealistic requirements for our yet-to-be-born problem child. This kid was definitely gonna have to jump through some hoops. We'd decided that our pathetic loser kid wouldn't receive one penny of our hard-earned money until he was at least thirty-five years old, had gotten through college with a 4.0 GPA, could bowl above 200 on a consistent basis, and had swum the English Channel while defending his doctorate dissertation from Harvard. For good measure I added a clause stating that the child should be able to juggle six pins. That way, at the very least, he would always be able to make money as a bowling ringer or in a sidewalk clown juggling act. Maybe by then he would have grown out of his slacker attitude and understand what it's like to be an adult.

Kids today don't know the value of hard work. Most people don't know this, but many of history's famous explorers or inventors were trust-fund babies, and also wouldn't have known the value of hard work if their parents hadn't stipulated their demands in the trust. Do you think they would have done what they did if there wasn't a financial reward? No, their parents knew that and stipulated in the trust exactly what they wanted. For some, their kid couldn't collect his trust unless he discovered a Northwest Passage. For others it was a lightbulb, a cotton gin, an airplane— the list goes on and on. Who would want to subject themselves to harsh living conditions and potential Indian attacks if it weren't for the trust fund?

Either way, just by holding this conversation, we had already undermined our baby's self-esteem. Though he was still in the womb, he was no doubt listening; forget the cost of setting up a trust, this was now going to cost a fortune in trips to the therapist. We really wanted to be able to trust that our child would have common sense, but I could understand the need for such precautions. If I had been left a large sum of money in my early twenties, I too would probably have squandered it all away. But even though you would have done that, you don't want to assume that your child would. You'd like to think that your child will be this bigger, better, brighter version of you. That your child is You 2.0, all the same fun with none of the failings. You don't want to think that the same mistakes you would have made are genetically transferable.

"The trust fund will ensure how your assets will be distributed," the lawyer went on. "It will minimize your taxes, expenses, and blah, blah, blah . . ." I hate having to focus this much on anything financial; I couldn't wait to get out of there. The lawyer droned on as I drifted off. I found myself thinking about my early twenties and how decisions I made probably would have been pretty different if I'd had a trust fund.

At twenty-three I moved to California to pursue a career in stand-up comedy. I wanted to become a stand-up for three reasons. Since I considered myself a people-pleaser, I thought stand-up comedy would be a perfect job for me because, most times, it presents the opportunity to please a whole room full of people at the same time. It's not that I work hard to make people happy because I *want* them to be happy, it's because it makes *me* happy to know other people are happy. It really is self-motivated. I guess I'm not so much a people-pleaser as I am a "me-pleaser." The second reason was because I enjoyed telling jokes, and the third and most important reason was to impress Roxanne Bellwood, the girl I had a crush on in high school.

Even though I had my sights set on being a stand-up, my first few years in Los Angeles seemed like they were spent pursuing a career in part-time jobs. As an aspiring stand-up, you needed your nights free, so I found day jobs through a company called Manpower, an employment agency that would find you temporary work paying minimum wage and then take a percentage of your earnings as a fee for finding you this work. Years later I would learn of more companies like this, companies that were called Creative Artists and Associates, William Morris, United Talent Agency, and so on. At the time I didn't mind the low wages and hard work because I was young and wanted to experience California, enjoy the beaches, and drink Coors, which was unavailable on the East Coast at the time. If I'd had a trust fund, this would have been the time that I would have blown through it.

Manpower found me all types of temporary work, most of which only lasted a day or two at the most. I sorted mail in the mail room at the Beverly Hilton Hotel, unloaded furniture trucks, and scraped acid off battery terminals that powered large banks of computers, just to name a few. Now, don't get me wrong, not all the jobs were glamorous. I spent one day crawling around the basement of an auto supply store picking up moldy, crusty guard-dog crap from piles of old mufflers. This, however, I did just for fun, and it had nothing to do with Manpower.

A year or so later, I worked for a car leasing company in Beverly Hills whose client list included quite a few movie stars. My job was to go to their homes, pick up their leased cars, and bring them back to be serviced. I would later return the car to the star's house. I was driving cars that cost more than the home I grew up in. I had never seen such amazing cars. There were Mercedeses,

Jaguars, and Porsches—not to mention cars I never heard of before, like Stutzes and Bentleys. Each one had that new-car smell and new-money smell to it. Getting into the driver's seat was like climbing into the cockpit of a fighter jet, with all sorts of gadgets, expensive wooden dashboards, and fine Corinthian leather surrounding me. I delivered these cars to many movie stars, including Barbra Streisand, Mel Brooks, and Jerry Lewis. Unfortunately, I never got to see these stars. I would usually just drop the car off in the driveway and hand the keys to the star's assistant, and then my friend and fellow aspiring comedian, Dan, who also worked for Manpower, would meet me out on the street and bring me back in a company car. We would take turns driving the priceless cars, depending on which one of us was less hungover.

After a few months, these menial jobs started to take a toll on my spirits—that, and the fact that the holidays were right around the corner and I would be away from home on Christmas for the first time in my life. I just couldn't seem to get out of my slump. I eventually diagnosed myself with an acute case of homesickness. The drab apartment that I shared with my friend John was minimally furnished; I thought it would have appealed to an assassin or some type of international spy who never accumulated too many material possessions for fear that he would one day have to leave everything behind at a moment's notice. We tried to brighten the place up with a pathetic three-foot-tall Charlie Brown Christmas tree, strategically placed in the corner and decorated with a string of empty Coors cans. That was what I came to call my low point. There was no way around it: I was definitely feeling sorry for myself.

It's funny how life sometimes throws you curves. As I accepted defeat and began reluctantly packing my bags to head back home, the phone rang. It was Anthony from Manpower with the temporary job offer of a lifetime:

"Would you be interested in working as a department store Santa Claus for the next month or two?" he asked.

Steady work as a department store Santa sounded pretty damn good. This meant that it would be a sit-down job in a climate-controlled Sears & Roebuck, with only minimal amounts of waste cleanup. That's not an easy offer to turn down when you'd spent a part of the previous months on your hands and knees, picking up dog excrement. Of course, I contained my excitement so they wouldn't offer me less than minimum wage.

"Sure, I guess I could do that," I said. It didn't occur to me until after I hung up that I was only twenty-three and looked nothing like Santa even with the padding, the suit, and the cheap beard and wig. Still, that was hardly enough to deter me. I welcomed the job as Santa primarily because at the time I was going on the occasional job interview. The Santa suit came free with the job, so I figured I could get the most out of this experience and have it double as an interview suit. I could just slap on a tie and be in business.

The Santa job went something like this: I sat on Santa's throne by the toy department for about eight hours a day, while kids climbed up on my lap or their parents put them on me. Once a kid was situated on my lap, the only thing I had to do was try to speak to her about the impending holiday, while my photo-elf, Elaine, snapped a photo that would then be sold to the parents for about twenty dollars. The area, of course, was cordoned off with plush velvet rope surrounding the red carpet and the stairs leading up to my throne, so that no errant children could get to me without waiting in line.

I must admit, after a while I got to be pretty good at being

Santa. I had the whole rap down: ". . . And have you been a good little boy?" I'd say in my best Santa voice. "And what would you like for Christmas?" I thought I'd sound more like Santa if I started each sentence with an "And." ". . . And have you been good to your sister? . . . And what else would you like? . . . And are you wetting your pants right now?" Since this job was in San Diego, most of the children who visited Santa were from the neighboring Tijuana and didn't speak English. They would just gaze at me with their big brown eyes trying to figure out what I was. *Click, click, click* went Elaine's camera.

Aside from the air-conditioning and the joy of sitting on my butt all day, there were other perks to this Santa gig. Elaine was a cute eighteen-year-old whose elf costume consisted of an elf's hat, a short green skirt, and a white blouse. Several days before Christmas, she showed up at my doorstep (I still had one back then) holding two handmade Christmas stockings with a bottle of wine in each one. It was that night that I discovered that Elaine was not really an elf but actually a minx.

That Christmas, John was also working across town as a Santa. A few nights before the holiday he wanted to go barhopping after work. I agreed that it could be fun. We decided that that night he would dress as Santa, and I would carry the candy canes and camera. I also agreed to be Santa's designated driver. Much like Santa's throne area, the club entrances were cordoned off with plush velvet ropes surrounding the red carpet leading up to the door. Instead of Santa being at the end of the carpet, though, there was usually a big burly, hulking doorman. Upon seeing Santa each discerning doorman invariably turned into a giddy little boy, allowing us to jump to the front of the line. We got in free to every club and were mobbed by throngs of tanned southern California girls. At the very last club Santa got picked up by a very attractive, slightly tipsy girl named Liz. Liz danced with

Santa for over an hour as I snapped pictures and handed out candy canes. As the bar gave last call, I looked around for Santa. He was gone. I went back to our tiny apartment, hoping to find him, but no such luck. I sat down next to our Charlie Brown Christmas tree and opened a can of Coors. I took a sip and smiled, knowing that Santa was probably giving Liz an early Christmas present, and it was all because I couldn't afford a plane ticket back east. It seemed I was going to survive my first Christmas away from home. (John and Liz eventually married and have been together for over twenty-five years, have two kids, and by the time you read this book will be grandparents for the first time. I guess you can meet the love of your life in a bar.)

Shortly after we met with the lawyer about setting up a trust for our unborn child, I learned a trust fund wasn't the only thing that would save my offspring from potentially having to barhop with a drunken Santa Claus during Christmastime. Apparently it was also an excellent idea to have a will in case something sudden or tragic should befall me. This way people would know what my wishes were if I became incapacitated in a terrible accident. Making out a will is a very unpleasant task because you have to make several decisions based on gruesome hypothetical situations. In the event of any unfortunate accident or illness where you end up in a vegetable state or simply unable to communicate, would you want to be kept on a life-support system? Would you rather they pull the plug? Or maybe just pull the plug out a little and then stick it back in? Who would you like to pull the plug? Would you like them to pull the plug or push it in? Where do you want to be buried? What clothes do you want to be buried in? Will you be checking bags? Maybe you would like a Viking burial? Do you even want to be buried, or would you rather be cremated? What type of lighter fluid? Maybe you'd just like to be lightly toasted and then buried? How about just freezing your head and using it as an ice sculpture centerpiece at future family reunions?

Deciding how you want your body to be disposed of when you die really is one of the more unpleasant decisions that you have to make in your life, the frustrating thing being of course that you don't even get to enjoy the fruits of this painstaking choice. At this point I am leaning toward cremation. When it's over, you can spread my ashes anywhere. I don't care. What difference will it make to me? For all I care, you can put them in a snow globe—something with a cityscape of downtown Los Angeles. During the holidays you could shake the snow globe to see my ashes dancing around in the water like snow, or for that matter smog. "Awww, remember Kevin? Merry Christmas, everyone."

I'd like some thought to go into where and how to spread my ashes, though, and so for that reason I stipulated in my will that the executors think before scattering. I also want the physical spreading of the ashes to be well thought out. If you've ever cleaned out a fireplace, you know that ashes can be a little unruly. A while back a friend of mine passed away, and his wish was to be cremated. He loved the sea and sailing, so his family and some friends took his ashes out on a boat. When they got a mile or two offshore they held a small vigil for him, and then proceeded to empty his ashes into the sea. These well-meaning mourners were obviously unfamiliar with the wind, and most of the ashes blew back onto them and all over the boat. To this day they are still picking pieces of him out of their teeth.

When it comes to being incapacitated, I feel it is important to work out some subtle signals to communicate with your loved ones in case you cannot speak, write, nod, or move and want to say, "I have changed my mind, don't pull the plug!" Maybe even just simple responses that will indicate a yes or no. The simplest one would be one blink of the eyelid for a no and two blinks of the eyelid for a yes. But let's say you can't move your eyelids. One should never discount the many possibilities of communicating through flatulence. First of all, you will probably have plenty of gas in your system, since you have been so traumatized. I am not suggesting trying to form words through farting, although I am sure there are some frat guys somewhere who can do this. I am merely suggesting that, like the eyelid technique, perhaps one simple *pppft* could indicate a no answer, and two *pppft*s could indicate yes. It may be worth it to start practicing that sometime in the near future. I think it could be a viable way to communicate, although to keep a pleasant setting in the room, very few questions should be asked in one sitting.

A lot of what-ifs go through your head during a pregnancy, and once thoughts of a will enter the picture, they only get magnified. What if, on the way to the hospital in a taxi, the baby can't wait and wants out, and we have to pull over? Will insurance cover the cost of the meter ticking away (plus tip) until the baby is delivered? What if the stretch marks don't go away? Will they gross me out? No, why should I be grossed out? The woman really has no control over them. Stretch marks are genetic. And besides, she's not grossed out by my skid marks, which, incidentally, are also genetic.

The night after we had our first will discussion, Susan looked at me fondly and finally said, "Please don't ever die." I assured her I wouldn't and that I would probably outlive both her and the baby . . . and probably even have another thriving family after them. That didn't sit very well with her, and I am sure that she now hopes that I go before her. Nevertheless, after that talk, Susan and I began warning each other to be more careful, especially while driving. We started worrying—what if one of us died before the baby was born? Since it is very dangerous to use your cell phone while driving, we made a pact not to. For the record,

I believe this pact was made over our cell phones while we were both driving on the freeway.

In some states it is illegal to use your cell phone while driving. I suspect soon it will be illegal in all states. As far as I am concerned, it is a good time to make your calls, especially the ones you have been putting off. I am always talking on the phone while in traffic, and that is because, once again, I deplore traffic. It's very frustrating to be wasting that much time. I consider myself a mover and a shaker, and if I'm not movin' I can't be shakin'. I suspect that one of these days it will get me into a terrible accident. I mean, I can just visualize it. I'm not only on the cell phone, but I am also multitasking. At the same time I'm also fiddling with the CD player, eating French fries from a bag in the passenger seat, a Starbucks decaf-soy-latte-grande between my knees, looking through the glove compartment for a map, then looking at the map, and I just know one of these days I am going to get into a wreck. But until that happens, I am getting *a lot* of stuff done.

Making out wills and trust funds is one of those responsible tasks that you only have to perform once in your life, and when you are through with it, you can put it away and forget about it. Here are some other unpleasant things you should only have to do once in a lifetime:

- Be toilet trained.
- Be fooled by a transvestite.
- Carry your drunken girlfriend back to her parents.
- Drink away a tequila hangover with more tequila.
- Be fooled by a transsexual.
- Retrieve a ring from the garbage disposal with your tongue.
- Be fooled by a cross-dresser.

Let's face it—life is short. In fact, I live every day like it's the last day of my life. Every morning I wake up very early, spend maybe three hours on the phone making funeral arrangements, and then just sit back and wait. I do that every day because you never know. Whenever someone dies, I am always curious as to how, why, and what the circumstances were. It may appear as if I am being compassionate and caring, but in reality I just want to make sure *I* don't have any of those symptoms, and it's not gonna happen to me. It's the same when someone absurdly claims they were taken aboard an alien spacecraft. No one believes them or cares about their story. But when they claim they were "probed" by the aliens, all of a sudden everyone is interested and wants to know how they got into that situation. Once again, it's not compassion—they just want to make sure it's not gonna happen to them.

I've had the same address book for the last eight years. The pages are held together in a small binder that allows me to add more pages if necessary. Of course, I tend to meet more and more people over the years, and I like to stay in touch with them, so for that reason, adding pages is necessary. I suppose I could upgrade to a handheld device like a BlackBerry or an iPhone, but there is something I like about having my old, worn paper address book. It is a sloppily written collection of friends, family, acquaintances, and associates. Some names are crossed out, and some names are added. The color of ink, pencil, or my handwriting seems to change with each one. I know exactly where everyone's name and phone number is, and what color pen or pencil I wrote it in. Some names are not in the right alphabetical order or legible for one reason or another, but I know where they are. It's so sloppy I can't ask someone to look up a phone number in it for me because they would never find it. Still, I would be lost without it. Some names are crossed out because they have moved or got married and no longer have that last name. Somewhere in the book, though, they have been re-added with their new name and address.

The only dilemma I have with my address book is what to do with the names of people who have died. I thought it would be insensitive and disrespectful to just cross their names and addresses out. It would be even worse if you just obliterated them by covering their names with Wite-Out. I tried that once and I felt like I had buried them in liquid snow. I'm sure with a Black-Berry or iPhone you could simply delete the names, but how insensitive would that be? It would be as if they never existed at all. Currently I am drawing a simple little frown face next to the person's name.

Incidentally, I find it quite unsettling to read the paper lately and see who is in rehab for heroin or who died of a heroin overdose. Aren't people smart enough these days to realize that heroin can kill you? It's the same with suicide. Don't these kids know that suicide can kill you? A fellow comedian I knew committed suicide. From what I heard, he was depressed with his career. I guess he felt that he should have been a lot further along by this point. Most comedians, in general, are fairly neurotic and insecure. They are always comparing their level of success to other comedians'. In my opinion, comparing yourself to anyone in any profession is not healthy. It will not help you or do you good in any way. When I heard that he had killed himself, I started thinking about his career. I was confused at why he took his life because I thought he had a pretty good career: he was successful, and I knew for a fact that he made a lot of money. I suddenly found myself comparing my career to his and thinking, "Hey, his career was a lot better than mine, yet he still took his life. Why didn't I take my life first? Why should he be getting all the attention, when my career wasn't even as good?"

I've noticed that people like to associate a deceased person's occupation or passion with what they are doing in heaven at that very moment. When beloved University of Michigan football coach Bo Schembechler passed away recently, one of the sports announcers during a football game spoke fondly of him. He reassured all the listeners that Coach Schembechler was in heaven now, probably roaming the sidelines and watching the game.

I've come up with a few others for different professions that you can use for your next eulogy:

FISHER: Frank loved fishing. I know Frank is up there casting his rod down from a cloud, and probably pulling up a big ol' bass.

POKER PLAYER: You always knew Hank was down at the club, playing cards. Well, I know that Hank is probably playing cards with Saint Peter right now, just outside the gates, and he's probably going all in even though all he has is a pair of threes.

DOCTOR: I know Dr. Sugarman is up there right now, asking God to turn his head and cough.

PILOT: I know Captain Holden is navigating his plane through the clouds in heaven right now, with splattered angels all over his windshield.

ACCOUNTANT: I'm sure Sal is up in heaven right now just . . . ya know . . . boring the angels to death.

I guess in a way it makes us all feel better to imagine that whatever it was that person enjoyed doing, he was still doing it—even though there is probably enough other stuff to do in heaven that no one should have to do the same old mundane things he did while he was alive. I've always been curious about what state you or your soul arrives at heaven in. What if you're drunk when you die, and embarrass yourself in front of God? Let's say you got tanked at someone's party and then tripped and hit your head on the sidewalk. Bam! You're dead. The next thing you know, you are standing, barely, in front of God, and you are hammered. You are staggering and stumbling over your words. You are hugging him and telling him how great he is, how much you've heard about him, and basically making a fool out of yourself. The angels eventually have to manhandle you away and quietly kick the crap out of you behind a cloud.

After we had decided on a trust fund and assembled our wills, there was one final piece we needed to get our fiscal house in shape for the baby: life insurance. While life insurance had never occurred to me before, it seemed perfectly logical now that I was about to have a family. Here's how it works: the insurance company charges you a certain amount a year based on how much coverage you want. The more you pay, the more your beneficiaries receive when you kick the bucket, meaning that you have to decide how much you are worth and what it would cost to replace you. I know that in New York City, after six in the evening, the taxicab drivers charge an additional fifty cents per fare, since it is far more dangerous driving at night. I don't know how they came up with this figure. I suppose they must have had a meeting and determined how much their lives were worth, and they came up with that fifty-cent figure. There's some low self-esteem for you. (Their parents must have used the same lawyer that Susan and I did.)

With life insurance, you basically have to decide how much money the surviving members of your family will need to be happy that you are dead. It's important to tread lightly here—you don't want too much coverage, since that might only entice your family to kill you and collect on the insurance. Incidentally, I ripped that article out of a magazine, shredded it, and threw it away. The goal is to find the happy medium between a big payday that would lead them to harbor homicidal thoughts toward you, and a paltry sum that would fail to support them adequately. Once you have secured an insurance company and chosen a suitable amount, you write them the check for your coverage, and they send a representative doctor to your house to perform an in-home physical. This last step is very convenient for a doctor to do at my house, since I already have a lot of medical equipment.

In order for the coverage to begin, you must pass this exam. Mine was scheduled around noon, so all morning long I just relaxed on the couch to make sure my blood pressure was not high. With an exam like this, even the slightest health problem can be a reason to charge you more or deny health insurance coverage altogether. Though I had yet to curb my Milano cookie problem, I knew I was in reasonable shape, and I didn't think that passing the physical would be a problem. I have a physical exam every year, and things usually turn out just fine, although my doctor always seems a bit tense when he calls me with the results on my bloodwork. It's not that I can hear real concern in his voice, but there's always this audible hesitation, as though he's about to give me bad news. Mostly because he begins each sentence by saying, "I mean," and then follows up with slight pauses. He also emphasizes words or phrases that end up making things sound more severe than they actually are. "I mean . . . your blood pressure isn't *that* high." "I mean . . . I wouldn't worry about your cholesterol *at this point*." "I mean . . . let's just *keep an eye* on it."

Despite my doctor's less than reassuring delivery, the numbers don't lie, and I'm usually in fine health. For this reason, I was not at all concerned about the physical for my life insurance, but after a few weeks passed, I began to get a bit apprehensive. What if the insurance doctor was better than my doctor, and he found something terribly wrong by using a more sophisticated test? What if my own doctor had been taking my blood from the wrong arm? What if my urine sample got mixed up with some dude from a rock band? What if the insurance doctor mistook the grapefruit on my coffee table for a tumor?

Then, just as it seemed like my neurosis was peaking, I heard back from the agents. It turned out that they were concerned about whether I smoked or not. On the application form, I checked that I didn't smoke, but they were concerned that I was not being entirely truthful. As it turned out, the insurance agents were big fans of the Showtime series *Weeds*, which is about a pot dealer in suburbia. On the show, I play the pot dealer's accountant, who also smokes pot, so my life insurance agents had seen me smoking in several scenes.

Before the agents would approve me for the insurance, they wanted to know exactly what it is I am smoking, and how often. I told them it was a honey-rose herb, and it is only the character I play, Doug Wilson, that smokes. I myself do not smoke at all. Unfortunately, they said that this assurance was not going to be enough; they would need more definitive proof.

As I thought about it, I had to admit that it was a pretty preposterous excuse. I mean, on paper the I'm-not-a-smoker-but-I-play-one-on-TV line sounds like something an unimaginative teenager would come up with when an adult catches her with a cigarette, something along the lines of:

"Honestly, I got a part in the school play, and they, like, want me to be able to smoke and stuff."

"There were these guys at school casting for an antismoking public service ad, and they gave me a pack."

"There were these guys in white lab coats doing studies about the correlation between cigarette smoke and homework, and it was either use me or a rat."

As our lawyer would have no doubt reminded me, in a few short years it would be my own unimaginative loser teenager who would be delivering the excuse. I thought about my future teenager and what I thought my future teenager would say. Then I thought about what I would have said as a teenager, and it came to me: I called my publicist and asked her to start telling people that I only took up smoking for a movie I was shooting.

A few days later my life insurance policy was one hundred percent approved.

ELEVEN

Irritable Gasp Disorder

Susan gasped. It was one of those sudden, open-mouthed, inhaling gasps that is usually accompanied at the end with a slight audible "Uhhh!" It's the same gasp someone would make if she were a passenger in your car and she saw a puppy suddenly dart out in into the street in front of you. Normally it's an instinctual warning of impending doom, and I react accordingly. Normally, this signal would put me on high alert, code orange. I would immediately tense up, do a quick scan of my surroundings for any abnormal occurrences, and then turn to the source of the gasp. All of which would take about two seconds. Normally, that's the signal that this type of gasp represents.

So why should anything be different when I hear a loud gasp coming from Susan in the passenger's seat? Was I about to hit something in the road? Had a sharp pain just shot into her heart? Were we about to slam into a semi? The answer is no to all of these.

"What?" I frantically demanded. "What is it?"

Susan calmly answered, "I just remembered it was Tuesday, and that means farmers' market in our neighborhood from noon to four." After pulling myself off the ceiling, taking a deep breath or two, and waiting for my heart rate to return to normal, I reprimanded her.

"Don't scare me like that! Those gasps should only be used for emergencies, not for remembering, forgetting, or noticing cool things!"

"I'm sorry," she said, and then turned to me and asked, "Do you think we can make it home before they close?"

This was not the first time this had happened. Sometimes it seemed like even the slightest thing could elicit a similar gasp. It could be anything: *Gasp!* "That woman has my favorite bag!" *Gasp!* "I forgot my sister Karen's birthday!" While these gasps had always caused a spike in my blood pressure, things only seemed to get worse after Susan became pregnant. One never knew what potential disasters were lurking around the corner, waiting to destroy our fragile happiness: each gasp carried more serious connotations, with more profound and rippling implications. Susan thought I was just overreacting.

Yet it was because of this exact gasp interaction that I failed to react days later when I heard Susan gasp again. What I didn't realize was that she was gasping because she had fallen off a step. We were moving some boxes into our condo. Actually, I was carrying a box full of crap that we had no place for, and Susan was carrying three cylindrical containers of Pringles: two original flavor and one sour cream and onion. There is a six-inch step that goes down to the front entryway, which I had actually twisted my ankle on a few weeks earlier. As we were approaching the step, I was about to warn Susan to be careful when I heard a gasp escape her lips.

Since I couldn't see past the box I was carrying, I assumed

that she had just seen a cute dog or remembered an upcoming birthday. As I peered over the box to see what was going on, she was already falling, in what seemed like slow motion, onto the hard tiles. The Pringles containers were tumbling in the air. All of a sudden, real speed caught up, and Susan had landed on her side with a crash. Crushed, synthetic Pringles littered the tiles all around her. Time froze for a few seconds as we both tried to understand the potential repercussions of this terrible misstep. She quickly went into a panic, thinking she might have broken her leg. She wanted to go to the hospital right away, but my initial thought was, Oh, my God, I have got to clean up these Pringles. The entryway is such a mess! I don't want our new neighbors to think we're pigs.

Having been a lifeguard at one time in my life, I was able to assess her leg, which I promptly diagnosed as a sprain at most. Susan sat on the floor while several other neighbors walked past, carrying in their plants and boxes of crap they probably didn't need. Patrick in Apartment 102 was nice enough to offer us a bag of ice. Susann in Apartment 304 suggested we use her couch. She also explained to us how the baby is so padded in the uterus, it would take quite a bit more to cause any damage. As she entered the doorway, she looked down, slightly irritated, and said, "What's going on with all the chips in the entryway?"

A desperate call to our ob-gyn squelched our worst fear. She said not to worry and to treat Susan's injuries as if she weren't pregnant. The baby would be fine. Had she been six months pregnant and really showing and landed on her stomach then there would be concern. "If you'd like, you could come in for a checkup," she said, "just to be on the safe side."

For twenty minutes, Susan sat on the tiles with shards of Pringles all around her, as she iced her ankle with her back propped up against the wall. Eventually she hobbled a few steps, then announced that it looked like it was going to be okay. Aside from a scraped elbow and a slightly twisted ankle, she was fine. When she was comfortable on the couch with her leg elevated, Susan related to me how during her fall her instincts were to protect the baby and not her. As we went back over the scenario in our heads, we realized that one of the Pringles containers had probably cushioned her fall. Had it not been for the sour cream and onion, there may have been more serious injuries. "Hey," I said later, "how 'bout naming our kid Pringles?" Pringles Nealon sounded tough—like an Irish gangster from the thirties. I put it on the list.

In the days after the step incident, I felt increasingly unnerved. What if I hadn't been there? What if it had been six months in? What if my reaction to the gasp could have made a difference in the health of our baby? My worrier friend Elisa would have seen this coming. She would have warned Susan. Having not reacted with the appropriate vigilance to a gasp that actually mattered, I resolved not to let another important one slip by. I was coming to recognize a troubling new reality: the course of pregnancy is littered with little scares. Most of the time they're nothing, just harmless little issues that a doctor can easily dispel, but every now and then it's something more serious, and I would have to react to each as though it was the big one.

Unfortunately, I did not have to wait long before testing my new resolve. Another scare came when I was on the East Coast performing at a club and visiting my parents. Susan was going for another ultrasound, and this time it would be without me. My cell phone rang, and my caller ID identified the call as Susan's. I quickly answered the phone, expecting to hear her bubbly voice telling me how cool the baby looked in the ultrasound—but instead, she was sobbing. My heart sank, thinking that we had lost the baby, or that the doctor had noticed some profound problem. Eventually she settled down and told me the baby was fine. She was upset because Dr. Glass had told her that she wasn't gaining enough weight. She was underweight compared to what most normal mothers gain at this point, and if she didn't eventually gain the weight, she would have to be confined to bed rest. If someone told me that I had to eat more or risk being confined to bed rest, I would have said yes to both, no problem, but for Susan, this felt like the first time something wasn't right with her pregnancy. It devastated her, and so to compensate and lead by example I started double-fisting bags of Milanos. She followed suit and began chowing down like an Irish wolfhound, eating everything in sight.

Two weeks and several empty bags of cookies later, we were in the waiting room of the ob-gyn, preparing for the big weigh-in. Incidentally, if you accompany your wife to the obstetrician, bring your own reading material. All they have in the waiting room are chick magazines and magazines about parenting. An iPod might be a good idea, too, to drown out the crying babies. Better yet, a DVD player with headsets and a portable booth where you can draw the curtains around yourself would be ideal.

When they finally called us in, Susan stepped onto the doctor's scale; the moment of truth had finally arrived. The nurse wrote down Susan's weight, and we were relieved that she had gained ten pounds in two weeks. There would be no bed rest for her. Following the checkup, we were brought in to get another ultrasound. This would be the baby's fourth, and a particularly important one at that, since it had the potential to lead to many serious gasps. The results of this ultrasound and subsequent tests would reveal whether or not our kid would be walking around wearing a helmet all his life and riding a special bus to school. That's the scary part, and what if that's the case? This is the time when you have to ask yourself a few difficult questions. Do you want to take the risk of a miscarriage? Will you keep the baby if the ultrasound reveals problems? These are some really tough decisions.

I can say this—from the first moment you actually see your baby on the ultrasound, you are already in love. There is nothing you would do to hurt it. You start to understand why some people are such pro-life advocates, and why abortion is such a touchy subject. Who knows what the right answer is. I think the big question is, When does life actually begin? Some believe that life starts at conception. If so, can the mother start using the carpool lane right away? What worries me is that a lot of people think life begins at forty! I mean, you really have to draw the line somewhere! After some serious soul-searching, we both agreed that if the ultrasound or blood work showed any problems, abortion would not be an option.

You also have to consider that there are some things an ultrasound can't pick up—disorders that may surface when your baby gets a little older. It's a lot like those metal detectors you see those nerdy guys using on the beach. They might detect something under the sand, and hoping for something valuable, the guys discover it's only a bottle cap. The disorders I am referring to are conditions like ADD (attention deficit disorder), OCD (obsessive compulsive disorder), or how about IBS (irritable bowel syndrome)? I want to know, who comes up with these labels? Personally, I don't believe some of these conditions need labeling, or even exist, for that matter. My friend Dave thinks he can't get a disease or disorder that he hasn't heard about. Occasionally I will tease him by yelling out rare diseases. "Spina bifida!" "Cystic fibrosis!" Sometimes to really throw him, I will make up a disease.

"Dave," I'll say earnestly, "I just read about some guy that came down with something called berallisis menintiteus. The body slowly turns itself inside out."

"Nooo! Don't tell me that!" he will yell, reprimanding me. But what if there really were disorders that could affect our child that we didn't know about? How about A-D-Didilly-D, for children who are tone deaf? How about HDTV, for kids who insist on sitting too close to the television? What about LED, for kids easily distracted by those lights on your gadget control panel? How about EJD?—embedded journalist disease—inspired by that pause we all know so well after the newscaster asks an embedded journalist in a faraway foreign land a question? Because of the audio delay, we have to wait those few awkward moments for the question to be transmitted and for the reporter to answer.

NEWSCASTER: Tell me, Christianna—what is the general mood of the soldiers in Baghdad right now?

(Pause . . . Pause . . . signal being transmitted . . . pause . . . finally:)

EMBEDDED JOURNALIST: Well, Brian, the mood is quite surreal.

I think EJD would be a great tool for a successful relationship or marriage. It would give the husband or boyfriend time to think over his answer and possibly even come up with an excuse:

WIFE: Why did you get home so late last night?

(Pause . . . Pause . . . thinking . . . then, finally:)

HUSBAND: I, uhh, was at Tony's playing poker.

After all the waiting and fretting, the tests revealed that the baby had no problems. With the latest positive ultrasound in hand, I went straight to our home away from home, Kinko's, to make some copies. As I waited to pay the cashier, I happened to glance up on the wall to see a framed poster of Clark Gable. What a cool last name, I thought. Why didn't we think of this earlier? Dead movie stars from the forties! I called Susan immediately and ran it by her.

"How about 'Gable' for the baby's first name?" I asked. She loved Gable. It's a good thing, too, because if she didn't like Gable, then I was going to return to the Kinko's idea. Whether it was a boy or a girl, we liked Gable. Not only was it a cool, swashbuckling movie-star name from the forties, it was also an architectural configuration. A gable is a very strong, three-sided structure, which we thought was symbolic of the three of us. Each side relied on the others for support, which I guess some people could perceive as being needy, but regardless I liked the ring to it. It got to a point where we were looking for every positive Gable-ism to justify naming our child after a Nathaniel Hawthorne book. We were going overboard: "A gable is a triangle, and pyramids are triangular!" "Clark Gable had the same first name as Superman's alter ego, Clark Kent!" We also discovered that in French, *gable* means "dashing," and even if it doesn't, who is going to look it up? In Hebrew it means "miracle." Don't bother looking it up.

Our exhaustive search was over, we felt. So long as no one stole Gable from us or inadvertently tried to discourage us from using that name, we were all set. This name became our big secret. We were determined not to tell anyone, lest they should shoot it down. We agreed, however, that we would keep accepting suggestions from our friends and family—just in case.

Even though we'd made it through important fetal tests and we had a name, we knew that the future held many potential scares and gasps. I found myself constantly on the edge of my seat. We had one such scare when our friend Rachael called to tell us that she and her husband were adopting a dog from the local animal shelter, and they just wanted to check with us before they named it. Since we hadn't told anyone our name choice, she didn't want to name the dog something that we might have been thinking of. She wanted to name her dog Mable. We couldn't believe how close it was to our one and only name choice, Gable. After considering this for a few minutes, we realized that although they sounded similar, they were pretty different. Besides, most people don't call their dogs by their real name anyway. It's usually "Good girl!" or "Bad girl!"

Everything seemed to be going along right on schedule now, but any subtle request from the doctor immediately put us on alert. A couple of weeks later, Dr. Glass asked Susan to come back in to have her amniotic fluids checked. The doctor had been looking at some recent test results, and she wanted to look into a couple of things. She stressed that it was nothing to be concerned about, and that all she wanted to do was "keep an eye on it," which sounded a bit like something an auto mechanic might say to you when you bring your car in and he knows that there is something seriously wrong with it.

Though our doctor claimed she was not just an auto mechanic with extra letters after her name, I remained skeptical, possibly from too many trips to car dealerships. There's just something unnerving when your doctor says she wants to "just check something out." That's like when your boss signals you over and says, "Can I talk to you for a sec?" That's usually not good. There are several phrases that are not good to hear. "I've got a bone to pick with you," "I need you to step into my office," "Nobody told you?" How about this one: "Now hear me out." I guarantee you, whatever follows that is not going to be good. "Now hear me out. We are going to lower you into the well by your ankles— No, please, hear me out! Bill and Chad, here, will be dripping battery acid on you— Will you please just hear me out, for God's sake?" Dr. Glass put Susan up on the rack and checked out her amniotic fluids. Everything was A-OK.

In the interest of avoiding these potential scares during the difficult and gasp-prone final days of pregnancy, we decided to take birthing classes. The goal was to get a clearer sense of what's "normal" as the pregnancy neared its conclusion, so that we could keep the gasp–false gasp ratio at a respectable level and thus avoid my having a heart attack before the birth of my first child.

Since husbands are expected to be more involved with the pregnancy nowadays, I did not make a scene when Susan asked me to attend the classes with her. As with my Weight Watchers meetings, I assumed that I would be one of the only men in the room, and I was okay with that. Fortunately, as it turned out, we didn't have to attend a birthing class with a bunch of other breeders in a church basement or VFW Hall. We were invited to join our friends Brad Paisley and his wife, Kimberly Williams, at their house with a private instructor.

On the first day, Liz, our instructor, arrived out of breath and anxious to get the class started. She had no idea what she was in for. With her notes and visual aids Liz proceeded to explain the whole birthing process and how to recognize the right time to go to the hospital to deliver. As far as I was concerned, the right time to go to the hospital was when there was no traffic, but according to her the right time to go to the hospital was when the contractions were consistent and about fifteen minutes apart. We agreed to disagree.

When we got midway through the class, Liz showed us diagrams of the birth process and videos of mothers at the hospital going through an actual delivery. Brad and Kim had a new high-def home theater system, and let me say this: you have not seen a woman giving birth until you have watched it in high-def. All those commercials during football games talk about how "real" it is to watch sports and movies in high-def, and I usually just ignore them. But after seeing birth footage, I was convinced. I don't think the real thing even looks that real. We could see every sweaty pore on the woman as she agonizingly pushed the baby out. My first reaction upon seeing this high-def delivery was "I think I know that woman!" Meanwhile Liz was getting annoyed with my questions, most of which pertained to picture quality instead of the birth. "Do you have any idea if the camera that shot this was formatted for wide-screen?" "Is there a way to tweak the color red a bit?" "Can we adjust the surround-sound levels a bit so that we hear the doctor's instructions from behind and the woman's screams in the front?"

While I was not prepared to see any of this actual footage, afterward not only was I ready for the birth, I thought it had already happened. I was shocked to find Susan sitting next to me, still pregnant as ever. Being a smart aleck, I asked yet another question of Liz, whose patience seemed to be wearing thin, and accordingly her answer was a bit curt: "Kevin, yes, she knew she was being filmed."

Although the footage was useful for learning about Susan's pregnancy and convincing me to finally buy a high-def TV, I was hoping that Liz would show some videos on Los Angeles traffic patterns and alternate routes to the hospital. Instead I was taught what my responsibilities and "birthing stations" would be as Susan went into labor. Since the woman is not always thinking straight when the contractions start, it becomes the husband's duty to be the responsible one. This is also the case during a sale at the mall. The responsibility for thinking straight falls on the husband. I had to know how to react to her contractions,

make sure she was staying hydrated, time the contractions' dura-
tion and frequency, walk her around, make sure she was eating,
and distinguish and gauge when it was the right time to leave for
the hospital; again, many of the same signs to look for during a
sale at the mall. When the contractions were fifteen minutes
apart, it would be time to roll.

Among other things, the girls were taught how to use the
sixty-five-degree inflatable exercise ball to help her prepare for
the delivery. These are those big, colored balls you see at the gym
that nobody really uses. Basically, I guess, they are there just to
add color and get in the way. For pregnant women, though, it
would become an excellent tool to keep things flexible "down
there." Two of the stretching positions were called the Camel Roll
and the Cat Roll. We watched the girls go through these exercises
and then, as a token of our appreciation, I stuffed a few single
dollar bills in a nearby glass as a tip. It was in this class that we
were also taught how the baby "lightens" or drops down into the
pelvis area.

"The baby is preparing itself for a vaginal birth," Liz informed
us. If it doesn't drop down, then the mother may have to have a
C-section. C-section, I thought. Hmm, I don't know if those are
good seats or how far back they are, but these days you have to
take what you can get.

Liz briefly covered another exercise called Kegeling. Kegel
exercises are really quite odd. They were originally developed as
a method of controlling incontinence in women following childbirth. These Kegel exercises are also now recommended for
women with urinary stress incontinence. If fact, a survey found
that $5.2 billion is spent on adult diapers each year. Coinciden-
tally, $5.3 billion is spent on laxatives (don't look that up). The
principle behind Kegel exercises is to strengthen the muscles of
the pelvic floor, thereby improving the urethra and/or rectal

sphincter function. Bor-ing. I found myself bouncing up and down on the big green ball as Liz continued her instructions. For me, the bouncing only made me have to go to the bathroom. The success of Kegel exercises depends on proper technique and is quite difficult for a man to perform, since the proper technique calls for you to place your finger in your vagina and squeeze around it. When you feel pressure around your finger you have located the correct muscle. She said it's the same movements you make if you were trying to have a bowel movement—but, of course, without actually having the bowel movement. I had no idea this was even an exercise. A whole new world was opening up to me.

Not only did we attend birthing classes, but my wife also went to a psychic to ask questions about our baby and our future. I don't believe in psychics, but I do understand their appeal. Where else can you sit across from someone and have her talk about you, nonstop, for a half hour? Even if none of the stuff she was saying to my wife was true, she was giving her a ton of attention, and quite frankly, that took some of the pressure off me. I could tell that this psychic didn't know too much about childbirth. "You will have a natural childbirth through C-section," she said as she held Susan's hand. "The baby will be very . . ." She looked closer at Susan's palm and continued, ". . . very young . . . and babylike." I was waiting for her, like my psychic, to tell Susan she had three children she didn't know about.

In my opinion, there was no reason for Susan to fork over money to a psychic to have her pay attention to her for thirty minutes. As far as I can tell, there are plenty of people who are fully willing to give that attention to pregnant women. From what I'd surmised during my time spent watching Susan's pregnancy, this is perhaps the best thing about being a pregnant woman: everyone is constantly doting on you. It's like the pregnant woman becomes the queen bee. It's fantastic for the mother during those nine months: everyone asking if they can carry your groceries, everyone giving you their seat, everyone fawning over you. People gasp along with you and pepper you with questions to make sure you're all right. I have never heard so many people caution Susan about the importance of using the handrail going down the stairs.

But pregnant women shouldn't get too used to all this personal attention. Once they deliver that package, it all goes away. All of a sudden they are no longer so special in the eyes of the general public, creating a feeling of loss that many celebrities experience during their first trip to rehab. Suddenly their adoring fans have abandoned them, and they are just mothers—no longer *expectant* mothers. I can relate to this because I experienced this adulation once myself. It was during the filming of Adam Sandler's movie *Little Nicky*. The character I played was called "Tit-Head—The Gatekeeper of Hell." I was called Tit-Head because in the story Satan, played by Harvey Keitel, got upset and cast a spell on me. He made two large breasts grow out of the top of my head. I was endowed with a pair of 38C cups, and Rodney Dangerfield's character constantly wanted to play with them. In the story they were my curse, but off camera they were magic.

Every morning during the shoot I would sit in the makeup chair to have these things put on my head. The makeup department did a fantastic job. Due to two water-filled condom implants in each one, they even jiggled when I walked. They looked real, felt real, and together weighed about ten pounds. I didn't realize how heavy breasts were! I have a lot more respect for woman now, having to carry those around all day. The point of this story is, I couldn't believe all the attention I was getting with these breasts! It didn't matter that they were on my head. Everyone—guys and women—wanted to ogle and feel them. My head became a sex object. Some people were polite and asked if they could feel my breasts, whereas others were more crass, and I would catch them staring. How rude, I thought. "Hello?" I would say. "My eyes are down here." The minute the breasts were removed at the end of each day, people no longer took an interest in me. I felt abandoned. So, yes, I do know what it's like to suddenly not be the center of attention anymore.

Incidentally, it was around this time that we decided that we would breast-feed our baby. A "lactation consultant" had been referred to us to help with any breast-feeding questions we might have. This was yet another job that I had no idea existed, and never would have if someone had not suggested we see one. These professionals know absolutely everything there is to know about this field, and they are *not* in this business just to see women's breasts. Susan had many questions: How often should the baby feed? What kind of food should the mother be eating? How do we know when the baby has had enough?—and so forth and so on. Of course, I had my own questions for the lactation consultant as well: How much cream should I put in my coffee? How long can I drink from the milk carton after its expiration date? Why don't women have expiration dates on the side of their breasts?—and so forth and so on. Breast-feeding can be naughty and lascivious, but apparently there are many health benefits for the mother and baby. Unfortunately, none of them involve making my cup of coffee sweeter.

There is such a stigma in our country about seeing women's naked breasts. It is such a non-thing in European countries. But then again, apparently it's also a non-thing for a married man to have a mistress in Europe. Almost any beach you go to in Europe, you will see women going topless. No one is gawking except for the American tourists. If a European woman's breasts are covered up, then it's probably by a baby latching onto it. European women think nothing of breast-feeding in public, and for good reason: it is totally natural. In America some women will breast-feed in public, but usually they will cover up while doing it. Now that's just selfish, not to mention a big tease. But I guess that's just the way our culture is. We are the sexual prudes of the world.

Ironically, it's mostly men who find women breast-feeding in public offensive, and that's because it makes them feel awkward. They feel awkward because they don't know where to look. Should they just keep constant eye contact with the mother? Should they just look off into the distance? What if the mother catches you inadvertently looking at her breast? Worse yet, what if her husband catches you? Why don't fat men with man-boobs have to cover up on our beaches? I mean, they are breasts, right? There are certainly women with smaller breasts who are required to cover up. And what about women who don't really have any breasts? They still cover up. What if a man had hormonal treatments to give himself breasts? Would he have to cover up? Maybe if there was a certain amount of hair on our chests, no one would have to cover up. That would be considered covered up—sort of.

What we consider sexual or private is very confusing to me. I personally find the act of eating, especially in public, to be much more intimate than, say, using the toilet. I mean, if you think about it, when we eat at a restaurant we are opening up a cavity in our body and inserting food into it. Anyone looking can see the inside of our mouth—the pink walls, tongue, and rows of teeth. The whole process is then capped off by swallowing the chewed food. This is socially accepted. To me, using the toilet is much less intimate and revealing. I think eating should be done privately, perhaps in a stall inside a designated area. Maybe instead of meeting for dinner, people should meet to use the toilet. These meetings may be social gatherings or just a business luncheon. There could be a restaurant full of tables surrounded by toilets. The condiments on the table would be toilet paper, air freshener, and maybe a plunger. There would be no waitstaff, just attendants. During your evening they could offer you your choice of air fresheners, a menu of various plies of toilet paper, newspapers, mints, and other sundries. Friends could plan to meet there at a certain time in the evening—preferably shortly after dinner and coffee. Just like during the dinner crowd, maybe an acquaintance would walk past all of you on your toilets, and you would call to him, "Hey, Fred! How've you been? Care to join us?" Fred might answer by saying, "Sure, Mark. I'd love to." Or he might say, "Thanks, Mark, but I had a good one before I left the house. Let's plan another time."

Just think of all the names for your "restaurant":

* The Bowel Movement
* Flushed
* Pull Up a Stool
* Anchors Away!
* I'm in Here!
* The Porcelain Bowl
* Jiggle the Handle
* Stinky's
* Number Two's

Make up your own. The possibilities are endless.

Nothing is private for a baby. They don't care. They will eat with their mouth wide open, have food all over their face, head, and clothes, and be pooping all at the same time. I am anticipating many sudden gasps from my wife during those times, most of them probably when she is changing the baby's diaper. I wish naming a kid were as easy as coming up with a name for an establishment where you can poop alongside your friends. Just remember that Gable is taken, and if any of you try to steal it, I will find you . . . but probably not approach you or mention it to you, since, once again, I hate confrontation. At the most, I may just start devouring a bag of Milanos or flipping a nearby light switch on and off. Hopefully that message will be loud and clear.

TWELVE

Gathering the Straw

I stood in front of the large viewing windows alongside several other excited men as our babies rolled past us. The waiting room held about ten comfortable chairs, but most of us opted to gather around the window, tapping on the glass. Who could sit back when we could be up close to see our pride and joy? We weren't allowed inside, for obvious liability reasons: primarily germs, health regulations, and insurance restrictions.

"That's mine!" the gentleman to my left said proudly as he pointed to the little black one. I tried to stay reserved, but found myself ogling and pointing to mine—"That's mine." Another man contentedly said, "Mine should be coming out in a second. They just brought her in." You could immediately tell that most of these guys had formed a strong bond. One after another our loved ones came into view on the other side of the window. For some of the newer ones, this would be their first bath. I noticed that each was being attended to by what appeared to be a mostly Mexican staff. Typically rollers slapped soap on them, and high-pressure sprays shooting from the side rinsed them off, but this was a gentler car wash. It was the only car wash on the west side that washed by hand. Nothing's too good for our babies.

It wasn't just the car wash that reminded me of the hospital nursery and the pregnancy; other situations or sights had also started to trigger connections. Everything about my life had begun to center on the pregnancy and its related issues. I seemed to be noticing a lot more pregnant women now. There were probably just as many pregnant women as always, but because it had become such a part of my life, I in turn was hyperaware of them. It's like the weeks before Christmas, when you start noticing all the Christmas tree lots. It seems like every block has one. The rest of the year you don't pay any attention and don't notice them. It's also like when you buy a new car; all of a sudden you notice everyone else that has your car. You beep at them and give them a friendly nod as if to say, "You got one, too, eh? We have good taste."

But unlike when someone gets a new car, I find it's never a good idea to ask a woman if she's pregnant. If she's not, you're in huge trouble. I don't care if she's eight months pregnant and is wearing a T-shirt that says "Baby" with an arrow pointing down to her extended belly, I still would not chance it. I would simply say, "Hi. How are you? What's up?" all the while thinking to myself, Nice try. Not falling for that. Believe me, it is not worth chancing it by asking. I don't care if she's in the delivery room and the baby is halfway out. I would just casually point and say, "Excuse me, you've got a little something on your leg there." Only when she tells me she's pregnant, I'm sure that I heard her right, I've seen the test results, and I've verified that they match her blood type, then and only then will I extend my congratulations.

With pregnant women there is also that comparison of belly sizes. Susan would feel inferior sometimes if we met another pregnant woman who was the same number of months along but had a larger belly. I suggested that she might compensate for these feelings of inadequacy by buying a fancy sports car.

What was even weirder than noticing more women with baby bellies was noticing more guys with beer bellies. You become an expert in the field and try to guess how many years along each is—whether that one was started in college and is just now, twenty years later, reaching full term, or whether this one started in his early thirties and is now only through the end of the second trimester. In reality it's easier and far less potentially offensive to guess how many beers along a guy is.

Like with the pregnant women, I started seeing strollers everywhere, and quickly found them to be a lot like cars. When people passed each other pushing the same stroller, there seemed to be the same kind of connection. They were a part of the same club. There was that same little nod of recognition: "Nice stroller, right? We have good taste." On one particular Sunday morning, a cluster of them was parked outside a nearby restaurant. I used to only notice motorcycles parked outside restaurants and bars, and they made me a little apprehensive about going inside. Now I see strollers outside the restaurants, and I *want* to go inside so I can talk strollers with the gang of mothers. This was one of those times when it was clear that I was taking on one of my father's traits. Susan would comment on how cute the baby was, but I would be looking at the stroller, asking questions about the model and how it was constructed.

"Do you like it? Any problems with it? Is it easy to fold up and put in the car? How does it handle? Are there any steering issues? Have you tried off-roading with it? How does it do on rocky terrain? How does it look covered in mud?"

Many people would have you believe that it's what you feed, say, and do to a baby that sets a tone for its entire life. However, if the stroller lobby has anything to say about it (and believe me, they do), it's how your child rides in the opening months of his or her life that will dictate whether your child will attend an Ivy League school. As we came to terms with this apparent reality, we concluded that we were in way over our heads. Go to any park, and you will see myriad strollers. Some are inexpensive and some are very, very expensive, but before this, I'd never had to actually know anything about them. All I'd had to do was avoid them on the sidewalk.

Now it was a different story. Now I had to make a decision that would matter. Would I let my child ride in comfort and style, or was the high-gloss approach the way to go? Growing up, I always pictured a baby stroller like the ones I always used to see in cartoons or in *The Little Rascals*—the big black deal with the heavy springs. The tough baby with a five o'clock shadow and a cigar in its mouth would pop his head up.

What kind of stroller you should get depends on what you want to use the stroller for besides pushing the baby around in it. Will you be jogging with your baby? If so, you want the nylon sport utility. Will you be traveling? If so, you want something light and easy to fold up. Will you be shopping much? If so, get one that has a good turning ratio, not one of those three-wheel jogging strollers with the stationary front wheel. Those definitely aren't good for navigating around aisles. Will you be transporting a lot of junk in the stroller besides the baby? If so, you're going to need a large undercarriage storage compartment. Will you ultimately be using your stroller to transport junk from your garage to the trash? If so, then get a sturdy stroller with four big wheels. Better yet, get a wheelbarrow. They also have the very wide strollers that can accommodate twins or one really fat baby. These strollers have two separate seats, side by side. I can't imagine how any mother can push this thing down an aisle without it becoming some kind of tractor pull.

I guess the jogging strollers are pretty popular because many new mothers are eager to lose their pregnancy weight. These have one wheel in the front and two larger ones in the back. Most of the body consists of lightweight nylon. One model called a Bob International (no, seriously, that's not a joke, that's actually a type of stroller) seems to be very popular. In California there is a six-month waiting list to get a Bob International, which surprisingly is even longer than it takes to wait for a Toyota hybrid car. I would like to get the Bob International, but I don't jog anymore, especially internationally. For years I used to jog domestically on asphalt, and then I read that it is bad for your knees and back. I read this while icing my elevated knees on the couch. Since then I have been using the treadmill at the gym. It is much more forgiving. So I guess I will be looking for the best stroller to use on a treadmill—something that would work well on a rotating rubber belt.

Apparently, the Bugaboo stroller brand is one of the premier brands in the business, offering some of the best all-around strollers. I heard that Britney and a bunch of other celebrities who shouldn't be having babies in the first place use them. The list price is around a thousand dollars. I have no idea what makes a stroller so expensive. Maybe this one has airbags? A roll bar? A stereo system with subwoofer? I mean, what kind of materials could they possibly be using that would allow them to charge so much? Maybe it comes with a baby? Incidentally, I had this same conversation with my wife over designer handbags. I wonder if you can buy a knockoff designer stroller from some Algerian guy on a New York City street.

Stroller manufacturers have gotten pretty savvy, too. They have come up with all sorts of interchangeable attachments for your baby's stroller. The car seat can be removed to snap into the stroller, or you can get something called a "Moses basket" that snaps into the stroller. Some of these are great ideas, but then again some are not so great. Probably the worst design is the coffee cup holder, which is mounted near the stroller's handles—almost right over the baby's head. Given the priorities of a good stroller, somehow this seems like a design flaw. Let's say you're jogging with your stroller, and your coffee is nestled neatly in the cup holder. Suddenly you notice an interesting stroller parked outside a restaurant, and you slam on the brakes—*spppuh-lash!* That's right. Can you imagine your horror? You will have gotten your five-dollar Starbucks caramel-vanilla-soy-decaf-cappuccino-vente spilled all over your thousand-dollar stroller. Is it washable? For that price, let's hope so. Of slightly lesser concern is that the coffee may have spilled onto your baby, scalding the child in a manner that will no doubt require thousands of dollars in therapy, and create a general aversion to strollers forever. And the last thing you want is for your baby to get a taste of coffee and get addicted at that early age. The next thing you know, your baby is telling you that she needs her bottle of coffee in the morning before she can do anything. "I'm sorry, but I can't work on that potty training until I've had my coffee." Or, "Please, don't baby-talk to me now. I haven't had my coffee yet."

Even before this stroller dilemma emerged, I've long had a fear of spilling coffee. In my early twenties, my father got me a job at the factory where he worked, and we used to drive into work together. I started there as the lowest-level factory worker and eventually worked my way up to the same lowest-level factory worker. For two years I worked in this dusty, loud overhaul shop refurbishing helicopter blades. Financially, it was a great job for me since I was trying to pay off my student loan and also collect some money to travel around Europe. One time the foreman asked me what a young guy like me was doing wasting his time in a factory. I told him I was just trying to save up enough money to pay off my college loan and to get a little traveling money to go to Europe for a few months. He gave me a less than reassuring look and replied, "That's what I said twenty years ago."

Most of our morning drives into work found us running behind. More often than not my father would end up rushing out of the house, bringing along a full cup of coffee for the ride. It was just an ordinary coffee mug from our cupboard. (This was before they had those insulated travel mugs with spillproof tops. Those things are like sippy cups for adults.) Every morning, he would set his piping hot cup of coffee on the dashboard and we'd drive off. Nine times out of ten that cup of coffee would slide off at a curve, spilling its contents either on him, the radio, or me. To this day, when someone brings a coffee cup in the car, I cringe. I firmly believe there should be mandatory coffee-cup holders for all coffee cups.

The stroller was the first and most logical place for Susan to begin her "nesting" period. Typically an expecting mother will begin her "nesting" several months into the gestation period. It is a natural instinct for a woman, just like it is for a bird. A bird will start gathering sticks, straw, and feathers to build its nest for its little one, unless it is smart—then it will collect bricks. I would imagine that a bird or animal doesn't even know it's pregnant or why it's building a nest. It's not like they have an early pregnancy kit or an ob-gyn to tell them they are pregnant and should be preparing. It must just be an instinct that they are going to be having company soon. For all they know, they could be getting a roommate or having an in-law visit.

This nesting and gathering process usually happens about midway through the pregnancy, but as with everything else, my wife was one step ahead. One morning she revealed a drawer full of "adorable" baby clothes she had been collecting since a few months after we started dating. I guess these clothes were *her* cradle. She had shown me one or two of the "adorable" outfits around the time we were first trying to conceive, but this was the first time she revealed that she had a whole stash. This did not surprise me about Susan at all. She has always been a planner and a stockpiler. She will buy Christmas presents in June, have them gift-wrapped by July, and stash them away until December. I'm pretty sure that even birds that nest early don't buy pajamas with monkeys on them two years before conception.

With the delivery date still three months away, Susan was adamant about finishing her nest. We decided that the upstairs back room would be the most appropriate location for the nursery. Since it had originally been our bedroom, I knew from experience that it would be difficult to hear the constant crying coming from within. Also, the front bedroom had balcony access from outside, which is obviously an invitation to kidnappers. It seems the most important focal point of your child's nursery should be its crib. A regular, everyday, run-of-the-mill crib could be purchased and delivered in two days at the most, but being that we still had three months, timing wasn't an issue, which meant that regular, everyday, run-of-the-mill would not do.

"That type of crib will have no place in our child's nursery," Susan said. She continued, saying, "Our baby needs something unique."

By *unique*, I immediately knew she meant *expensive*. I guess the natural gestation period for a baby is ten months, because that's how long it takes for your new nursery furniture to arrive. The arrival of the nursery furniture was the one thing we wanted to know the due date on. Finally the crib that she'd ordered months back arrived, and she was pleased with her special selection: a hand-painted crib, custom-made at a farm outside of Copenhagen.

"The baby is going to love this!" Susan exclaimed. "The armoire and changing table will be coming tomorrow, and the baby is going to just flip over this!"

Honestly, the baby doesn't care what it looks like. The baby is going to lie in that crib and cry a whole lot, all while it's crapping its pants. It doesn't care that the crib was custom-made, complete with a canopy, carved rabbits on both ends, and a reversible mattress. I read somewhere that in the 1800s, babies actually slept in dresser drawers. Then again, could it be that I didn't read that, but saw it in a cartoon? I often confuse what I believe to be historical events I've read about with something I've seen in cartoons. Anyway, a drawer is obviously much cheaper than a designer crib. For the amount we spent on that crib and how long our child was actually going to be able to fit in it, we'd better have at least five more kids so we'd get our money's worth.

It turns out that while a crib is one of the pricier items, there are still plenty of other things that can really set your wallet back, and some of them are even essential. It is mandatory now that children under a certain weight must ride in a car seat. Luckily, there were no Danish custom-made car seats that Susan could find. The options were pretty basic: there was an infant car seat for babies up to twenty-two pounds, and then the baby car seat for babies weighing up to fifty pounds. I believe these are also required for fashion runway models. We were made aware that we would need to have an infant seat installed in our car before we could leave the hospital with our baby. Supposedly it had to be done perfectly, or the hospital staff wouldn't let us take our child home. According to rumor, the hospital would actually have someone follow us to our car and make sure that the car seat had been installed to the correct specifications.

Needless to say this caused me a great deal of anxiety. It was nerve-racking enough that we'd be leaving with our newborn child; what if the hospital staff member delayed us endlessly by forcing me to keep readjusting the position of the seat? What if that staff member cruelly scrutinized my work, looking over my shoulder as I attempted to adjust everything to the proper specifications? What if it was cold out, and our baby was struggling to stay warm, and this was my first chance to do the right paternal thing by my child, yet I was incapable because I couldn't get the car seat to the required angle because I had forgotten how to read a protractor?

Like lots of other baby information, we learned through word of mouth that there was a woman in Santa Monica who, for fifty dollars, would come to your house and install your baby's car seat to the exact specifications. We contacted her, and she arrived with her tools of the trade, which consisted of a Cabbage Patch doll (to simulate the baby) and some Styrofoam tubing (to simulate my brains) to get the angle just right. It took her about two hours to educate us about how many people don't install their car seats properly, and then it took her another fifteen minutes to install the car seat.

I was glad to have cleared this hurdle, but then the unfortunate side effect was that I had to drive around with an empty car seat in the back of my car for three months. I soon realized that it made a great holder for groceries while returning from the supermarket, especially the baby squash. Even if I were in an accident, they would probably survive.

Aside from word of mouth, most baby products and services can be found on the many Web sites sites floating around out there in cyberspace. People are always recommending Web sites to visit—sites that tell you what to expect almost every day of your pregnancy and thereafter. Here are a few that we heard about:

- Busybaby.com
- Ineedababy.com
- Idreamofbaby.com
- Babycenter.com

I'm even thinking about creating my own:

- Babypoopsmells.com
- ImadeamistakeandnowwhatdoIdo.com
- Ineedsleepdamnit.com
- Doessomeonehaveadirtydiaper.com

These sites are also a good source of information for baby clothing. I've learned it's very important to have a good supply of "onesies" for your baby. Onesies are the little one-piece cotton outfits that fit over your baby. You don't need a separate shirt, pants, and socks; you just slip the onesie over your baby and close the snaps down the front, and the baby is covered from neck to toe. Much easier to change when the baby throws up after a feeding. I believe this is also why Elvis wore those jumpsuits in his later years. You will find that most of these onesies have cute little sayings on the front. Interestingly, a lot of them are somewhat suggestive. Here are a few I've seen;

- Lover Boy
- Lock Up Your Daughters!
- Stud Muffin
- Babe Magnet
- You Had Me at Hello

- I'm a Boob Man
- Hunk
- My Mom Is Hot
- All My Mom Wanted Was a Backrub
- I Tore My Mom a New One

Here's a few I came up with that might be a tad too suggestive:

- Horn Dog
- Petite Perve
- Disease Free
- You Know You Want It
- Breast Connection
- Circumcised and Ready
- I Want to Gum You Up!

These Web sites have everything you need plus more. It's incredible how many products we decide we absolutely need, since they are available. One is a six-foot-long cylindrical pillow that helps support the woman's body while she sleeps. It comes with an instructional brochure that, through a dozen pictures, demonstrates the many ways to wrap your body around this thing. I believe it is called "Bob." Apparently, Bob is a popular name for baby products. This particular Bob, unlike the stroller, is not international. He must be local. Bob will become your wife's new sleeping pal. After a few nights you realize that Bob is providing more support to your partner than you ever could. You find yourself feeling a little inadequate. You also might become a little jealous of Bob. Not only jealous, but a little suspicious. I actually hired a private eye to trail Bob to find out if anything was going on between him and my wife. I was shown the pictures of them sleeping together. After several sessions of couples therapy, I accepted that it was a harmless relationship—purely platonic. I have since moved on. Bob now works as a door liner, keeping the heat from escaping from the bottom of our bedroom door.

There were also Web sites that advertise various services to the expecting parents, including agencies that charge a ton of money to come over and "babyproof" your house. If you ask me, it's a waste of money. I thought the best way to babyproof our house was to just stop paying the electric bill and water and power. Right away you are reducing the chances of your child getting hurt by 70 percent. In reality, the idea is to do away with anything in the home that may potentially harm the baby: sharp edges, electric wall sockets, glass vases, etc. These babyproofing people know of every possible accident that could happen. They also have different rates. "I could do it for $200," the man said, "or we can pull out all the stops for $1,100." I was thinking, why would anyone only spend the least amount to have their house babyproofed? What would they do for $200? Remove the knives from the counters? We also didn't want to go crazy with it and have them take needless precautions. When a company starts suggesting putting up a gate across the nearest on-ramp to the freeway, then that is excessive spending. You should really only limit the precautions to your home.

We could actually save a lot of money if we hired our friend Ray to babyproof it. Ray is a friend who drinks a lot and has a history of falling over furniture and injuring himself on the most mundane objects. We could get him drunk, follow him around the house to see what he hurt himself on, and then remove that object. It would only cost us a fifth of Grey Goose and a six-pack of Corona beer. If that didn't work, then we could bring in our worrywart friend Elisa.

I read somewhere that Indians never warned their children about impending harm. They felt that getting hurt was the best way for children to learn not to do whatever they did again. Back then, that was all fine and well. What's the worst that could happen? Fall out of a tree? Get a slight burn from the fire? Cut your finger on an arrow? Get war paint in your eyes? Nowadays I don't think that strategy would work. There are too many electrical outlets and fast-moving, heavy metal objects that you really shouldn't crawl in front of. From what I am hearing, parents are always overprotective with the first child. If the pacifier falls on the floor, they will boil it before they give it back to the baby. With the second child, they just stick it right back in its mouth. If the dog snags it, they will take it out of his mouth and put it right back in the baby's. Dirty diaper? No problem: just empty it out and slap the same diaper back on.

And what if your baby does get hurt? You will definitely need a good pediatrician. I started asking around for pediatricians, and apparently there was one right in our neighborhood, which automatically made me suspicious. I have a thing about going to a health provider whose office is too close to my house. I know it would be a lot more convenient, but for some reason I felt like she must not be very good if she is nearby—even if I live somewhere that's nice. I feel in order to have a good dentist or doctor, I need to drive at least thirty minutes. A doctor would be especially subpar if I could walk to her office from my home. The converse is that the very same dentist or doctor I had to drive thirty minutes to get to would probably not be the best dentist for someone who lives near them. We found the perfect pediatrician, except that she was only twenty-five minutes from our house. No problem—we could take some back roads that would add another five minutes to our trip.

With all these things to buy and health concerns, I found myself becoming overwhelmed by considerations and preparations. I wasn't just thinking about the baby's life in its first year, but worrying about its life six years down the road. What type of schooling will our child get? Will he be safe at school? Safe, that is, from his teacher? I didn't want to be that father who put a bumper sticker on his car that read "Our Child Is the Proud Parent of His Teacher's Baby." I was concerned. It seems more and more teachers are having sexual relations with their students. And what about being safe from other students? It sickens me that most public schools require their students to pass through an X-ray machine to detect knives or guns. I for one believe that guns don't kill people, people kill people, and that is exactly why I don't keep people in my house. And if I did, I would keep them locked up.

I suppose there is the option of homeschooling, which I, personally, am not a fan of. I think it's important for the child to have the experience of socializing with other children and races. Homeschooling seems like such an insular and lonely way to be educated. I was in Florida once, and I went into a hotel lounge. There was nobody else in there except some kid sitting at the bar. I said, "What's going on?" He replied that he was on spring break from home school. How much fun could that be?

And so it was, with the threat of home schools, expensive strollers, potentially attractive nannies, and perilous local doctors all looming on the horizon, I turned to the one place certain to help: a bookstore. There, in the self-help aisle, I found tons of books covering every topic of pregnancy and child rearing. Ironically, self-help is not always the easiest section to find. In fact, I was in a new bookstore recently and asked the cashier, "Would you please tell me where the self-help section is?" She looked at me sternly and said, "I could, but wouldn't that be self-defeating?" Obviously she was hormonal.

When I read a book, I like to mark certain pages so that I may refer to them later. Sometimes I will underline a specific sentence or paragraph with a pen or, better yet, use yellow highlighter. The highlighter, however, can sometimes present a problem. One time I had highlighted what I thought was an important passage, and later read it to a group of people. After reading it, I couldn't understand why I had highlighted it. It was neither interesting nor informative, and my audience was not even remotely impressed. After several perplexing minutes, I closely analyzed the page and discovered that the actual sentence I had highlighted, and meant to read, was on the other side of the page. The highlight had bled through to the backside of the page, sending me in the wrong direction. This also may have explained why the highlighted sentence was so short and uninteresting. The sentence read like this: ". . . off of the middle shelf."

Sometimes if there is too much good information on a page, I will mark this page by simply bending over the top corner. This is called "dog-earing." It is called that because once you have made the fold, with some imagination, you can see it as the ear of a dog. I initially was not a fan of dog-earing pages, and that's because I wasn't going about it the right way. I was drawing a picture of a dog's ear on the corner of the page. That's all fine and well, but it doesn't really help you find that page later. I dog-ear pages for different reasons. Besides noting a passage that I might like to refer back to at a later time, there might be a word that I'd like to remember so I can look it up later, find out what it means, and then try to impress someone by incorporating it into a conversation. One such word I recently came across was *crouton.* I also dog-ear a page so I can find where I left off the last time I was reading the book. There are even times when I dog-ear a page to cover a greasy food stain.

I returned from my trip to the bookstore with what turned out to be a particularly good baby book. After the first chapter, I noticed that I had large groups of pages dog-eared. I felt bad because, somewhere, I imagined, there was a pack of paper dogs running around without their ears. I squelched my emotions to the size of a crouton. The book had so much information that I had eventually dog-eared every page, which actually defeated the purpose of a dog-eared page. As a result, I started to dog-ear the bottom corner of each page, which is really saying something, because usually there's not as many noteworthy things written on the lower half of the pages. Authors know that people don't like to read past the first half of any page, so they don't usually waste useful information by putting it there. The one problem with the dog-earing is that you are limited to folding the page to one side or the other. You will need to make a difficult decision about which side of the page is more important. This is an ongoing pet peeve of mine. I long for the day that publishers print on thicker paper, so if you need to dog-ear both sides of the page, you can use your fingernail to split the corner of the paper in two and fold it down on *both* sides.

After dog-earing every top page of this book and many of the bottom pages, I determined that one page was actually just a little more important than the others I had marked. I decided to add a little yellow Post-it note to the dog-ear as well, with just enough of the yellow sticking outside the pages to see it. Eventually, though, I had too many Post-it notes on too many dog-eared pages. It now became necessary to dog-ear the more significant Post-it notes. I say "significant," but in reality I ended up dog-earing all of the Post-it notes as well. It got to the point where I would also double-emphasize a certain page of importance by throwing in a bookmark. I then started using the book's jacket flap to mark pages. You do this by extending the flap and inserting it between the two noteworthy pages. Don't forget that you have the ability to dog-ear the flap as well. The only foreseeable problem with this option is that you run out of flaps after marking only four pages.

By the way, it's not out of the question to use an additional jacket from another book to add to the mix.

I would narrow down the most notable pages by adding those little sign-here stickies as well. You know the ones I'm talking about; when your accountant sends you a bunch of wordy papers that he wants you to sign shortly before April 15, he knows you're not going to read through it, so he just has a little sign-here sticky stuck to where you are supposed to sign each page. Literally, they are about the size of a crouton. If that weren't easy enough, the sticky also has an arrow pointing to the line you're supposed to sign on. If your accountant is really on the ball, he will also dog-ear those pages for you.

It actually got to the point where the book was becoming difficult to close because of all the folds, dog-ears, Post-it notes, sign-here stickies, paper clips, and bookmarks. When I set the book on end, it would spring open like a shark's jaw, revealing the folded corners as if it were a killing machine of noteworthy information. All this may sound excessive and even borderline obsessive-compulsive, but it sure does beat highlighting every single sentence of a book. And if you think that's the direction you are going, then save yourself some time—put down the highlighter and just dip the entire book in yellow paint. I suggest you hold it by the dog-ears.

THIRTEEN

The Expiration Window

I don't know when you became so unfunny, but your days are numbered," read the first line of the next fan letter I removed from the small stack. He continued, assuring me, "I swear to God, I am going to put a bullet into your big *fat* Mick head." I wasn't sure if the writer of this death-threat letter was making a derogatory reference to my head as being from Ireland, or simply implying that my head was a menu item at McDonald's, in which case he should have spelled it "McHead." I believe the letter was in response to a joke I may have made at the Weekend Update desk during my stint on *Saturday Night Live*. At any rate, this letter made me incredibly neurotic. For the next week I walked around the offices at 30 Rockefeller Plaza asking everyone, "Do you think my head is McFat?"

Large heads run in my family, and according to our first 4-D ultrasound, our baby would not be breaking tradition. The 4-D is a much more detailed image of the baby that allows you to see the curves and the actual features. According to this image, our baby's head size was in the ninety-seventh percentile. The results of this ultrasound were understandable because Susan and I both have large heads. In fact, we can only wear hats that are XL. The one-size-fits-all doesn't apply to us either. Susan had to have a special graduation cap made in college, since the largest one was too small to fit her. Following tradition, at the end of the ceremonies the entire graduating class, in celebration, threw their caps up in the air. When Susan threw hers, it was like throwing a blanket. For a moment it blocked out the sun, creating a gray overcast. Incidentally, I also have trouble finding shoes to fit, since I am a size fifteen. More often than not, when I like a shoe, it doesn't come in my size. The salesman typically brings out another style, the only shoe they have in fifteen, and hopes I like it. Usually it's the ugliest style in the store, a pilgrim shoe with a big buckle.

We studied the images of this 4-D ultrasound in the hope that it might unlock the secrets of our baby's proportions. The picture is taken by sound waves, and unfortunately the results were not as clear as we had hoped they would be. In fact, the baby sort of looked like a crude clay sculpture. It wasn't cooperating to give us the best shot either. Its big head was turned away and hidden behind a big pile of placenta. The ultrasoundist used two or three fingers to gently push and manipulate Susan's belly in hopes that the baby would shift and become more visible. The baby finally cooperated and came into view on the screen. She snapped away, giving us a few different images, but since the baby was bigger than it had been during the previous ultrasounds, it appeared uncomfortably crammed in the womb. This resulted in some very unsettling and almost frightening images. One looked like it had a smashed-in nose and a swollen eye. It looked as if it had just gone ten rounds in a heavyweight fight. In another, it looked like a tough thug that worked down at the docks. The other three looked like a tough alien that just started his shift working down at the docks after a ten-round heavyweight fight.

The best of these was one of the baby's face with its foot planted against it. We kept this best shot and took an oath to never ever show anyone the others. Foot or no foot, Susan could already tell that it was "ultra" cute—so cute that she was already thinking about notifying the leading podiatry magazines to start a bidding war.

Brad and Kim sent us two of their baby's ultrasound pictures, and Susan and I noticed that the quality of theirs was much better than ours. Ours were black and white and grainy, while theirs were clearer, with more of a brownish tint—almost sepia-toned. As is natural for every parent, we immediately began to compare our baby to theirs, even though neither had been born yet. Their baby's head was much smaller than ours, but we decided the upside was that our baby would probably win in a fight. Some of my family and friends thought that in the pictures from the last ultrasound the baby looked more like me, and I wasn't sure how to take that, since it looked like the baby had a foot growing out of its head. Of course a lot of people think someone they know looks like me. A complete stranger will sometimes come up to me and say, "Dude, oh my God! You gotta come into my restaurant. Our bartender looks just like you. We always kid him about it!" He'll drag me in, and I'll see the bartender, and in my opinion, he looks nothing like me. Sometimes it's almost insulting. It will be some guy that maybe has the same eyebrows as me, but the rest of him couldn't be further from looking like me.

I guess we always perceive ourselves as being better looking than we are. I used to have trouble watching myself on TV because I was so critical of how I looked. I couldn't believe how bad my posture was. I started yelling at the TV, as if I could fix my appearance: "Stand up straight! Pull your shoulders back! Fix your hair!" Since I am pretty tall, I've always had trouble with my posture. I usually try to make a conscious effort to stand up straight and keep my shoulders back, but I always forget. Besides, it feels so unnatural. If I walked into a room full of people with my shoulders back and my chest out, I would feel like I was some combination of pompous and aggressive, as though I should accompany that posture with a tough comment like "Who wants a piece of this?"

Yes, most of us perceive ourselves differently than how we actually look, and I think that is an ego survival trait. I once remember watching a street artist sketch a picture of a woman. The woman was quite unattractive, almost a real-life caricature. I watched to see how accurate the artist would be. As he sketched her, I saw that he was being very forgiving. He was clearly an artist with many years of experience of sketching people. He cleverly reduced most of her unfortunate features and made her look fairly normal. I stayed around to see how happy the woman would be about the finished sketch. He signed it, tore it from the easel, and finally showed it to her. She looked at it for several seconds, then immediately crumpled it up and yelled at the artist, "This doesn't look like me! You made me look like a goon!"

Earlier in my career, after I'd attained some minor celebrity status, people started to recognize me. Most of the time, though, they weren't really sure who I was. They would think that they knew me from their bank, or I was a regular customer at their store. Other times they would approach me and say, "You look a lot like that guy on *Saturday Night Live*." I would usually respond by saying something like, "I know. I get that a lot." Or, "I wish I had his money!" They would then go on their way. Eventually, when I got comfortable with being recognized, I would admit that yes, I was in fact that guy.

For several years I lived in Lake Tahoe, Nevada, and one snowy winter day my hot water heater decided to stop working, so I called a plumber. An hour later, he arrived, and I opened the door to find him covered in snow and winded from trudging up the eighty-nine steps to my house. He looked at me for a few moments, and in between his frosty gasps for air, I could see him trying to process whether it was actually me. There was that beat where he finally realized it was me, and accepted his mental computation. He finally said, "Well, I guess everyone has to be somewhere." He then brushed by me with his toolbox and asked where the water heater was. Another time, in the Dallas airport, a well-worn man with a beer belly and a Texas drawl approached me. He said, "I know you. Man, you are a lot better looking on television." I was waiting for him to laugh at his bad joke, but he just kept sizing me up. I guess I was a little insulted, and even more surprised when he asked me for my autograph for his kid. I agreed and scribbled on the paper, "Your dad is a big loser!" and then signed it. I handed it back to him. Without looking at it, he stuffed it in his pocket and took off.

Most of what we learned from the 4-D ultrasound had more to do with us than with our baby. Suddenly we found ourselves disappointed that there were no more ultrasounds to look forward to. Even with the grainy image, the feet finally looked like feet; you could distinguish the legs and some of the nooks and crannies. It was our way of communicating with the baby—our window to what was going on in there. The only communication after the 4-D was feeling it kick or punch Susan's stomach from the inside, which is pretty one-sided. There would be these slight raps that periodically emerged from inside her stomach, leading me to believe that it was trying to communicate with us by kicking in Morse code. My brother Mike thought it would be a boy because it was only kicking; he said if it were a girl, it would be kicking, scratching, and using pepper spray.

No more checking in on it. No more voyeurism. The baby would finally have a window of privacy, at least until it was born, and then all bets were off. One of the gifts we got recently was a baby monitor. Apparently these are quite essential. You set up the base unit in the child's nursery, and from anywhere in the house you can hear the baby through your walk-around unit, which picks up any noise your baby makes. It is reassuring to the parents, but also the earliest violation of your baby's civil liberties. Not only may Big Brother be listening in, but also Big Parents. The baby is totally unaware that every little move or sound he or she is making is being monitored.

I am a little sensitive when it comes to the invasion of privacy, since a few years ago I was unwittingly part of several different wiretapping scandals, courtesy of Anthony Pellicano, the Hollywood private investigator who was indicted on racketeering and conspiracy charges. Pellicano apparently thought I might have some useful information that could help one of his clients, and as a result, I made his infamous list of wiretapping victims.

"What did you get?" the infamous Pellicano must have asked as they stood in the Dunkin' Donuts parking lot. The crooked cop who he had paid off to check the L.A. police database probably handed him a coffee-stained manila envelop. Pellicano probably continued hopefully, "Is there anything in there that we can use against him in court?" It would be at least a year or more later that I would learn that they could very well have been discussing me.

Was I surprised? Did I feel violated? Did I feel resentment? The answer is no to all three. I mean, why shouldn't I have my phone tapped? I am a big player in Hollywood and hold a lot of power. Anyone who has seen my cameo in *Joe Dirt* will attest to that. I also learned that there was a possibility that the police database was searched to dredge up "embarrassing material" to be used against me if I ever decided to testify against an "enemy."

Is this something that surprises me? The answer again is no. Since I am clearly a "somebody" in this town (did I mention my cameo in *The Wedding Singer?*), this comes with the territory. Although I have to say I wasn't aware that I had an enemy.

I first discovered I was involved in this fiasco when one morning I opened the *New York Times* to discover a picture of me sandwiched between two other unwitting victims: Sylvester Stallone and Garry Shandling. I actually liked the photo they used of me. It was taken at a golf benefit I participated in. I was wearing my favorite bucket cap and was only ten pounds over my ideal weight. Never in my wildest imaginings did I actually ever think "Kevin Nealon" and "wiretap" would appear in the same news article. But, I must say, I was elated to have made this group. It made me feel important. You're nobody in Hollywood until you get on a list. I missed out on the Heidi Fleiss client list, Mr. Blackwell's "Worst Dressed" list, and even the "Where Are They Now?" list. And the only reason I'm not on that last one is that Mr. Pellicano, apparently, always knew where I was.

It wasn't long after that that I learned that the Ringling Bros. and Barnum & Bailey Circus had apparently also hired someone, several years earlier, to wiretap my phone. That would explain all the clowns with binoculars outside my house, squished inside that little car with the tinted windows. This particular allegation was probably the result of my involvement with animal rights demonstrations in the nineties. I remember protesting with my former wife and other animal activists outside the circus in New York City. We had also been criticizing the circus's inhumane treatment of animals in radio interviews and print—not to mention doing some stickering.

Most of us grew up loving the circus and never entertained the notion that its animals were being treated inhumanely. We watched the elephants as they paraded around in a circle, each holding the tail of the next elephant with its trunk. If you've ever been forced into a conga line at a party, you know how humiliating this could be. The trainer would poke and prod the elephants to sit down and lift their legs or whatever. The fact is, the elephant is a beautiful, sentient creature. Circuses keep them chained almost twenty-four hours a day, except for the hour or so when they are forced to perform degrading tricks for an audience. They are transported around the country in small train cars and trucks with little or no room to move. Above all, if you've ever seen any footage on how an elephant is "broken" so that it will be submissive to its handlers, you would cry. It's not just the elephants, either; it's all the animals they use.

In hindsight, I should have known someone was eavesdropping on me. There were obvious signs. The peephole in my front door had been reversed. I was sold a paper shredder that made copies. "Homeless" people went through my garbage before I even threw it out. I was issued license plates with my PIN on them. Most upsetting to me, though, was discovering that my diary was missing. It was the diary I've kept since I was seven. And before you hear it from someone else, yes, I did have a major crush on Mary Barker in third grade.

Susan found it very exciting to be with a man who has been wiretapped. The intrigue, the mystery, and the secrecy were all very alluring. All of a sudden I was a bad boy, and believe me, I milked it for everything it was worth. We'd be strolling at night, and I would quickly pull her aside and look back, concerned. Frightened, she would ask, "What's wrong?" I'd reassure her and say: "Probably nothing. I just thought . . . no, nothing."

What did I do to protect my future privacy and to ensure my security? Not only did I change all the locks in my house, but I also moved the doors. As an added measure of security, the doors would now swing out instead of in; we all know how frustrating it is to push on a pull door. To add to the confusion, I installed one of the doors horizontally, so the only way you could enter was by rolling in. I also switched from telephones to walkie-talkies. (Is it possible to "tap" smoke signals?) When I would leave the house, I started turning on the garbage disposal, so everyone would think I was home. (Much cheaper than an alarm system.) Finally—and I know I may be going overboard with this—I recently got a bomb-sniffing dog, and apparently I've got explosives in my crotch.

It's not easy being in the public eye—or the private eye, for that matter. For years I have told my therapist that I suspected my phone was being tapped. She said that was ridiculous, and I was just being paranoid. Well, these recent revelations finally prove me right. Now maybe she'll believe me about the bogeyman in my basement. The bogeyman who also probably wants to put a bullet in my big fat Mick head.

With the passing of the 4-D ultrasound, we were within what I came to refer to as the "expiration window"; that is, our baby would be born before most currently stocked items on grocery store shelves pass their expiration date. Of course, that was true for Twinkies before we even got pregnant, or for that matter, before we even got married. I remember when I was starting out in stand-up comedy, and my name would be listed in the *TV Guide* as appearing on the *Tonight Show* that coming week. It really made my appearance official, and I thought to myself, Uh-oh, now I have to do it because I'm listed in the *TV Guide*. Everyone was expecting to see me now. I was within the expiration window.

Our life was already beginning to change. Instead of the traditional trip we would make back East every Christmas to visit our families, this year we stayed in California. Susan, being in her last trimester, was too pregnant to fly, and I was in the final stages of pregnancy brain, which was now affecting even our friends. We had a small Christmas get-together at our house, and due to my pregnancy brain, I inadvertently served everyone glasses of Eggbeaters, mistaking the carton for eggnog—actually an easy mistake to make, since the cartons and contents look similar. Luckily our friends didn't notice, since each glass also had a few shots of rum in it. I accidentally came up with a new drink, the Rum Beater.

Since the due date was rapidly approaching, we decided to take a tour of the hospital's maternity ward to get an idea of where it would all be going down. As we entered the lobby, we looked in through the glass window of the hospital nursery. On this particular day, there was only one baby.

"Great, maybe there won't be so much traffic sixteen years from now," I said to Susan.

The lone baby's father held it briefly, then handed it back to the nurse, who unswaddled it and gave it a once-over. She weighed it, measured it, and gave it a sponge bath. Sort of like a mini Ellis Island for the newborns.

As she reswaddled the baby in the blanket, the father stood nearby, seemingly uninterested, almost as if he were waiting for the store checker to bag his groceries. The trend nowadays is to get the husband to be more actively involved in the delivery. I was wondering if me being curled up in the fetal position, sucking my thumb, in the corner of the room would be considered "actively involved." You can basically have whomever you want in the delivery room with you, too. You can call them a "support group," your "posse," your "lawyers," or whatever. We decided that we would probably have several people in there with us. Susan wanted her mother, her mother's friend Betty (to take video but not of her business), possibly Heidi, who is a wonderful massage therapist we love and is very spiritual, and me. Oh, yeah, and also the doctor and however many nurses and anesthesiologists would be needed.

It seemed like maybe a few too many to me, but I went along with it. Don't get me wrong—I like having people around. It reminds me of when my friends and family would hang out in my dressing room during my last season on *Saturday Night Live*. The room was very small, and eventually, by the time my ninth and final season was winding down, it wasn't unusual to have about ten people in there partying it up. This wasn't after the show, mind you—this was while the show was being shot "live" a short way down the hall in the studio. I would occasionally come back to my dressing room, in between sketches, for a rest and barely be able to fit in. Everyone would have to squeeze into the room so I could open the door. There would even be some people in the mix I didn't know, probably some friends of Chris Farley or David Spade, who both had dressing rooms just down the hall from me. My friend Grant would usually bring in a blender and make his specialty, frozen margaritas. The TV monitor on the wall was airing the show, but no one would even be watching. They were all too busy talking about other things, laughing, and getting tipsy. I'm not sure but one time, while out in the studio performing a sketch, I think I heard the whirring of the blender.

I think on some level I imagined live birth to be similar to live TV. I pictured all these people squeezed into this small delivery room; someone would have a blender mixing drinks, and everyone would be laughing playfully, not really paying attention to the real action at hand. Perhaps the sound of the blender would distract from Susan's repeated requests for painkillers. If nothing else, the bystanders would be comfortable. In the end, whatever scenario made Susan feel comfortable was okay with me. Besides, maybe we wouldn't need some of the nurses.

Thirty-five years ago mothers didn't have as many options as they do now. When women gave birth they were usually knocked out (not literally), and the husband or future ex had to hang out in the waiting room until someone came to tell him he had a baby boy or girl. In her inimitable fashion, one of Susan's biggest concerns was whether the room would be comfortable enough for our guests and me. Here she was, about to push a baby out, and she wanted to make sure the room had a seating plan. Sandy, one of the nurses in the maternity ward, showed us the rooms. The traditional hospital rooms are much homier now. They have plasma TV screens on the walls, a nice easy chair, soft, indirect lighting, a cushioned bench/bed for your partner to crash on, and, most important, beautiful blond hardwood floors. Hardwood floors are such a big seller these days. All of the homey features, though, can't disguise the nearby monitors that Susan will ultimately be hooked up to. Too bad they couldn't paint them to look like a jukebox or something.

On our way out we made our usual stop at the hospital's pharmacy for snacks for the ride home. It's amusing the things you come across in a pharmacy, especially the pharmacies at the hospital. We discovered one particularly unique item: the Travel-John. The TravelJohn is basically a reusable plastic bag for you to urinate into in case you are stuck in traffic or in a tent in the middle of a rainstorm. One of my pet peeves, besides being stuck in traffic, is to have to pee while stuck in traffic. You simply keep the TravelJohn in your car in the event you have to urinate and can't pull over. The box says that men, women, and children can use it. Somehow, once you pee into it, it freezes the urine. There are even lots of testimonials on the box's cover about how this product saved folks from extremely uncomfortable and potentially embarrassing situations. I had never seen one of these before and had to have it. Susan picked up two additional ones for stocking stuffers.

At that time, Susan's pregnancy was making her take more trips to the bathroom during the night. It finally got to the point where she was almost getting up to use the bathroom at night more than I was. I am a light sleeper, so I had no problem waking up to help push her out of bed when she needed to get up, but when the bladder of a healthy woman in her thirties starts acting like that of a fifty-year-old man, that's when you know it's bad.

Maybe it was Susan's bladder situation, or maybe it was the trip to the hospital that allowed me to envision precisely how the whole thing would go down, but for some reason, it was around this time that the truth became undeniable: this baby was happening soon. That realization brought a new level of stress to the situation, and in response, I found myself making many last-minute prebirth preparations. As I tried to anticipate problems that might come up, I took the precaution of protecting our new mattresses from any bodily discharge in the coming weeks. This way we'd be protected against everything from Susan's water breaking all over the bed to the baby throwing up, peeing, or pooping on it. It would even protect the mattress from the excessive moisturizing cream I was using at night. Bed, Bath and Beyond carries large waterproof covers for mattresses. They slip over the mattress like a large condom, except this one has a zipper at the end.

But my adjustments were not all practical. *"Your life will change"* kept echoing in my head. *"Get sleep now when you can." "Do the things you want to do now, because once the baby comes, well—"* In response to this chorus of anxiety, I decided to turn over a new leaf, to buckle down and make the most out of my life. At last I was going to get some work done—specifically, I was determined to write more. The rumor was that soon I would have less time, so now, mere weeks before Susan was supposed to deliver, seemed like as good a time as any to start some major projects that I had no hope of finishing before the baby was born. But hey, until that water broke, I'd be as serious as ever—no more goofing around. There would be no more distractions. Life was too short, and I had not accomplished nearly enough before my first child was born.

As my new regime of prefatherhood discipline emerged, I got a call from my friend Jay, who asked me if I wanted to go surfing with him. "Nope, can't go surfing," I told him. "I'm buckling down, and I need to get work done." I explained to him that this was the new me. He expressed his disappointment that I wouldn't be able to join him, but said he understood. I then found myself asking him what time he was going. I had never been surfing before, and it seemed unlikely that I would have another time to try it in the near future, since I would soon be a father with no time for frivolous things like surfing or sleep. Though surfing was not explicitly part of my getting-serious routine, it was something that I'd be unable to do in a few weeks' time. I'd lived in California for years and never done it, so why not try it out now before it was too late? "Hey, I live in California," I said to myself. "I have to at least try surfing, otherwise it would be a waste." It would be like going to Vegas and not getting a hooker. That new leaf I was going to turn over wasn't going anywhere. I could always turn it over the next day. The leaf would not be disappointed.

It seemed that this would be as good a day as any to try surfing. As it turned out, this would not be as good a day as any. My first time surfing was a horrible and painful experience. I actually hit a deer, or at least I thought I did. It turned out to be a big wad of kelp. But like a deer, it came out of nowhere. That's what people say when they hit a deer: "It came out of nowhere. I was coming up your driveway at about a hundred and fifty miles per hour, and this deer came out of nowhere!" Everything comes out of nowhere when you are doing a hundred and fifty miles per hour. "That McDonald's drive-thru came out of nowhere!" "That family of tourists came out of nowhere!" There is probably no greater disappointment than when you take something's life. I'm sure the deer was disappointed and shocked as well. "Disappointed and shocked"—now there's a tough comment to handle. I have enough trouble withstanding someone telling me they're just disappointed with me, but when I shock *and* disappoint them, well, that's really a knife in the heart.

Even though surfing proved to be something of a bust, it didn't put an end to my fears that suddenly I would find myself unable to do all these things that I'd always wanted to do, and even things that I didn't really want to do but sort of wanted to do. Now I would have a very good reason not to do them. And not just midlife crisis things like base jumping or surfing, but legitimate these-are-important-things-to-do things that somehow I'd avoided for my whole life. Prior to this, I had never been one of those people who asked, "Won't a baby take up all my time? I may not have time to do the things I really wanted to do." To me, the answer always seemed clear: You will still have time to get your stuff done and continue all your silly hobbies. After all, let's face it, some people just have too much free time on their hands. A friend of mine was telling me about a performance artist who paints by squatting over a canvas and shooting paint enemas out of his butt. I said, "No way!" He then showed me a picture of the guy in *People* magazine, and I actually knew him! He was the guy that painted my car! No wonder it took him so long . . . and a crappy job, too! I realized that this guy had too much time on his hands.

My assumption was always that a baby wouldn't stop me from pursuing my lofty ambitions of, say . . . joining a drum circle, transferring my address book to my iPhone, learning to complete a sentence while burping, or looking for Nicole Brown Simpson's real killer. But let's be honest, I probably wouldn't have done these things to begin with. The baby just makes for a good excuse. We live in a world of distractions, and at least now I can blame my failure to succeed on my baby.

But being on the cusp of the actual birth brought me to doubt my earlier assumptions about how my life would not change. Since I was a lot older than most new fathers, I had many age-specific concerns about what this meant for me. Many expectant fathers in their early thirties can dismiss fears of not being able to do things by saying, "Oh I'm young, I still have time for that." As a fifty-three-year-old, I knew this to be either a poor rationalization or denial. There won't be and never would have been any skydiving or celebrity boxing matches. Furthermore, I had additional concerns about the everyday stuff that I had enjoyed doing for the last fifty years. When you have a kid at thirty, you're not so set in your ways because you've only had these ways for thirty years. When you have a kid at fifty, it's a different story. Extra time digesting meals, fondling the TV remote, naps, working out kinks in my joints—these would all be disrupted. I'd been afforded twenty additional years to become a slave to my habits and schedules, and once the baby was here they'd all be moot, rendered instantaneously irrelevant by this new person. There would be no time for me, me, me.

In the end, I had to believe that if I wanted to get something done, I would. I would get the necessary amount of work done, and anything that I didn't accomplish probably wasn't all that important. The problem was that no one is a bigger procrastinator or more easily distracted than I am, and over the course of fifty-three years I had put off a lot of things in the name of one excuse or another. I really don't believe I'm lazy—I think I just wasn't quite ready to do those things. Of course, I can't underestimate the role that laziness played. Lately, I have been saying no to a lot of job opportunities. I have been hearing myself say, "That seems like a lot of work." No matter what it is, I imagine the workload and think, "That seems like a lot of work." Sometimes I will also begin to tell someone about something that happened, and not too far into the story I find myself saying to the other person, "Ahhh, it's too long a story." I completely bail out of it. Why? Because it just seems like a lot of work.

This newfound anxiety was no different: I'd had plenty of time to worry during the course of the pregnancy, but I had procrastinated on my worrying and now it was too late. I never used to worry about doing well on tests in high school until I was taking them. Then I would say to myself, "Damn, I should have studied for this." Then I would start worrying that I wasn't going to pass it. By then it was too late. It was the same with worrying about my life after pregnancy. I was beginning to realize that yes, my days *were* numbered. Maybe I put off worrying because it was too much work. Was that possible? Maybe I thought Elisa had done enough worrying for everyone.

Most men procrastinate on doing things that they don't really need to do, like buying a $90,000 sports car or trying out for the Olympics. In fact, whenever the Olympics are on TV, I get extremely motivated and think, "I gotta start working out," but then I never do. I know that I have another four years before the next Olympics, and then before I know it, I've let time slip by, and the next Olympics is airing. I've come to accept that the only sport I could possibly try out for at my age and shape is the bobsled event. Even that may be a tall order, since I don't think there is a helmet big enough to fit my big fat Mick head. Also, I would have to be the guy in the front of the sled, since I'm not big on having to push. Once again, it just seems like too much work.

Some of us are just suited to certain roles, and for some that's not being a father. I'd always believed, though, that I was suited to the father role. I had confidence that everything would be okay, and I needed to embrace it. I needed to keep surrendering. After all, I still had a pot to pee in—and even if I didn't, I'd always have the TravelJohn, which one of these days I'm gonna figure out how to use.

FOURTEEN

Girlieman

This might be a good time to start packing a bag to take with you to the hospital," Susan suggested one morning. She must have picked up on my nervous energy as I paced back and forth in the kitchen, cramming Little Debbie Snack Cakes into my mouth. "Pack enough clothes and toiletries to last you about three days," she said. Good idea. It's important to do this now, because once your partner starts going into labor, it will be very disrupting for you to pack. Not only will she be distracting you with her wailing about her contractions but also she probably won't be much help to you with gathering your clothes. The scenario would be something like this:

HER: Aiiiiiieeeeeee!

YOU: Honey, have you seen those soft green socks of mine?

HER: Ohhhhhh! Oh, my God!!

YOU: They were in the hamper last week, and now I can't find them.

HER: (*Labored breathing.*)

YOU: Do you think the hospital will have a blow dryer?

HER: Make it stop! Make it stop!

The job of a stand-up comedian, especially in the early years, requires a fair amount of travel. After years of traveling, I thought I had developed a pretty good system of packing my suitcase. It usually turns out that you forget things, or you pack too much. It's gotten to the point now that I just line the inside of my suitcase with Velcro and then toss it into my closet. Whatever sticks, I take with me. Sometimes this method doesn't work. Last year, I went to Hawaii, and I ended up bringing a sock and a scarf. I ended up not even using the scarf.

More often than not, I will check the extended weather forecast in the area I am traveling to. In the case of going to the hospital, though, odds are the weather will be the same. I used to check the weather map in *USA Today.* You get a little better insight on what clothes to pack by referring to their color-coded temperature shadings. For example, last summer I had to go to the Midwest, and I noticed that that whole area of the country was shaded in red, so I packed all my red clothes. Again, here is a great example of working smart, not working hard.

But the most important item to bring to the hospital was my iPod. During the final weeks of the pregnancy, I spent a good amount of my time ignoring Susan's gasps and the baby's "wanting out" while selecting songs for our stay at the hospital. I created two separate playlists for those few days. One I labeled

"Susan's Soft Birth Songs"—mostly gentle, soft songs either for right after she has delivered or to help me sleep. No Enya, though, because one of the nurses not-so-subtly let on that she was sick of hearing her. I thought, The last thing we want is the nurse avoiding our room because she doesn't want to hear Enya again. The other playlist I made was called "Susan's Rock Birth Songs," and this one had more hard-driving songs, in case she needed more motivation while she was pushing. These were songs with anger, mostly Alanis Morissette. I liked the idea of these songs because I knew they would drown out the potential screams.

By the way, it's amazing how much you can tell about someone by checking out the playlist on their iPod. I had someone do it to me once, and I must say it was somewhat unnerving. I felt like I was being judged me and sized up as hip or square (the fact that I just said "square" probably tells you which category I fall into). What would they think of the Tony Robbins motivational series I had downloaded? What about the various Books on Tape? I did have an Anne Murray song that I hoped no one would notice. I have a bookshelf in my living room that my houseguests seem to check out while they are visiting, as well. Again, I feel like they are judging me as they scan each shelf. For that reason I have loaded the shelves with classics, poetry, and other thick books, none of which I have read. I should probably do the same for my iPod—maybe more Miles Davis and less of the Carpenters.

When your bags are packed and your playlists are sorted, you know you're getting close. You also know that most likely none of the clothes you packed match because you've been so tired recently. At this point in the pregnancy it is difficult for the woman to get a full night's sleep. This in turn means it's also difficult for the man to get a full night's sleep. Some of these sleepless nights may likely be attributed to the anxiety stemming from the imaginings of the upcoming and probable bloodbath during delivery. This is understandable for you, but why she is having difficulty sleeping is another story.

In Susan's case, I had no doubt that a large part of her concern was coming from the fact that her stomach had grown to a substantial size, which, from what I gathered, was pretty uncomfortable. Her belly was so large that she hadn't laid down on it for months. Then again, neither had I, but I'm not a big lying-on-my-belly kind of guy, so I didn't miss it. It wasn't that Susan ever spent a lot of time lying on her belly, but it was like anything else—just knowing she couldn't do it made her want to do it more. I told her if she really wanted to lie on her belly, I would take her to the beach, dig a hole in the sand the size of her belly, and she could then lie facedown, but for some reason she didn't find that funny.

This total lack of sleep might have explained Susan's fit of hysteria that she had one day toward the end of the pregnancy. Following some intense false labor pains, I had said something that made her laugh. I was enjoying the laugh with her until I noticed that she was laughing almost a little too hard. It became a guttural, almost maniacal laugh. Her maniacal laughter started scaring me, and I tried not to encourage it. I tried to distract her by changing the subject and asking her boring questions.

"Did you watch *American Idol* last night?" I asked. Her laughter continued. "We have to bring the car in to be serviced this week," I added. She ignored me and continued her out-of-control demonic laugh. The laughter soon turned into sobbing and then returned to laughing. I was quickly getting dressed, thinking this might be a sign that I had to drive her somewhere—to the hospital or an asylum, I wasn't sure. Regardless, I scurried around throwing last-minute things into my suitcase in case we needed to leave the next moment. She eventually settled down, and the false labor pains subsided. She later told me that because of her false labor pain, she felt out of control. Okay, I get it, but what about me? I had no idea what was going on except that I couldn't find my iPod to throw in the bag.

Though we felt that we could see the light at the end of the uterus, we soon learned that the due date is a lot like the window of time they give you for your cable-guy appointment. It's usually not the exact time, so you have to wait around all day anyway, just in case. Just like, I resolved that I need to do something constructive while waiting in traffic, so one morning I exercised to Susan's Kegel workout video for two hours. I worked up a pretty good sweat and didn't think I'd have to go to the bathroom again for another month. Feeling lighter, I snuck out to the garage, stripped down, and weighed myself. My weight had gone up two more pounds. A neighbor saw me standing naked on the scale, and I reminded myself that this was all for the baby

It was around this time that Susan's mom, Sally, and her friend Betty arrived from Nashville. Sally is a fertility specialist, but she had nothing to do with our becoming pregnant aside from the fact that she created Susan. Because she is the kind of woman who's always prepared, Sally brought her surgical/delivery equipment, in the event that Susan doesn't make it to the hospital in time. On the night that they flew in, Susan and I were about to go to bed when we heard a knock on our back door. When I looked out, I saw Sally and Betty standing in the hallway with a suitcase. Embarrassed, they explained that they had grabbed one of the wrong suitcases from the baggage claim back at the airport. The suitcase looked exactly like Sally's, but the tag said it belonged to a John Garrent in Buena Vista. Luckily, they discovered their mistake before Sally needed any of her surgical equipment. She might have had to deliver our baby with a heavily starched businessman's shirt instead. On the other hand, some disgruntled businessman in Anaheim might have been pulling on sterile latex, surgical gloves, and scrubs to go to a morning meeting.

I took Sally and Betty back to the airport that night, and they made the exchange. As it turned out, Sally and Betty were a big help to us. They both encouraged us to do ourselves a favor and hire a night nurse. A night nurse's job is twofold: to help the mother recover from the labor, and to keep an eye on the baby in the nursery for the first few weeks. In reality, a night nurse takes care of the parents, so they can take care of their baby. It takes a lot of pressure off the parents; they can catch up on sleep and not have to worry that the baby is not breathing, getting kidnapped, developing SIDS, choking on the mobile, or any other trouble. By "any other trouble" I mean not being quiet.

We followed everyone's advice and found a wonderful night nurse. Her name was Greta, and she came highly recommended. She came and checked our nursery and told us that we had almost everything we needed. We were only missing a few things. For starters, Susan would need a breast pump. This is an electrical pump that has two clear, funnel-like attachments that fit over the mother's nipples. One of its jobs is to pump milk from the mother's breast to be stored for future use. The other reason to pump the breast is to release, or "express," as it's known, some of the milk from a breast that is too full. All great things to know if you work at Starbucks. Sometimes breasts that are too full, or become engorged, can be very hard and uncomfortable. The only other thing that we would need, she said, would be something for her to sleep on. I'm thinking to myself, "Why does she need to sleep? Who will be watching the baby while she is sleeping?" I eventually gave in and found her a very uncomfortable, plastic, nineteen-dollar air mattress from Target. I figured it would be very difficult for her to sleep on this, and thus we would get our money's worth out of her, since she would be up most of the night listening for our baby and trying to fall asleep.

Even with our night nurse lined up and a resident fertility expert living in our guesthouse, we still had a few questions for our doctor, and most of them involved getting the epidural shot. This is the medicine that numbs the mother from the waist down so she doesn't have to experience quite so much pain. "How soon can we get it? Why do we have to wait? When does it take effect?" Susan asked. We had other questions, too, but mostly from me: "Is there a place I can stand where I won't hear the screaming? Can I get cell phone reception in the hospital? Is there a TV nearby? What about Internet access? Most important, what about a blender for margaritas?"

A common concern with many pregnant women is that they will have a bowel movement while they are trying to push the baby out. Let me tell you something, an involuntary bowel movement can be quite unnerving. Have you ever been so scared that you accidentally pooped in your pants? It's not a pretty sight, but I'm not ashamed to admit that it has happened to me. When I was fourteen years old, my friends and I were ringing doorbells a few days before Halloween. The guy who lived in the house fooled us and came running out full speed after us from around the back of the house. We barely had time to get away. I don't know where he was from originally, but I think he was swearing at us in Romanian.

After a few blocks of him gaining on us I decided to make a left turn hoping that my three friends would follow. They decided to run straight. The Romanian chose to follow me. It was like he singled me out of the herd like a lion does, recognizing the weak link. When I turned around, I saw that he was right behind me—but that's not when I pooped. Not yet. As he started reaching out for my shirt I quickly darted behind a house. It was pitch-dark out, and I was running aimlessly in a panic. I began to hit clothes-lines and trip over lawn furniture. I finally slipped and fell to the ground. As I desperately tried to catch my breath, the irate Romanian came running up behind me, grabbed me by my collar, and literally lifted me off the ground. Right then, a little turd came out. It just "pushed cotton," though, and then it went right back inside again. It was totally involuntary. I don't know why it went back. I guess it didn't see its shadow. It was like the angry poop came out and said, "What the hell is going—WHOA!" And then at that very moment it saw the angry Romanian, got scared, and made a U-turn. I have not seen that poop since.

So, as with many of Susan's concerns throughout the pregnancy, I could relate to this one. I wasn't so old that involuntary bowel movements had become a thing of the present, but I was aware that they were looming somewhere on the horizon. I wasn't wearing adult diapers yet, but I did need a regular fiber boost. I could understand her anxiety, and I knew that it wasn't going to go away until this thing was finally over. Someone asked me if I was going to be in the delivery room when the baby was delivered. In the early stages of pregnancy, I thought, Sure, of course I'll be in there. I'll be giving all the support I can. By this point, though, I wasn't so sure I wanted to be anywhere near there. For that matter, Susan decided she didn't want to be there either. Instead, we were considering paying someone to go in there and wail like a madwoman for about eight hours—perhaps a "surrogate wailer"?

We were both quite prepared for the pregnancy to end and parenthood to begin. We were ready to take on this responsibility. In fact, I knew that Susan was totally qualified because she had been very responsible with valuable items in the past: more specifically, a few expensive designer handbags. With a handbag, like a baby, before you make the decision to have one, you need to think hard about whether you really want it or can afford it. When Susan is carrying one of her Hermès or Dolce & Gabbana purses she is very protective of it. She is very selective as to whom she lets hold it or watch it. Some women are envious; others would never think of owning one. Unlike a baby, though, the only stretch marks involved are on the wallet and, oh yeah, some screaming from the husband.

In order to really prepare for the parenting stage, we attended one final class with Brad and Kim called Child Caring. As this was to be the last class, I tried to cram as much information as possible into my big fat Mick head. The whole point of the Child Caring class was to teach us how to care for our baby once we'd brought it home from the hospital. Our teacher was a very pleasant twenty-something woman named Chanin. She had a soft cast on her foot, which was the result of a skateboarding accident. I loved the notion that a skateboarder was instructing us on how to care for our baby.

She was very good, though, and she went over how to change diapers, bathe the baby, and swaddle it. Apparently swaddling is very important to a baby's sense of security. The idea is to wrap the baby in its blanket to get a very secure and snug fit, a fit that resembles the tightness of being in its mother's womb. There was a method to doing this. Certain corners had to be folded over first and tucked into certain areas, blah, blah, blah. It was all very hard to follow. Instead I suggested, "Why not just put the kid in a straitjacket?" It seemed logical to me; after all that's where our kid was going to end up anyway, according to our lawyer. We continued to practice our swaddling and diaper changing and by the end of the class we were pretty confident. We figured if it worked on Brad, it would surely work on a baby.

We were also taught how to hold the baby. You think you'd know the proper way to hold a baby, but there have really been some inroads on the best way to do it. I remember several years back running into Arnold Schwarzenegger while skiing in Sun Valley. At the time one of his kids was only a few months old, and I remember being fascinated by the way he carried her—like she was a football: facedown on his massive forearm. In fact, I wasn't quite sure if it really was a baby on his arm or just another muscle—a screaming muscle wrapped in a diaper.

I wasn't convinced that this was the proper way to hold a child, but when you see Arnold Schwarzenegger, your first instinct is not to criticize the man—I don't care what your politics are. I had originally met Arnold several years earlier while I was at *Saturday Night Live*. Dana Carvey and I had come up with a popular sketch about two pathetic-looking bodybuilders who claimed to be distant cousins of Arnold Schwarzenegger named Hans and Franz. We wore outdated gray sweatsuits stuffed with foam padding to simulate muscles, although none of our muscles were anatomically correct. We also wore flat-top wigs, darkened a space between our front teeth, and spoke with Austrian accents.

At one point these characters became so popular on *SNL* that Arnold himself wanted to be in a sketch with Hans and Franz. When we heard this news, Dana and I looked at each other, perplexed. Concerned, I said to Dana, "Doesn't he know we're making fun of him?" We couldn't understand why he would want to have any part of this. After contemplating this for most of the day, we came to the only reasonable explanation, which was that he wanted to come on the show to rip our arms off.

The day Arnold arrived at the SNL studio, Lorne Michaels, the creator of the show, came to Dana and me on the set and told us Arnold was in his dressing room, and he wanted to see us. Dana and I began to quietly panic. We were like two schoolkids sent to the principal's office. We were blaming each other: "You came up with it!" "No, I didn't, you did." "You wanted to do the

Austrian accent. I said not to." "You wanted to do the 'Girlieman' thing!" "No, I didn't." We rounded the corner to find Maria Shriver, Arnold's wife, waiting outside his dressing room. She smiled and said hello, but I thought I detected an undertone of distrust. We said hello back to her and then anxiously approached the door of Arnold's dressing room.

As we peered in, we saw that it was full of cigar smoke. Through it all, we could make out Arnold sitting on a little chair across the room. In hindsight, it was actually a regular-sized chair, but Arnold made it look small. In one hand he held the script that we had written for him, and in the other he held a big, fat cigar. He looked up through the thick smoke and said to us in his familiar Austrian accent, "Hello fellas. Now how am I supposed to do this accent?" It was right then that Dana and I realized he had a great sense of humor. We all laughed and had a great time working with him that week. I got to know him over the years, although to this day I don't think he knows my real name. Anytime I run into him he greets me by saying, "Hello, cousin Franz! How are you?"

Aside from the birthing and child-care classes, we also took a class in CPR. I had learned CPR in my early twenties when I was a lifeguard at Seaside Park in Connecticut, but had forgotten most of the details. Actually, I'm not really sure I ever really knew the details to begin with, since mine was probably the easiest lifeguard job anywhere. The beach was on Long Island Sound, and as a result, the water was always very calm, mostly because the pollution kept waves from forming. Not only was it calm, but it seemed that a swimmer would have to wade out almost a mile to get in water deep enough to drown in. By then, the swimmer was halfway across the sound and more than likely in the jurisdiction of a Long Island lifeguard. Typically, the only first aid we had to administer was Band-Aids for cuts. On a rare occasion some of us, but never me, had the opportunity to perform mouth-to-mouth resuscitation on a drunk partyer. They would usually pass out and fall facedown into a foot of the murky salt water. You would have to drag them out of the water and start the mouth-to-mouth immediately. More often than not they would be revived, but only after they vomited water into your mouth. They would then stagger back to their picnic/drunk fest.

Perhaps I would have been more attuned to the details of CPR had I not also been working the late shift at Dunkin' Donuts. Thankfully, I never had to use CPR there either. I took this job from ten at night until five in the morning because I desperately wanted a Marshall amplifier for my guitar, and the smell of doughnuts was more alluring than some of the other late-night possibilities. I had to be on the lifeguard chair by ten in the morning, so needless to say, I wasn't the most alert lifeguard. It was probably the worst occupation, aside from parent, to have, if you're so tired. I knew it was time to quit making doughnuts when most of my days were spent sleeping on the lifeguard chair. And besides, how awkward would it be if I woke up on the chair in my swimsuit, and it was the middle of the night?

From one of these baby classes or books or skateboarding "experts" that we met during the final countdown to baby, we learned one of the best ways to care for your child is to care for yourself by saving the umbilical cord after the birth for the purpose of stem cells. Later in life, if your child or you or your partner ever gets sick and needs stem cells, you will have them available. This is called cord-blood banking. There are companies that will store the cord for you for the rest of your baby's life for around fifteen hundred dollars. Great, more stuff to put in storage, I thought.

Even if we hadn't learned of the umbilical cord's future organ-harvesting value, Susan probably would have saved it anyway because she's never really been big on throwing stuff out. It was probably this fact that led me to start cleaning up some clutter while waiting for the cable guy/contractions to come. People had been reiterating to me that we would need plenty of space for the baby's toys. I didn't really see the point, since the only toy we were going to get the baby during its first year was a roll of wrapping paper and some boxes that used to contain toys. I'd heard that's all babies really play with anyway. But cleaning up the clutter was more symbolic than necessary. If creating the nursery was the result of Susan's nesting, my nesting was going through the house and getting rid of all the junk that had been idling for far too long anyway.

It was amazing how much had accumulated in just a few months—boxes we couldn't throw out, receipts that needed to be filed. On the plus side, our baby would not need a rattle, as I had uncovered plenty of half-full prescription bottles that would work just fine. I hate clutter. You can only put so much crap out in the garage and still be able to get into the car. Because of this, I graduated to renting a storage unit a few years ago. I was surprised at just how many people use storage units. This is a well-kept secret. No one ever talks about them. From what I understand, most people store their clutter in them and then years later throw it all out. Storage units are really just expensive Dumpsters. People are a lot like squirrels. We take our nuts and bury them somewhere just so that we may have access to them later. The difference is that squirrels are smart; they don't bring the nuts they find back to their home in the tree. They take them directly to their storage unit, which is a hole in the ground somewhere. Somehow they remember exactly where they buried them. For Susan, me, and most everyone else I know with a storage unit, the nuts we keep in the unit are nuts that we don't like and will never eat, use, or wear, but still can't manage to part with.

Nowadays, its not just physical clutter we store but also digital clutter. Every day I find myself spending heaps of time discarding junk e-mails from my computer and deleting stored messages on my cell phone. There are also the recorded TiVo programs that I have to delete. I refer to all of this as digital pruning.

I've noticed that most of my nondigital clutter comes from my closet. I have tons of T-shirts that I never wear. On many occasions I've attempted to thin the herd. I take them all out and pile them on the bed. I start pulling out some that I don't think I'll wear again. One time I gave a T-shirt away to a friend, and it looked great on him. I regretted giving it away and wished I could have it back. Every time I saw him in it, I felt as though he was with an ex of mine. There are other T-shirts, too, that I haven't worn in years, but can't get rid of because they have special meaning to me. Some of them are from concerts I went to or events I attended. Some of them were even nerdy and corny. I hesitated to give those away, because you never know when you might be invited to a nerd concert or event.

Ultimately I ended up putting all the T-shirts back in the closet, which is generally a routine I do about every two years. At least it was an opportunity to fold and stack them all neatly. Generally I would have more space in my closet, but somehow my wife's clothes seem to be making their way over. In an attempt to free up my closet from her increased infringing, I offered to turn our very small spare bedroom into a walk-in closet just for her. This would be a perfect closet to hold some of the clothes and shoes that were crammed into her closet and the stray ones that were ending up in mine, much like an overflow valve. At least, I assumed that that would be the case. Instead, it was just an invitation for her to buy more clothes and shoes, since she knew there would now be more available closet space. I guess I had forgotten about additional needed space for maternity clothes, too. And these clothes will only be temporary. Eventually they will be moved out of the walk-in closet and transported to our regular storage unit.

As I dismissed the clutter, I devised a convenient way to store stuff without paying the monthly storage fees: put the items that you want stored out by your driveway. On each item, in a discreet place, attach one of those LoJack tracking devices. Eventually each one of your items will be stolen from your property. Then, when you need that item again, call the police and report it stolen. They will track it down using the LoJack, and you will have your item back again with no storage fees. Problem solved.

Of course, that doesn't work for everyone, and there are some skeptics out there who like to know where their stuff is at all times. And then there are also those of us who get so overwhelmed by the amount of junk in our storage unit that we rent an additional one so that we can clean out the original. I was in my storage unit doing precisely that in the days before Susan delivered, when I came across some brochures of a trip we took to Scotland a year or so ago.

As I flipped through it, I saw the beautiful Loch Ness. *Loch*, in Scottish, means lake. I didn't know what *Ness* meant, but I thought it sounded beautiful, especially following the name Gable—"Gable Ness." That way, our child would definitely be bound for a future in law enforcement. While I contemplated how having a virulent anti-bootlegger in the house would impact my life, I called Susan and asked her what she thought. She liked it—didn't quite love it, but liked it for now. I found out later that *ness* in Aboriginal means "strong." By the way, you can't look that up, because there is no Aboriginal dictionary. Don't even try. My cousin knows an Aboriginal bushman who told him the meaning. Besides, their language is all clicking and clucking noises. We were going for a nice phonetic-sounding name, not so much a name from our family's history. I was just glad we didn't need to find a name that fit well with Schwarzenegger.

FIFTEEN

Birthquakes

I wanted to be in the room for the conception, and I was. A lot of guys don't like that, but I really didn't mind. And I figured that since I was there at the beginning, I might as well be there at the end, so I would go to the delivery room with Susan. I wanted to help—as long as manning the iPod would be considered helping.

I got home at two in the morning to discover Susan in our bedroom, curled up on the bed—going into labor. She told me she'd woken up at one thirty in the morning with severe contractions. Earlier that evening I had attended the Screen Actors Guild Awards, and originally Susan had planned on going with me but then decided against it, since she didn't want to chance having the baby on the red carpet. Had that happened, though, it would have been the best color carpet to have a baby on. She encouraged me to go, since I was part of the ensemble on the nominated Showtime series *Weeds*. "Make sure you leave your cell phone on," she yelled to me as I left.

Honestly, I am not a big fan of award shows. It seems like it has gotten to the point where there are so many award shows airing on television, there's no time for regular TV programs. Award shows are now getting awards for being the best shows. I must say, though, walking down that red carpet is quite exhilarating. It really makes you feel like a big shot. Ever since my first award show, I have considered putting one in my hallway in my house. That way, every time I get up to go to the bathroom at night, I'll feel very important. The only downside would be to have to stop for fifteen minutes each time to talk to Joan Rivers. I stayed at the SAG Awards just long enough to have a few pictures taken on the red carpet, and also long enough to accept not winning in our category.

Since Susan's contractions were consistent and lasting, we called her mother in from the guesthouse. Sally came with her sterile latex gloves, ready to check the progress. She examined Susan's cervix and determined that it had dilated to almost two centimeters. Upon hearing this, my jaw dropped, dilating my mouth to over ten centimeters. She was definitely in labor. I have discovered that there is a direct correlation between the size of the woman's cervix dilation and the size of my mouth opening up to gasp. A wide-open-mouthed gasp, which equals about ten centimeters, is enough for a baby to come out of it. I changed into my green T-shirt and green sweatpants that I had laid out. These would be my scrubs. I had seen enough episodes of *ER* to know that this was as close as I would come to looking official. If I was going to be in the delivery room, at least I wanted to fit in fashion-wise, but with the T-shirt and sweatpants I resembled more of a med-school dropout who'd been practicing south of the border somewhere. I believe the last time I wore this outfit was the previous Saint Patty's Day, when I had accidentally sat in someone's vomit. I decided against wearing the leprechaun hat.

We waited at home, keeping an eye on the timing of the contractions and their intensity. As we learned in our birthing classes, these consistent contractions indicated that it would soon be time to leave for the hospital. I checked the clock and hoped for an earlier than later departure time—I just knew Susan was going to hit me up for a ride. Sometimes you can just tell when someone is going to need you. I was fine with that, but I didn't want to get caught in the morning rush-hour traffic. As I mentioned earlier, I absolutely hate traffic, and most of my day is planned around trying to avoid it. Thankfully, at four thirty in the morning Sally said, "Okay, I think it would be a good time for us to go." My mouth dilated another centimeter. Wow, this is it! After over nine months of waiting, it was "go time." I would finally be a dad. I would soon have a baby as an excuse to get out of doing things I don't want to do. I braced myself. We were making that long-awaited trip to the hospital. The reality of it all hit hard. As I gathered our things, I realized, "I'm really not ready to go, it's just time."

There was not a single car on the road as we drove, and the scene was absolutely surreal. The orange glow of the rising sun shone down upon us, filtered by the smog, as we traveled north along the coast. Still—no traffic. As I looked over to Susan, I was flushed with a wave of exhilaration. Here she was, sitting next to me, pregnant with my child, on our way to the hospital . . . about to deliver. I thought, This is such a miracle—*no* traffic! Not one other car! God must be watching over us.

As I pulled onto the freeway, I was thinking how similar the birth process is to a surprise birthday party. When the baby comes out of the womb, it has no idea that we will all be in some room waiting for it. We will all wait anxiously until the guest of honor arrives. The doctor will even probably give us a heads-up as he or she arrives. We'll all get giddy and excited. And when the baby does enter the room, we will all jump up and down and open a bottle of champagne. If the baby had a choice and knew all the attention it would be getting—and more importantly, that someone would be cutting off its umbilical cord, its food source—it might have had second thoughts. I can only imagine the cold shock the baby must feel when first entering this world. One minute it is in the dark solitude, security, and warmth of the mother's womb, and the next minute it's pushed into this bright, loud world. It's probably the same sensation a winning football coach experiences when his players sneak up behind him and dump a bucket of ice-cold Gatorade over his head. The truth of the matter is, there's no longer any room for the baby. It's the same cramped feeling you might experience when you've outgrown the small apartment you'd been living in. You just start accumulating too much junk and have no option except to move out and find a bigger place. That or get a storage unit—and a baby might have difficulty doing that.

We arrived at the hospital at dawn and left our car with the valet. (I know—it's such an L.A. thing.) I tossed him the keys and jokingly told him, "Keep it running. We won't be long." We checked in, and as we approached the maternity wing of the hospital, my heart rate seemed to spike again. I honestly didn't know if I would have the courage and wherewithal to be in the delivery room when the fireworks started. I don't like blood, and I don't like placenta. Both of them together, tag-teaming me, would not be good at all.

We were led into a private room on the third floor—the room where our long-awaited surprise would be unveiled. Outside our window was a beautiful view of a new wing of the hospital under construction. The room's double-paned glass windows shut out most of the cacophony of the worker bees and their jackhammering. The nurse left us briefly to settle into the space where we would be welcoming our baby into the world. Before things got too crazy in the room, Susan and I were able to spend a few intimate moments together, one on one, reminiscing about how little traffic there was.

"I don't think I've ever seen the pavement in Los Angeles before," I said. "And we hit most of the green lights, that was great."

She didn't have to respond for me to know she agreed. That she was gripping my arm tightly, and her piercing stare, said it all. Susan slipped into her hospital gown and climbed up on the bed, and I began to do my job. I professionally removed the iPod from my overnight bag and hooked it up to the mini-speakers. As I was doing that, the nurse proceeded to hook Susan up to several monitors. Yep, we were both doing our jobs, prepping for the arrival of the little bundle. The gauges and LEDs on the nurse's monitors revealed that Susan was definitely in labor. The LED on my iPod revealed that all of our songs had been properly downloaded and were ready to go. I was trying to savor every moment of this experience. Sometimes, though, you just can't savor each moment. You need to experience the whole thing at once and then look back on it. It's a lot like being on a roller coaster. You can't stop it every two seconds and savor just that small distance you traveled. "Wow, that little two-foot segment was fun . . . can't wait for the next two!" You need to complete the whole ride, nonstop, to really enjoy it. It's the collective day. The whole row of dominoes needs to be knocked down to enjoy the effect.

After checking my own blood pressure, I double-checked the connection between the iPod and its mini-speakers. We couldn't have that coming apart during all of this. The iPod was my monitor, and my job was to keep an eye on the playlist, making sure each song fit the mood. It was also my crutch, my Dramamine to get me through all this. I would be fine as long as I kept direct eye contact with the iPod or Susan's face. As Susan had requested,

George Harrison's "Here Comes the Sun" would be the song played as the baby was coming out. Right now, though, all she had on her mind was the pushing and the impending epidural. Though she knew the epidural would make giving birth a lot more bearable, the idea of a two-foot needle (or however long it is) going into her spinal column made her extremely anxious. It really is amazing how we can worry ourselves silly sometimes.

The nurse who was to administer the epidural made us all leave the room. I felt terrible for Susan because she was incredibly apprehensive about this procedure. I don't blame her. All through the pregnancy she had told her doctor that she was the biggest wimp in the world, had no pain threshold, and dreaded the notion of any pain. By her own admission, if she were a contestant on *Survivor* she would be the one sitting under a tree crying and wanting to go home at the end of the first episode. The nurse told us to come back in a half hour. I felt anxious for Susan the whole time I was out of the room. Once again, I thought, Why me? Why do I have to go through these uncomfortable situations? And once again, I got through it. I accepted it. When the epidural had finally been administered, we were allowed back in the room. Susan had a totally different attitude now. It was like she became a Stepford wife. Everything was just fine. "It's all going to be great," she said. "I'm just going to push this puppy out and . . . how are you doing?" I closely examined her to make sure this was still my wife.

From the indications of the contractions showing up on the monitors, it appeared that Susan would be pushing the baby out at around five o'clock. As it got closer, Susan started getting the shakes. Our doctor said it was nothing to worry about, very normal, and referred to them as "birth-quakes," an uncontrollable shaking of the body and chattering of the teeth. It was the body shifting into the delivery mode. Some people experience it, others don't. Nevertheless, I planted myself under the nearest door-frame. As it got closer to delivery time, some type of incredible fortitude came over Susan. The birth-quakes stopped, and she was resigned to get through all this. She no longer feared it. When she finally started pushing, she was like Braveheart running into battle. She rose to the occasion.

"Push!" the nurse instructed Susan. I immediately noticed that our doctor was not in the room and became a little concerned. I didn't want to insult our nurse, but, I asked where was our doctor? She informed me that the doctor would be coming in soon. She then instructed Susan to push to the count of ten, three times, during each contraction. We all counted in unison with the contractions. Once again, I anxiously asked the nurse where the doctor was. The nurse informed me that she would come in just before the baby was about to come out.

Oh, I get it, I thought. The doctor is like the headliner at a rock concert. She will be introduced at the height of the evening. I imagined her waiting for her cue right outside the room, as if it were backstage, smoking a cigarette and polishing off a bottle of Jack Daniel's while pacing and trying to remember her song list. After Susan had been pushing about twenty minutes, the nurse was confident the baby was ready to make its appearance, and Dr. Glass miraculously appeared and assessed the situation.

She asked Susan how she was feeling and then turned to me. "Would you like to help with this?" she politely asked.

"Yes, I am helping. I'm working the iPod," I said.

"No," she said, "do you want to help deliver the baby?"

No, no, no! I *don't* want to help deliver the baby! Don't you understand how I feel about blood and placenta? But instead I said, "Yes, sure, I would love to help. That would be a wonderful experience." I couldn't believe that came out of my mouth.

I didn't think this was the time or place for a confrontation. I was hoping that she would read between the lines and realize my discomfort level and let me off the hook. Didn't she understand that yes meant no? She just wasn't listening to me. She handed me a pair of sterile latex surgical gloves, which I nervously pulled on. In my haste I realized I had pulled them on upside down. The contour of the latex pushed my fingers back and up, making it very difficult to close my hands. I would not have time to put them on correctly now, since they were already full of sweat and the doctor needed me. As Dr. Glass expertly pulled on her own latex gloves, she instructed me to hold up Susan's left leg. She then instructed Sally to hold up the other. I couldn't believe that I was this involved. I thought my job would be to either keep an eye on the iPod or, at the most, sit next to Susan, keep eye contact with her, and just cheer her on—never seeing any of the actual birth stuff. I mean, that is what the husbands were doing in the birth videos that we watched. But there I was, holding up her leg, which, by the way, is how I got in this position in the first place.

After a few more minutes of pushing and deep breaths, mostly from me, Dr. Glass casually commented, "Look, you can see the top of the baby's head. See?" She continued, "It looks like a bulging purple rock with skin and hair on it."

I didn't want to look, but I did, and just so I didn't have to focus on it, I discreetly said, "I don't know, I think that's always been there."

I quickly turned my eyes away and looked at the iPod. Susan's requested song was not timed to come on yet, which meant only one thing: I would have to induce it. I definitely should have hired a DJ. I could have had *him* hold Susan's leg, while I manned the iPod. But I hadn't, and it was too late now. I thought to myself, If I start freaking out with all the blood, placenta, and screaming, I can disappear into my own fantasy by imagining that I'm churning butter with Susan's leg. Or if things got really bad, I could imagine her leg was the control stick of an old World War II fighter plane, and I could get the hell out of there. With one hand still holding Susan's leg up, I reached with my other to the iPod. I clumsily scrolled down the playlist with my latex glove to George Harrison's "Here Comes the Sun."

"The baby's head is making its way out," Dr. Glass said. I clicked on the song and quickly went back to my station at her leg, focusing now just on Susan's face.

Everything was unfolding. Suddenly the room was full of applause—coming from the iPod. Unfortunately, I realized that I had downloaded a live, in-concert version of "Here Comes the Sun." As the baby's head was coming out, there was now some patter from George. He was talking about adjusting his microphone or something. His patter was followed by about fifteen seconds of more spirited applause, which lasted long enough for the baby's head to completely poke out. "The head is out!" Sally yelled. As if it was a bad car accident, I had to look. I couldn't tell what was up and what was down. Where was the face? Finally, as the rest of the head emerged, it turned, and there I saw its little face. The doctor asked me if I would like to pull the rest of the baby out. I didn't hear her at first, since I was so transfixed by the baby's head. I was actually rubbernecking in the delivery room.

"Kevin, would you like to pull the rest of the baby out?" she asked me again.

Absolutely not! Not on your life! But I said, "Sure. I'd love to."

With my inverted latex gloves I nervously grasped the soft, goo-covered head the best I could and gently started pulling. It wasn't coming out. The neck just seemed to elongate, and this terrified me. I anxiously told the doctor that I was afraid I was going to pull the baby's head off. She told me not to worry, that wouldn't happen. Under the stress, I quickly snapped back, "Okay, but if it does, I'm gonna be really mad at you!" Oh, yes—I really let her have it by telling her that. She was now well aware of my threat and what my feelings would be should the baby's head come off. I had the urge to run over to a light switch and flip it on and off a solid five times, with my other hand simultaneously tugging the windowshade up and down.

I needed to get this baby out, but it was not budging. It now seemed that it would be my turn to run to the pharmacy for Susan and buy some Fleet—her turn to call my cell phone every five minutes from the delivery room, frantically asking me, "Where are you now?" I eventually thought that I might need to apply a headlock to get this kid out, but instead I gently tugged some more, and suddenly the rest of it came spilling out. Glorious Jesus Explosion, how amazing! Have you ever seen kids rocketing out of the end of a water slide? Well, it was something like that, except it was covered in, yes, blood and placenta. As it slid out, the doctor guided it into my hands. The baby and I immediately let out a quick wail . . . no slapping necessary. It looked perfect. Everything was intact.

I held it up and immediately saw that it had a penis. What a great surprise! I'd always said I didn't care if it was a boy or a girl, as long as it had a penis. In my excitement, I announced to the room, "IT'S A PENIS!" I excitedly yelled it out again, "IT'S A PENIS!" The doctor suggested putting him on Susan's chest. Susan, through tears of joy, looked down at him and emotionally proclaimed, "I have a penis! I have a baby penis!" And George Harrison sang, "It's all right, da dadada, dadada, dadada, da da, da, da . . . It's all right."

The doctor then asked if I would like to cut the umbilical cord. Jeez, I thought, doesn't anyone want to work around here? First it was the night nurse wanting to sleep, and now it's the doctor wanting me to do her job. Maybe I should have asked her to come to my house and cut my grass, or better yet, bring her latex gloves and wash our dishes. Wouldn't that be a good experience? After helping to deliver the baby, I had no problem cutting the umbilical cord. I said, "Sure, I'll cut it. Gimme the scissors."

By now, "Here Comes the Sun" had ended. That song selection was really quite prophetic except for the misspelling of "son." The iPod was now on to the next song: Lee Ann Womack singing about her cheating boyfriend. I really should have put more thought into the playlist. I quickly scrolled down to the next song, pushed play, and returned to my station. The doctor handed me a pair of scissors and then stretched and clamped the umbilical cord. She pointed between the two clamps to where she wanted me to cut. I felt like a dignitary cutting the ribbon at the opening ceremonies of a mall. I expected someone to then hand me a bottle of champagne to smash over the end of the bed. I couldn't believe that I had helped deliver this beautiful baby. It was, hands-down, the most incredibly wonderful experience I'd ever had. In fact, I felt so good about it that two hours later I went across the hall and delivered two more babies as well as performing a C-section—which I botched, but still a great experience.

After we had some time to bond with the baby, I walked down the long hall to the waiting room to deliver the fantastic news. I pushed open the door and now stood before my son's grandparents and our good friend Paul Reder. I paused, relishing this moment as they patiently anticipated the news. I smiled and finally announced, "It-is-a-boy!" I savored each and every word of that sentence. My parents beamed and then were overcome with joy. As we all hugged, the others in the waiting room cheered and applauded. I continued by telling them the mother and baby were both healthy and doing fine. I brought my parents in to meet their first grandchild—another moment I will forever savor. I will never forget the look on their faces as they gleamed down at him adoringly. Several hours later, the doctor had to perform a special surgery to break their loving eye-lock. They were absolutely crazy for this kid. It was now time to announce the closely guarded name that Susan and I had come up with.

I said, "Okay everyone, his name is . . . ," and in unison Susan and I slowly counted to three and then clearly said, "Gable Ness Nealon." If anyone had disapproved of the name, they kept it to themselves. Besides, it was too late now for anyone to complain. Our plan had worked.

Bringing Gable home from the hospital was quite frightening. We had prepared our home and ourselves as much as we could for his arrival, but taking him out of the security of the hospital and its staff and into this crazy world was pretty nerve-racking. We were totally responsible for his safety and well-being. This was so much more responsibility than a designer handbag. Our son was born at exactly 5:20 PM, January 29, 2007, and we were checked out of the hospital two days later at 6:00 PM. Before leaving, I insisted that we sit in the hospital's pharmacy for two hours until the evening traffic let up. When it finally did, we carried Gable along with an additional TravelJohn to our waiting car. We then loaded the little guy into the car. As I strapped him into the meticulously installed infant seat, I couldn't help notice how adorable he looked in his first ever onesie. It read "I-pood" on the front. I thought, what a way to start him off in life. Let's completely humiliate him with a clever, yet embarrassing logo.

As we pulled out of the hospital driveway, I noticed our gas tank was just about on empty. Apparently the valet didn't know I was joking when I said we would be right out and to keep it running. Thankfully it was a hybrid and had enough gas left to get us home. On the drive home, as a safety precaution, I kept it to just fifteen miles per hour under the speed limit. I also found it more soothing for the baby to hit every pothole and bump on the road, as well as turning up the static white noise on the radio. Thirty minutes later we were back at the house, completely exhilarated and exhausted from three nights of minimal sleep—not to mention the headache from the potholes and radio static. Paul had put a large banner over our front door that read, "Welcome Home Gable!" Our friends Jane and Mark had wrapped nearby telephone poles with blue and white crepe paper and hung balloons in our walkway. If only Gable could read and appreciate this!

An hour later we were relieved to have Greta, our night nurse, arrive at our door. She would be helping us out for the next few weeks, and we couldn't wait to get a solid night of sleep. She met Gable and then, rather quickly, asked again about the sleeping situation and whether or not we had something for her to sleep on. Something was telling me that she only took this job to come here and sleep. I told her I was totally prepared and had made sleeping arrangements for her. I took the air mattress out of its bag and unrolled it on the floor of the nursery. I then removed the electric air pump/compressor from its box. I had prided myself on planning thoroughly and paying a little extra for the compressor. It used to be that you could blow up an air mattress with your mouth, but these days you really need a good manual pump or a small electric compressor. I guess people just don't have the lung capacity they used to. The last thing I wanted to be doing after coming home from the hospital with our baby was kneeling over an air mattress and puffing air into it for forty-five minutes. I plugged the compressor in, knowing within minutes I would finally be in my own bed for a good night's sleep. I pushed the on switch, and nothing happened. I checked that the plug was securely in and pushed the on switch again. Nothing. I took out the small, single instruction sheet and held it under the nightlight. It directed me to plug it in and push the on switch. In smaller words at the bottom of the sheet it said that the compressor would need to be charged for ten hours before it could be used. Damn.

I told Greta not to worry. I would drive down to the gas station with the mattress and get it filled there. I assured her it was not a problem, and that I would be back in a few minutes. That's another thing I got from my family: the ability to underplay things. Even if someone had to drive over an hour to get to our house, we would often say, "Why don't you swing by?" or "Why don't you pop over?" It really makes it seem like a shorter drive. I ended up driving around for thirty-five minutes with the air mattress until I found a gas station that had an air pump. The gas station was closed, but the air pump, which was right next to the water pump, was coin-operated and always open for business. I removed the air mattress from the car and laid it down on the pavement. I reached into my pocket, looking for change. Unfortunately, I came up empty-handed. I started to pilfer from the car, looking for loose change. I finally found three quarters, a dime, and an old scratch-and-play lottery ticket under the passenger seat. I didn't have the right valve to fit into the cheap plastic mattress, so I just shoved it all the way in and tried to seal the opening around it with my fingers. With my other hand, I pumped the three quarters into the machine.

Some air was going into the mattress, but some was also coming out. After a trip to 7-Eleven and twelve dollars in quarters later, I had the air mattress 75 percent filled, and had been away from my wife, my newborn baby, and my sleep-concerned night nurse for an hour. I was hopeful that there was now enough air in it to keep Greta off the floor. For a brief moment I did consider filling it with water from the nearby water pump. Waterbeds worked well for some people in the seventies—why not a water/air mattress? When I returned home with the limp air mattress, Greta looked at it as if to say, "Is that all you got?" You see, she was looking at the glass as 25 percent empty, and I was looking at it as 75 percent full. I remembered that Paul, who lives down the street from me, once mentioned that he had an air compressor that came with his car. It worked by fitting the attachment into the car's cigarette lighter. I told Greta that I would call him to borrow his compressor to top off the mattress.

"Only if it's not a problem," she said.

It was a huge problem, but I said, "Not a problem at all. I'd be happy to."

I was exhausted and desperately wanted to be in bed. Susan was already sleeping, and Gable was probably already in school by now. At eleven thirty in the evening I called Paul, awakening him from a deep sleep. Groggily, he said he would leave the compressor near the front door of his house for me. Once again, I took the air mattress with me, picked up Paul's compressor, and brought it back to my driveway. My car was parked directly under the window of the guesthouse, where my mother-in-law was sleeping. When I plugged the compressor into the cigarette lighter it made a very loud, clattering noise. I didn't want to wake up my mother-in-law or the other neighbors so I quickly unplugged the compressor, put the air mattress back in the car, and drove about three blocks away from my house. I found a parking spot on the main street and tried again. The clattering of the compressor was competing with the noise from a nearby bar. The mattress was not inflating any more than it had been already. In fact, it had now lost 20 percent of its valuable air, leaving it only 5 percent full. For some reason the cheap valve on it was not letting air get in.

After a half hour of the clattering compressor failing to do the job and drunks poking fun at me on their way home, I gave up. At least the mattress was now 45 percent full. I threw it back into the car and headed home. As I approached the back door, I came up with an idea. Why not use Susan's breast pump to finish the job? It worked like a charm. Greta was pleased and got herself a good night's sleep.

That night, with Greta asleep on a sagging air mattress, I crept into my son's room. Looking at him, I found myself wondering where he came from. Why did he pick us? Was he the reincarnation of someone—possibly someone who had recently died? Over the next few days, I started looking through the obituaries to see which notable people had died recently. I was troubled when I remembered that the humorist/journalist Art Buchwald had died just before Gable was born. What if the cute little baby we were swaddling and kissing nonstop was really the reincarnation of Art Buchwald? Sometimes it doesn't pay to let your mind wander like that. I was now a father. I was that guy showing everyone pictures of his new son. I was that guy walking around with his kid over his shoulder, burping him and pulling extra pacifiers from my pocket.

Several weeks later, as our families were getting ready to head back to the East Coast, we stood by the car and hugged each other. The glare from the streetlight revealed the tears welling up in my parents' eyes. Out of habit, as I was hugging my father good-bye, I actually found myself trying to burp him. I patted him on the middle of his back and worked my way up. I didn't get anything out of him, indicating that the tears weren't the result of gas, but of happiness.

By the time our families had cleared out, and Susan, Gable, and I were alone, I didn't need my machine to tell me my blood pressure was sailing at a smooth 120 over 80. We were now comfortably nestled in our own bed in our own house, and I realized that I finally had a family. As we were all about to drift off to sleep, delirious with joy and gratefulness, I heard the base notes of a Kanye West song blaring from across the street.

"Can't you do something about that?" Susan implored.

I thought about it for a minute. Yes, I could do something about it. I had to do something about it; I was a father now. I got up, walked over to the phone, and called the cops . . . anonymously.

Afterbirth

The photo of the father on the beach with his son sleeping on his back now hangs in our living room. Only now that father is me with *my* son on *my* back.

It has been almost a year now since that brisk early morning with no traffic. I remember it fondly: barely one other car on the road. I still regale people with that rare phenomenon and how wonderful and surreal it was. Our friends were right when they predicted our lives would change. It did . . . and it was for the better. The time I spend in traffic now is not as annoying as it once was. In fact, I've discovered a shortcut into Hollywood that circumvents the 405 Freeway, cutting almost ten minutes off my travel time. I'm no longer in a hurry, no longer worried about wasted time, and no longer concerned with overpopulation. Instead of me being more uptight about things, I find myself much more relaxed. It's not essential that I pick clutter up off the floor right away, and I no longer apologize for a room smelling like a waste treatment plant. My blood pressure is at a constant 122/78 and I no longer need my dental guard at night. Perhaps this is all the result of the feeling that my life is finally complete.

Of course there was an adjustment period. Old habits died

hard, and you don't stop your behaviors overnight. It's difficult not to let the little things get to you from time to time. For the first few months, when the baby cried in the car, I would try to steer over every pothole or series of bumps to get him to sleep. In the last year I have gone through two full sets of Goodyear tires and three front-end alignments.

Then of course there are some things that haven't changed: our bright yellow house has not faded one bit. I still work out of town, but now I consider it rest. We still travel but bring the baby along. In almost the span of one year, the baby has visited three countries, been on thirty-two flights, two high-speed trains, four boats, and a bicycle. He is not crazy about his passport photo but who is?

My iPod is loaded with baby songs now. If anyone were to scroll through my playlist today they would think that I was a big baby. Instead of finding cat hair on my clothes from what seems like another lifetime I am finding crusty baby puke from several months ago. I still notice strollers on the street, but I don't scrutinize the new, fandangle gadgets and designs like the strollers that swivel around, or car seats that unfold into a stroller and then back like a Transformer. I also notice soon-to-be fathers by their anxious eyes. I want to tell them that it will all be okay—in fact, better than okay, but it's just one of those things they can only come to realize on their own.

My surrender is official. All of my concerns about the possibility of me being an inadequate father are dissipating. I find myself just going along with everything and making do. We're out of diapers? No problem—a washcloth with duct tape will work . . . for now. The baby is messing up the television remote by using it as a hammer?—no problem, I just take away the nails. The baby is screaming on the plane—no problem—Starbucks gift cards for everyone in the vicinity. As I put the childproof gate across the top of the staircase I find myself fascinated by how it fits tightly with the use of a spring-loaded mechanism. I find that the baby has a better grip while barefooted than while wearing socks or a onesie. I find traits of my mother and father creeping into my parenting, causing me to say things like, "Sure, the baby is crying but at least we know he's alive." It dawns on me that I do have parenting skills and I am using them pretty well. Like Dorothy in *The Wizard of Oz*, I finally realized that I had these powers all along.

I don't think anyone is ever totally prepared or feels completely adequate when it comes to parenting. All my worries during the pregnancy were totally legitimate at the time, but they became moot the second Gable was born. The baby has not asked me any questions yet that I don't have answers for. Actually, he probably has but I just couldn't understand what he was asking. My guess is that most of his questions involve the future location of breast milk and if I can make his diaper work better. I don't have answers to either of these, but I've been practicing how to divert his attention to another topic. Even at a full speed crawl he has been unable to penetrate our baby-proofed home and not one of our mattresses has gotten soiled.

In fact, I've become so relaxed that I've started to lose weight. This morning I came into the kitchen excited to show Susan how I could almost fit into my fat jeans again.

"Suz?" I yelled, "Check this out." There was no answer. Gable looked up at me, smiling from his high chair with a mouth full of Cheerios. "Suz," I shouted excitedly again, "you're not gonna believe this."

The door of the bathroom slowly swung open and out came Susan looking somewhat puzzled. She walked over to the counter and set an e.p.t. stick on the counter and said curiously:

"Does that look like two pink lines to you?"

Acknowledgments

First and foremost thank you, thank you, thank you Susan for sharing this most wonderfully amazing gift with me, for your patience and for allowing me to expose so much of your personal journey through pregnancy. To Mom and Dad, thank you for showing me what good parenting looks like, for instilling confidence in me, and for giving me the best childhood any kid could hope for. To Sharon, Mike, Kimberly, and Christopher for your companionship and teaching me how to share; to our ob-gyn for her expertise and for calmly guiding us through this entire experience without our having one panic attack.

I would be remiss to omit some of my very funny friends for greasing the comedy wheel: Garry Shandling, Eric Idle, David Mirkin, Tony Desena, Mike Brown, John McEuen, Matt Harper, Mel Sherer, and Gavin de Becker. Also to the ever-inspiring Beth Lapides and Greg Miller for fanning the fire under my imagination. Brad and Kim, thanks for letting us piggyback onto your private child-birthing classes.

I'm also indebted to all of our families, friends, and strangers who shared their advice on child rearing and parenting, and of course our lifesavers, Heike and Carmen. Without you guys I wouldn't have found the time to finish this project. I will forever be grateful to Sally Yeagley, Betty Harper, Paul Reder, and my parents, Emmett and Kathleen, for staying close in those final hours.

I should mention my peeps at Brillstein Entertainment Partners, Marc Gurvitz, Amy Weiss, and Bernie Brillstein for not laughing at me when I said I wanted to write a book.

The opportunity to write this wouldn't have been possible had it not been for Judith Regan. Thank you, Judith, for appreciating my sense of humor and encouraging me to write a book in the first place even though I kept telling you that I thought it would be a lot of work.

To my editor and oddly my mentor, Matt Harper—who is probably young enough to be my son had I accidentally knocked up someone in high school—for holding my hand through this writing experience and squeezing every last drop of creativity out of me.

Oh, and since we haven't had time to send thank-you cards, yet, I'd like to take this opportunity to thank all of you for the really cool baby gifts, especially the Evenflo Exersaucer and the giant stuffed giraffe.

And last but not least, thank you, Gable, for choosing us as your parents.